PRAISE FOR RONNIE BURKETT

Tinka's New Dress

"Remarkable… complex, and stimulating. The theatre that is so much about humanity has (apart from Burkett the puppeteer) no human in it. We need a show such as Burkett's to remind us that in the hands of a master puppeteer, old-fashioned string marionettes can make you laugh, weep—and even think."
—*The Guardian* (UK)

"Burkett uses his proven and superb control over his medium to score some telling points about the nature of art and dissent." —*The Toronto Sun*

"Ronnie Burkett is one of the world's geniuses… seeing his troupe every few years has just become a necessity of civilized theatergoing." —*The Village Voice*

"Pushing the limits of illusion and the perfection of the art of the marionette, *Tinka's New Dress* is an intricate work where drama and comedy, improvisation, advocacy, and intellectual questioning for the sake of discussion all interact with intelligence." —*Le Devoir*, Montreal

"If theatre festivals are intended to represent the best international theatrical endeavours of imagination and style, then this show was in the right place. This is art as politics in its subtlest form; the call not to arms but to that most powerfully subversive weapon, imagination."
—*The Sunday Tribune*, Dubli

Street of Blood

"What is remarkable about this show is the emotional and stylistic range it achieves… profoundly touching… hilarious… chilling… this puppeteer provocateur is one of the most daring theatre artists in Canada." —*The Globe and Mail*

"*Street of Blood* is by turns mordantly satirical, gently humorous, deliciously bitchy, sad, dirty, despairing, hopeful, lyrical, tender, and moving. Even for the jaded playgoer, Burkett's work is a triumph of theatrical illusion. It's bloody brilliant." —*The Calgary Herald*

"Ronnie Burkett is a national treasure and *Street of Blood* should not be missed… you will be challenged, moved and, in a final redemptive scene, uplifted. If you've never seen one of his shows, be prepared to be astonished."
—*The Edmonton Sun*

"Never one to be accused of lacking chutzpah or vision, Burkett reigns over an exotic stage universe awash in rage, lost faith, and blood. His artistry is beyond question. It's a tour de force of imagination." —*Winnipeg Free Press*

"It is a remarkable mixture of the gothic and the homespun, the camp and the heartfelt, the outrageous, the acidly funny, and the quietly touching. It nuzzles at your heart and takes a great big bite out of it." —*The Guardian* (UK)

D1500701

Happy

"Alternately profane and poetic (and sometimes both simultaneously), *Happy* emerges as the gentle voice of reason in Burkett's examination of the power of memory to both heal and imprison."
—*Toronto Sun*

"There are quite wrenching moments of exquisite sadness—others of such exultation that you can feel your heart beating in your chest." —*The Edmonton Sun*

"*Happy* is, quite simply, the richest, most emotional experience I've had at the theatre all year. It contains so much humour and yet so much pain, so much theatrical inventiveness and yet is governed by such a sense of humanity that, even though it's a play about death and loss, it's executed so beautifully that it becomes an affirmation of the glory of being alive."
—*Vue Weekly*, Edmonton

"Ronnie Burkett creates a world on stage that is urban, surreal, and deeply emotional all at once.... In short, Ronnie Burkett is stretching the possibilities of theatre and puppetry with every new work. *Happy* is just the latest step in what will hopefully be a long journey of experiment and innovation."
—Becky Johnson, www.MyTo.com

"...in the hands of this master showman we are privileged to enter a remarkable Lilliputian world peopled by creatures with big, beating hearts."
—*Edmonton Sun*

Provenance

"Burkett's status as a true theatre renegade is confirmed with *Provenance*."
—*Edmonton Journal*

"With Burkett you always have the sense of a prodigious talent fretting about, worrying, testing the nature of that gift. He never takes it for granted, and that is beautiful."
—*Edmonton Journal*

"In this world premiere of his latest work, *Provenance*, Burkett immediately establishes his singular relationship with his audience. 'Follow my voice,' he invites and then takes us on an incredible journey that probes the meaning of love, beauty, and obsession."
—*Edmonton Sun*

"There is a bewitching delicacy about these puppets, even in repose; they have been carved for character."
—*National Post*

"The logistics are mind-boggling, the execution flawless..." —*Vancouver Sun*

"...he pushes aside previous boundaries to expand the universe in which he labours."
—*Toronto Sun*

"It's theatre magic!"
—*The Globe and Mail*

STRING QUARTET

Four Plays by Ronnie Burkett

TINKA'S NEW DRESS

STREET OF BLOOD

HAPPY

PROVENANCE

Playwrights Canada Press
Toronto • Canada

PLAYWRIGHTS CANADA PRESS
The Canadian Drama Publisher
215 Spadina Ave., Suite 230, Toronto, ON Canada M5T 2C7
phone 416.703.0013   fax 416.408.3402
orders@playwrightscanada.com • www.playwrightscanada.com

For professional or amateur production rights, please contact:
John Lambert & Associates Inc.
2141 Boul. St-Joseph E. Montréal, Québec, H2H 1E6 Canada
514.982.6825 fax 514.982.6118 info@johnlambert.ca.

The publisher acknowledges the support of the Canadian taxpayers through
the Government of Canada Book Publishing Industry Development Program,
the Canada Council for the Arts, the Ontario Arts Council,
and the Ontario Media Development Corporation.

Cover and interior photos by Trudie Lee, except "Stephan and Tinka," "Tinka and Mrs. Van
Craig," "Carl and Tinka," "Tinka and Dress," and "Carousel Set" by Cylla von Tiedemann.
Cover Design/Typesetting: JLArt

Library and Archives Canada Cataloguing in Publication

Burkett, Ronnie, 1957–
String quartet / Ronnie Burkett. -- 1st ed.
Four plays.
ISBN 978-0-88754-820-8
I. Title.
PS8553.U639S87 2009   C812'.6   C2009-905617-8

First Edition: February 2010
Printed and bound in Canada by Hignell Book Printing, Winnipeg

For, and with, the army of women behind the "one-man show"

Terri Gillis, Cathy Nosaty, Kim Crossley, Iris Turcott,
Angela Talbot, Dina Meschkuleit, and Eileen Burkett

Table of Contents

❧ Introduction ❧

"Some people might think that my reach exceeds my grasp. Well, pardon my French, but isn't that the whole goddamn point of being alive?"
—Happy in *Happy*

Ronnie Burkett's remarkable puppet play *Happy*, which was first produced in 2000 and is the third of his "Memory Dress Trilogy," is named for a mysteriously positive old geezer.

Happy is an aged war vet and homespun philosopher of apparently limitless resilience who lives in a rooming house full of solitary misfits, each with their own secret story. Some are locked forever in the grey rented room called memory; time has stopped their narrative at a loss, a regret, a consuming sorrow, or a missed opportunity. Not so, Happy. He sees creative possibility. He owns his memories; he doesn't lease them by the week. "The higher I swing the clearer it becomes," he says of his dreams of flight, "behind all the gray."

In this respect at least (and only), Happy is like his creator, a questing spirit in hot pursuit of a complex, nuanced, and emotional full-colour response to life. And if Happy—followed, in a close second, by Burkett's plump prairie sage Mrs. Edna Rural of *Street of Blood*—is the most inclined to the homely epigram, he's not the only Burkett puppet to ponder the mysteries of his universe.

Everywhere in Burkett's unique marionette theatre are living, breathing characters with metaphysical doubts—about free will, about their place in the human drama, about who's pulling their strings… and why.

No wonder. To be a puppet-actor in the intricate, multi-character dramas created by Burkett is to be an existentialist, with strings attached. Burkett's diminutive, exquisitely crafted marionettes are only human, after all. And, as they create expressive, full-blooded characters you can care about, they insist on a life of their own. Which means that their relationships with their cast mates are complicated, sophisticated, and meaningful: sometimes subversive, sometimes confrontational.

In Burkett's landmark 1994 puppet fable *Tinka's New Dress*, the first of the "Memory Dress Trilogy," and inspired by the underground puppet cabarets of Nazi-occupied Czechoslovakia, the relationship between puppet and puppeteer takes on a dark, political palette. As illustrated by the plays in this volume, Burkett loves framing shows within shows. In *Tinka*, the puppet characters are themselves puppeteers, manipulating their own marionettes in this haunting theatrical meditation on the co-opting and marginalizing of artists by repressive regimes. Set in the darkening shadow of an Orwellian regime called, ominously, The Common Good, two puppeteers, childhood friends and proteges of the same old master, chart very different artistic courses in dangerous times. Fipsi conforms, and prospers. Carl resists, creating his own subversively topical versions of the classic "The Franz and Schnitzel Show."

Carl's defiance as an artist colours Burkett's spirited originality, his zest for experiment, and for his bravery about giving his small-scale actors the biggest ideas to work with. At a moment of eerie comedy in *Tinka*, tiny Schnitzel tackles the thorniest of existential questions face on. He takes it in his head to fly. Against the advice of his surly stage cohort Franz, he scrambles up the brocade curtain of his little puppet theatre to glimpse the face of his puppeteer/creator. "Maybe I am but a vessel to be filled with another's thoughts. Maybe I'm being controlled from on high," he wonders. "Why are you jerking me around like this?" The question, so puckishly presented, gets to the heart of the way characters come to life, and commandeer the stage in all forms of theatre.

This question also resonates in a unique way through the marionette canon of Burkett, a Canadian theatre renegade of startling originality and theatrical exuberance, who combines breathtaking technical virtuosity and obsessive craftsmanship with an artist's vision—as a playwright, director, and actor. The wayward artist from Medicine Hat, Alberta, has not only single-handedly wrested his diminutive actors from the grip of children's entertainment and side-show freak-dom, he's compelled them to be as large as life... and as dimensional. Burkett has given them a home on the adult stage, as expressive characters armed with compelling, human stories to tell, in challenging, full-length, multi-layered dramas.

The question remains: Who is this much-awarded international artist who has given papier mâché, string, and wood a human pulse and temperature, along with the mysterious capacity to make us care—and, not coincidentally, achieving the first-ever international recognition for the puppet as actor? Ronnie Burkett is the Canuck Prairie kid who become fatally fascinated, at seven, when the family *World Book Encyclopedia* fell open at P for Puppet. A strange and wonderful career was born in that moment.

Burkett is the prodigious, young self-educator who read *everything* about puppets, and wrote letters to the best puppeteers everywhere, claiming the right to be mentored by the artists he still calls the "old boys." By twelve he signed up for a correspondence puppetry course with the late Martin Stevens (Burkett still tucks a tiny portrait of Stevens into all his sets). By fourteen Burkett had become a touring puppeteer himself, a kids' entertainer no older than his audience, with a repertoire that came to include *The Patchwork Girl of Oz*, *Triple Fun For Everyone*, and *The Plight Of Polly Pureheart*, available at fifty bucks a performance. By nineteen the kid from Medicine Hat had moved to New York and landed a job performing with Bil Baird's company in Greenwich Village, the only permanent Equity puppet theatre on the continent.

Three years later, Burkett walked away from the big-money world of TV puppetry, and its big-mouth Muppet mafia. He moved back to Calgary, aspiring to be a *theatre* artist. Soon, he's creating, stringing, and dressing the most astonishing marionettes the country has ever seen. He's giving them individual voices. Most astonishing of all, he's reinvented the marionette body language in every subtle shoulder adjustment and flick of the wrist, in order to set them in motion in outrageously virtuoso, X-rated, multi-entendre *tours de force* that blithely break—no, explode—the ancient puppet theatre commandment about never appearing onstage with puppets.

Until then, no one had seen anything quite like the high-camp brio and flamboyance of *Fool's Edge*, a giddy *commedia* marionette musical—with Burkett as an outsized cameo player, and a banquet scene where everyone talked at the same time. Similarly, *Virtue Falls*, a raunchy, Victorian operetta with a ringleted heroine, a Mountie hero, featured Burkett as a wiseacre stage manager. Later, there would be a preposterously dexterous gothic romance/thriller/murder mystery/musical called *Awful Manors*, set in a gloomy Victorian mansion where the puppeteer, in a sly Burkett joke, was the butler, at the beck and call of seventeen characters and forty-three marionettes.

Burkett now calls this his "bad boy period," which blossomed in the Fringe venues and theatres of Edmonton, then toured, to instigate amazement across the country. As he's described it, "the desire to dazzle" by "jiggling the dollies" was giving way to other artistic impulses—with refinements of an already unparalleled technique to match. What he was after, he's said, was dramatic power, subtlety, and characters who engage their audience.

There'd been signs, of course. The emotional palette was becoming increasingly multi-hued. In Burkett's nostalgic *The Punch Club* of 1989, we're backstage with a road-weary company of thespians in the last gasps of a Punch and Judy tour that is sabotaged by a Uzi-wielding guerrilla warrior, one Bettina Tofu. Neville Newton, a classic actor/impresario of the nineteenth century mode, expired as the puppeteer released his strings. It was a powerful, dramatic moment in a piece full of ambivalence about the new order. Likewise, in *Awful Manors* (1991), the hectic energy, genre spoofing, and high-camp humour of a piece crammed with grotesques (like fey designer Nicky Naque and the sole Canadian, Phyllis Stein of the Canada Council) was shot through with moments of real heart. Mostly they had to do with the lyrical relationship between Beatrix Poppers and the love of her life, "jewel of her bosom," Eudora Bladderpots.

Then, in 1994, came *Tinka's New Dress*, "the start of what I really do," as Burkett puts it. And what he "really does," as audiences worldwide have discovered, is dramatically, theatrically, and emotionally urgent and charged performances. International recognition, such as the Best International Show Award at the Dublin Festival, an OBIE in New York, the Siminovitch Prize in Theatre, as well as Dora and Sterling Awards in Canada, alongside multiple citations in the marionette realm, confirms that the ebullient Canadian from Medicine Hat is a unique, multi-sided theatrical talent.

At the outset of *Tinka*, Burkett enters, threading through the gilt horses and rabbits, people old and young, slowly revolving on a twinkling, tarnished Victorian carousel. We watch Burkett's thirty-seven puppets, including a pair of contrastive puppeteers, explore dissent and the price of resistance in the shadow of the Holocaust. The virtuosity is as remarkable as ever, with longer-limbed marionettes that are physically expressive in every incline of head, tip of shoulder, or bend of knee. What's new is our connection with the drama. A playwright's voice and vision had emerged to cohabit the stage with a master performer who was, we suddenly realized, a bona fide actor among actors.

Soon we would see, in Burkett's *Street of Blood*, a wildly audacious "Prairie gothic epic" that embraced religion, gay terrorism, vampirism, AIDS, and the blood supply. We'd engage with an amusingly conservative matron, Mrs. Edna Rural of Turnip Corners, Alberta, as she transcended the limits of her jellied salad vision of the world, to achieve a kind of grace. And we'd watch the puppeteer/provocateur as Jesus, attacked by a vampiric showgirl for his policy of non-intervention in human affairs.

In *Happy*, we'd wonder, along with the characters, about grief and the mysterious human capacity for happiness. And we'd watch as Antoine Marionette presides, as MC, over a "Grey Cabaret" of memory that includes such morbid acts as Miss Cleo Paine (Queen of Denial), or tragic cellist Jacqueline Dupressed. Burkett's humour, as always, is quicksilver. But the elegant sparseness in stagecraft and design—the stage as a kind of cabinet, with memory "drawers"—speaks to a more austere notion of the puppet as actor, and performance as fully formed theatrical production.

Provenance, which premiered at Edmonton's Theatre Network in 2003, opens with an instruction that could hardly be more radical in the boldly visual marionette world: "follow my voice." Thereafter we follow plain Jane Pity Beane, a Canadian art history grad student who is inspired by a mysterious painting of a boy, and embarks on a quest through old Europe with its legacy of war, age, and loss to find the object of her desire. What she's truly after is an understanding of our attachment to beauty.

Ah, the beautiful. Burkett's attachment to beauty—and his sense of a full human spectrum of the beautiful that includes startling ugliness and homely insight—weaves through his theatre, linking the stage to the carpentry shop and the costume studio. Always we see the gorgeous, witty detail of Burkett's impeccable craftsmanship in sculpting and dressing his cast, down to the last fishnet stocking, sneaker lace, ball cap, and lacy knicker. The aristocracy of Canadian theatre artisans and craftsperson's labour come together to execute Burkett's designs, from tiny green room divans to mirrored boudoirs.

We see the amazing refinements of a technique that has redefined the time-honoured art of the string-puller. It can not only make a monkey skate, a cellist hurl down her instrument, and a marionette pull the strings of her own tiny marionette show, but make us forget about technique altogether. As you read the plays in this collection, that virtuosity is something you'll have to imagine, and then forget to imagine as you turn the pages.

If your average marionette has nine strings, Burkett's typically have sixteen. There are Burkett's unique hip and neck joints, and his custom-modified German airplane controls (created by Vancouver's Luman Coad) that are designed for the dramatic requirement of a marionette in each hand. As the plays in this volume indirectly reveal, virtuosity is never an end in itself. In a wonderful love scene between Tinka and Morag, for example, the drag queen who presides over the demi-monde of outcasts, Burkett simply releases the controls, backs off, and watches. The characters continue to live and breathe.

Burkett's sophisticated and simple magic breaks every rule in the Puppet Bible, a measure of the dramatic dimensions of his playwriting. Burkett's more recent works, *10 Days On Earth* and *Billy Twinkle: Requiem for a Golden Boy*, reveal a continuing dramatic momentum started by the plays in this anthology. But the turning point for this restless talent is here, in the "Memory Dress Trilogy" and *Provenance*.

As Morag, the transvestite cabaret singer of *Tinka's New Dress,* so memorably advised his puppeteer friend, "make the bastards laugh. That way they won't know you said anything important until it's too late."

It's too late. We've found out.

—Liz Nicholls, 2009

Tinka's New Dress

Note

Two sections of the play are improvised at each performance. These are the character Carl's underground "Franz & Schnitzel" puppet shows. Ronnie assumes the human portrayal of Carl for these, working on a small stage within the larger set and manipulating a cast of separate characters designed to look decidedly more puppet-like than the naturalistic marionettes in the dramatic body of the play.

The title characters are Franz, a grotesque psycho-clown and his innocent sidekick Schnitzel, an elf-like child who longs to grow fairy wings. Their debates begin each improv section, and usually centre around social and political happenings of the (present) day. Sometimes these debates are silly, bawdy, or just comic, other times they carry significant satirical bite, depending on the news of the day, the audience, and certainly the performer's whim.

There is also the "fat lady who sings" in the form of Madame Rodrigue, the resident diva. She usually makes an appearance in the first section to berate and bully the audience, training them in the fine points of how to greet a star. In the second improv she sings a song, written that day and commenting on topical news, to one of five standard bedtracks composed by Cathy Nosaty.

Other characters include the critic (usually brought onstage to comment on any particular reviewer not in the performer's favour that moment), Schnitzel's spiritual guide, Larry the Fairy, and The Judge. Interestingly, in over two hundred performances to date, The Judge has never been used.

While there is commentary on Carl's performances throughout the play, these two improvised sections have the performer playing to the audience by his wits, and serve to illustrate that Carl/Ronnie is in constant danger of crossing the line. The first section is introductory, light, and funny, while the second sequence later in the play is darker and risks a true emotional connection with the audience.

The improvs bring the struggle of the artist as commentator vividly to life and relate directly to the audience. To merely describe them, or the impact of Schintzel on the audience is impossible, but it is profoundly strong and real, and gives the struggle of Carl and Tinka within the play a deeper resonance for those watching their journey.

For the purposes of the published version of the play, the general structure and content of the improv sections are written down.

Notes On Staging

The set is a carousel, somewhere between human and puppet scale. There are twenty-one animals in two rows on the centre ring, which is flanked by an "acting ring." The entire set floor is a circle, eighteen feet in diameter. The carousel ring, thirteen feet in diameter, is set into this, but upstage of the outer ring. Therefore, the acting ring is greater at the front of the set. The entire puppet cast, including duplicates, hang from the centre poles of each carousel figure, "riding" on the animal. The carousel is faded, almost ghostly, painted in sepia tones like a faded photograph.

At the stage left side of the set, on the acting ring, is the puppet stage for "The Franz & Schnitzel Show." The cast for this segment hangs behind the backdrop of the small stage, except for Franz and Schnitzel who hang on the miniature stage. This stage unit rides around the acting ring on a fixed castor system. By simply pushing the unit, it can be moved to centrestage front, and off again, to either side.

On the front curve of the stage decking, which is one foot high, are wooden cutouts of letters reading "JAKO SVEDEK A VAROVÁNÍ." This is the Czech translation of "As a Witness and a Warning."

Present on the acting ring, and in front of the set, are seven figures, referred to as The Officer, Mother, Thin Woman, Fat Man, Thin Man, Little Boy, and Little Girl. They are self-standing, made of cloth, and completely natural in tone with no shading or colour detail. This is "The Populace." During the course of the action these figures are moved around the acting space as silent extras playing a variety of roles.

Stage directions herein are kept to a minimum. The play is performed solely by Ronnie Burkett, and reference to him is throughout the stage directions.

When a number appears after a character's name in the stage directions, such as "TINKA #3," it indicates a character represented by duplicate marionettes. This is most usually for costume changes, which require a separate figure for each. Tinka, for example, is represented by seven different marionettes.

The play progresses from light to dark emotionally, and each scene is assigned a palette dictating colours and tones for costumes to further enhance this.

Cathy Nosaty's score and Brian Kerby's lighting are integral to the overall design and performance, although lighting and sound notes within this text are referred to only when necessary to the reading.

The play is performed without intermission, with a running time of approximately two hours and twelve minutes.

Tinka's New Dress, produced by Rink-A-Dink Inc./Ronnie Burkett Theatre of Marionettes, premiered at Manitoba Theatre Centre, Winnipeg in November, 1994, with the following company:

Written, designed, and performed by Ronnie Burkett

Music and sound designed by Cathy Nosaty
Lighting designed by Brian Kerby
Stage managed by Leo Wieser (1994–1997) and Terri Gillis (1997–2002)
Movement advisory by Denise Clarke
Voice of The Common Good by Dana Brooks
Marionettes, costumes, and set designed by Ronnie Burkett

Carousel built by Martin Herbert
Marionettes built by Ronnie Burkett
Costumes and soft sculptures built by Kim Crossley
Marionette controls by Luman Coad
Puppet workshop assistance by Angela Talbot and Larry Smith

Subsequent runs include the Canadian Stage Company, Toronto; the National Arts Centre, Ottawa; the Belfry Theatre, Victoria; Theatre Network, Edmonton; One Yellow Rabbit, The Secret Theatre, Calgary; Festival de Théâtre des Amériques, Montreal; Das Meininger Theatre, Germany; Usine C, Montreal; Henson International Festival of Puppetry, New York City; Dublin Theatre Festival, Dublin; Images Festival, Holland; queerupnorth, Manchester; Festival Theaterformen 2000, Hanover; The Barbican Centre, London; and The Melbourne Festival, Australia.

Characters

STEPHAN, an elderly puppeteer
CARL, Stephan's protege
MRS. ASTRID VAN CRAIG, a wealthy patron
TINKA, Carl's seamstress sister
MORAG, a transvestite cabaret performer
FIPSI, Stephan's other protege and Carl's rival
HETTIE, a radical poet and writer
BENJAMIN, a friend of Hettie's
ISAËL, Mrs. Van Craig's nephew

Setting

A vaguely European city and an internment camp on the outskirts.

Time

Ostensibly mid-twentieth century, although possibly the present or future.

❧ Tinka's New Dress ❧

Once the house is open, and until the beginning of the play, the soundtrack consists solely of sporadic announcements from The Common Good. These are referred to as THE VOICE, and are heard throughout the show as well, seemingly with no direct relation to the action. It is intended simply to be the omnipresence of the government.

THE VOICE "For The Common Good, please have your identification card available for inspection at all times. Thank you. This has been a message from The Common Good."

"Compliance is the core of civilization. Resistance to The Common Good results in chaos. Thank you for your civility. This has been a message from The Common Good."

"Remember to travel only in those sectors as indicated on your identification card. This has been a message from The Common Good."

"Non-family groups of three or more must obtain assembly clearance from their zone commander. This has been a message from The Common Good."

"The Common Good represents the best of us all. Please feel free to report those who do not embrace our collective cause. This has been a message from The Common Good."

Once the house is full and the doors are closed, we hear a final announcement:

"This area is now secured. Movement will be monitored and discouraged. Thank you for your co-operation. This has been a message from The Common Good."

Scene One

The Park—Yellow Palette

Music begins. The house lights and stage are pre-set, fade to half, and then to black. After a brief moment in blackout, lights up revealing the faded carousel. Ronnie is standing stage right looking at the carousel. With a change in music, he notices the soft sculpture figure standing beside him. She is referred to as Mother, the only figure off the acting ring. She is standing downstage centre facing the carousel. With the music now playing the carousel theme, Ronnie places Mother on the set. He moves from figure to figure, moving them to their opening positions. The carousel does not move during the beginning of the play, however during the following scenes when the carousel is moved, the animals which have stopped centre front hold the marionettes for the scene. This is what happens on the now static carousel animals centre front. Ronnie takes the puppet of STEPHAN #1 and presents him with the final flourish of the music. It is spring. The music and leafy texture of the lights reveal this. Ronnie walks STEPHAN through The Populace. They do not speak, although he answers them as if they had. Music out.

STEPHAN   Thank you all so very much for coming. The puppets and I appreciate the generosity of your applause, and your pockets.

STEPHAN bends over to talk to a young girl:

Well, look who's here today! Tell me my dear, did you enjoy the show? Oh yes, that is funny, isn't it? When Schnitzel tries to fly, it always brings a great laugh. Yes, I will be sure to tell Schnitzel that you love him. I'm quite certain he loves you too.

To the child's mother:

It is remarkable, isn't it? How the puppets—mere wooden dolls—become so real to the children.

He turns, as if reacting to the Thin Man figure:

Oh yes, we'll be here again next week. With each spring comes a new season of The Franz and Schnitzel Show.

To a Fat Gentleman:

Oh yes, same place. I've performed in this park for… well, for almost fifty years now!

To the Thin Woman figure:

Really? You're little Zina? That precocious girl who would sit in the front row and yell every time Madame Rodrigue began to sing? And now look at you my dear. My dear! Thank you so much for coming to visit me and my players once again. Oh, I see.

He stoops down to address the Little Boy beside the woman:

So, your mother brought you to see my puppets. What did you think of them? Well, Franz isn't really a bad clown, he's just naughty. You're naughty once in a while yourself I would imagine? Yes, I will be sure to tell him that he ought to be nicer. Thank you very much for your thoughts on the matter.

A figure standing stage right of the others is illuminated by light. There is a strain of music, The Common Good theme. Until now this figure has been somewhat in shadow. Once lit, we see that he, while still in neutral cloth like the others, is more erect and official in appearance, with his hands clasped behind his back and feet astride. This is The Officer.

STEPHAN reacts to him.

No, no Officer, this is not an unsanctioned assembly. I was simply chatting with some of my audience. The puppet show. The Franz and Schnitzel Show. Yes, that's right, I am Stephan. Oh yes, sir, I do have an amusement vendor license. I keep it over here with my puppet stage, if you'd care to see it. Thank you, Officer; thank you very much. That's very kind of you. Yes, I will be sure to avoid creating any such disturbances in the future.

The special on The Officer figure fades. On STEPHAN's following speech, he is hung centrestage as Ronnie moves The Populace to stage right and stage left.

Well, my friends, I'm afraid that we must now part company. Thank you all so very much for coming to see me and my players today. I do hope that I shall see you all again very soon for another performance of The Franz and Schnitzel Show!

Ronnie takes the marionette of CARL #1 from the carousel and walks him toward STEPHAN.

CARL	Well, it appears that even the genteel and beloved Stephan is not immune from the watchful eyes of The Common Good.
STEPHAN	It was nothing, Carl. A simple misunderstanding.
CARL	It's a good thing you had the appropriate papers, Stephan. Or was that business about the amusement vendor license merely a bluff?
STEPHAN	Carl, I would never bluff The Common Good.

CARL	So you actually went out and registered yourself as an amusement vendor?
STEPHAN	Well, it is the law.
CARL	It's an insult.
STEPHAN	Oh Carl, it changes nothing. I still perform my shows. What insult is there in that?
CARL	You're an artist, Stephan! This is theatre.
STEPHAN	Carl, this is a park. And I am merely an old puppeteer performing for children on a sunny day. There is no shame in being an amusement vendor, and if that is how The Common Good needs to classify me…
CARL	Then that is where The Common Good will keep you, Stephan.
STEPHAN	Carl, I'm old. I've had a happy career. And I've been proud to share it with you and Fipsi. Soon, Franz and Schnitzel and all the other characters will belong to you both. To do as you will, and to keep our traditions alive. But I can only pass it along as I know it, Carl. Please, don't ask me to march alongside you in your cause.
CARL	I only want to take what you taught me, Stephan, and make it mine.
STEPHAN	The puppets become tangled in your ego, Carl. It's not your soapbox. It's just a puppet stage.
CARL	No. It's more than that.
STEPHAN	What then?
CARL	I… I don't know yet.

> *CARL is hung in position. STEPHAN puts his arm around CARL's shoulder.*

STEPHAN	Sweet David, do not engage Goliath in a battle unless you know that God is on your side.

> *Ronnie reaches for MRS. VAN CRAIG #1, seated on the carousel.*

MRS. VAN CRAIG
> My word, Stephan, how bold you are! How revolutionary!

STEPHAN	Mrs. Van Craig, you startled me.

MRS. VAN CRAIG
> On the contrary, Stephan, 'tis you who startles me. Public discussion of God! My word, you are more daring than I would have imagined.

STEPHAN   Thank you, madam, but really, since when is discussion of God a public offence?

CARL   Since last month, Stephan. The Common Good has forbidden public utterances of God by those not classified as Disciple Brethren or Holy Army Officers.

MRS. VAN CRAIG
    It's true, Stephan. Didn't you know?

STEPHAN   No. No, I didn't. How could I? The Common Good swept to power as God's government. Why would they now ban him?

CARL   It's us they've banned, Stephan. The Common Good has made God in their image. But they don't want their poster boy to be too common.

MRS. VAN CRAIG
    Bravo, young man! I see you've an opinion on our ruling party.

STEPHAN   Carl has an opinion on everything.

MRS. VAN CRAIG
    Carl. Yes. Your celebrated protege. Your performance of Franz in this afternoon's show was very interesting. One might almost say… bloodthirsty.

STEPHAN   Others might say out of control. Forgive me, madam. Carl, this is Mrs. Astrid Van Craig.

CARL   I know who she is. Slumming, Mrs. Van Craig?

STEPHAN   Carl!

MRS. VAN CRAIG
    Please, Stephan. I am not one who takes offence at the umbrage of youth. No, Carl, I often take the sun on days such as this, and for many years I have found enjoyment in the company of your mentor's beloved characters.

CARL   Oh brother…

MRS. VAN CRAIG
    Does it dismay you to learn that an old woman finds kinship in the antics of a few puppet players?

CARL   It puzzles me, Mrs. Van Craig, that a wealthy person would find anything in folk art. The voice of the common people.

MRS. VAN CRAIG
    I see. You praise the common man, yet you condemn The Common Good?

CARL   It's a convenient slogan.

MRS. VAN CRAIG
> The common man?

CARL
> The Common Good.

MRS. VAN CRAIG
> They are both slogans, Carl. What makes yours the more noble of the two?

CARL
> Well I… I think that it's… what I mean is, the struggle of the common man is mirrored by the… no, the good of the common man is no way reflected by the will of the… what I mean is, the common man and The Common Good… well, are… what I mean is… shit…

STEPHAN
> His militancy is still somewhat embryonic.

MRS. VAN CRAIG
> Then I await the maturity of your ideals, Carl, and the opportunity for the ensuing debate.

> *CARL and STEPHAN are now hung in position. Ronnie reaches back for TINKA #1.*

TINKA
> Carl, shouldn't we be going? Oh, hello.

MRS. VAN CRAIG
> You must be Stephan's other pupil. Fipsi, isn't it?

TINKA
> No, Fipsi is beautiful. I'm Tinka.

CARL
> My sister.

STEPHAN
> Our seamstress.

TINKA
> The puppets' seamstress.

MRS. VAN CRAIG
> My dear, are you the one responsible for Madame Rodrigue's stunning new concert gown?

TINKA
> Why, yes.

MRS. VAN CRAIG
> Well my dear girl, you are significantly more than just a seamstress. Tinka, you are a couturier. Tell me, do you ever design for people?

TINKA
> No. Well, not other people. Just myself I mean. This one is my good dress.

> *MRS. VAN CRAIG admires TINKA's dress.*

MRS. VAN CRAIG
> Just one? Well, the results are lovely. Now, I really must be going. My driver will be wondering what happened to me.

CARL	Held captive by the deviants, no doubt.
MRS. VAN CRAIG	
	Held captive? No, Carl. Captivated, perhaps.
STEPHAN	Allow me to walk you to your car, Mrs. Van Craig.
MRS. VAN CRAIG	
	Oh Stephan, do you really think I should be seen on the arm of a known revolutionary such as yourself?
STEPHAN	Why don't you risk it, madam?
	She giggles like a schoolgirl.
MRS. VAN CRAIG	
	Oh Stephan, how you talk! Well, a pleasure to meet you both. Carl. Tinka.
TINKA	Goodbye, Mrs. Van Craig. Carl.
CARL	Bye.
MRS. VAN CRAIG	
	He's quite eloquent, isn't he? Let the revolution begin!
STEPHAN	This way, madam.
	CARL and TINKA are left hanging stage left and stage right as STEPHAN and MRS. VAN CRAIG exit, seated back on their carousel animals.
TINKA	Carl, did you really have to be so rude?
CARL	Yes, Tinka, I did. She needs to learn.
TINKA	What? That you're rude?
CARL	That her wealth is no longer an asset. It's a vulgar handicap.
TINKA	Carl, stop it. You need her, people like her.
CARL	I don't need anyone like her. I don't want my audience to be fat and pink and polite. I'm not a court jester for the rich.
TINKA	Carl, you're a performer. And a performer needs an audience who will pay to see them.
CARL	Tinka, didn't I promise to take care of you? Haven't I always taken care of you?
TINKA	Yes, always, but…
CARL	But what then, Tinka?
TINKA	Carl, I worry about you. It's not a good time to be controversial.

CARL   It's the times that have made me controversial. Oh, Tinka, I can't explain why I need to do it this way, but I know you understand. Don't you?

              TINKA nods.

              Then let's leave it at that. Please. I can't talk about it. Not now. Not before I have to go and do it.

TINKA   Did you tell Stephan?

CARL   I was about to, but that woman interrupted us. Look, if it's a success, I'll tell him about it. And if it's a complete failure, he'll never know.

TINKA   I'm quite sure he already knows.

CARL   How?

TINKA   Fipsi.

CARL   How did Fipsi hear about it?

TINKA   Carl, you're doing a midnight puppet show in a cabaret. It may be offbeat, but it's certainly not a covert activity.

CARL   Yet.

TINKA   You wish!

CARL   Do I, Tinka?

TINKA   Sometimes I wonder.

              Carousel music begins and lights on the acting ring dim. Both puppets are placed in their original starting positions on the animals. Ronnie kneels at centre and pushes the carousel into the second position. Once this is completed, the music and lights shift, becoming more "cabaret" in tone, suggesting the world of the nightclub into which we are now being drawn. It is late night, and the lighting reflects the entrance to a seedy club. The Populace are moved into their cabaret positions, children off to the side, the adults by the carousel pillars.

Scene Two

Outside the Cabaret—Red and Blue Palette

MORAG is obviously male, but dressed in a turban and an elaborate feminine dressing gown. Underneath the loosely-belted gown we see men's boxer shorts and a singlet; fishnets and flat slippers. Ronnie takes the puppets off the animals on the carousel. CARL #2 is placed face out, slightly downstage. MORAG #1 walks toward him as the music flourishes and ends.

MORAG	Darling, there you are! Carl, what are you doing out here? You're on after my next number.
	CARL looks at MORAG.
CARL	In that?
MORAG	Let me be the bitch, Carl. I've had far more practice.
CARL	Shouldn't you be padding something, Morag?
	MORAG looks at CARL's crotch.
MORAG	Some of us opt for a more subtle approach.
CARL	Sorry hon, no padding there.
MORAG	*Mon Dieu!* A genius, and he's hung! Which will bring you the greater fame, I wonder? Strange, Carl, well-endowed men usually lack ambition. They don't need it. No, ambition is for their admirers. Alas, darling, it's those of us who are genitally challenged who strive so for success.
CARL	You call this success?
MORAG	I'm my own man. I call the shots around this dump and I do things my way.
CARL	Well Morag, that's all I'm after.
MORAG	Well then darling, big or small, I suppose we meet somewhere in the middle.
CARL	And isn't that what society should be?
MORAG	Carl please, I've got to put on a wig, a dress, and enough makeup to sink a battleship. Don't get profound on me now.
CARL	Sorry, I'm a bit nervous.
MORAG	Well darling, it's natural to be nervous on one's big opening! Take a tip from the pros. Some do deep breathing exercises backstage, others say a prayer, most smoke. Me, I pee. I always make a little tinkle before going onstage. And voila, darling! I'm a star!
CARL	"Tinkle, tinkle little star…"
MORAG	You really are a hateful man.
CARL	I love you, Morag.
MORAG	And I adore you, old friend. Welcome to the club, Carl!
	They embrace. MORAG looks at The Officer figure, stage right.
	Wouldn't they just love this little tableaux? Mister and Mister Common Good.
CARL	You be the common, I'll be the good.

MORAG You'd better be, darling, you'd better be. I'm risking my swan-like neck putting you on the bill tonight. What was I thinking? A puppet show. By an unknown. And worse, an unknown with ideals!

CARL And I appreciate it, Morag.

MORAG Well then, just remember. If they run us out of town, Carl, there's nowhere left to go.

Cabaret music from within, MORAG yells back.

Keep your knickers on, luvvies, I'm coming! There's my cue, darling. I've got to get into my drag. I'm doing the dance of the six veils tonight.

CARL Six?

MORAG Cutbacks darling, always cutbacks. Be brave out there tonight, Carl.

He starts off.

And remember, darling, make the bastards laugh. That way, they won't know you said anything important until it's too late.

Turning upstage.

Coming! Oh, and Carl, please don't flush in the middle of my number. It's one thing to play in a sewer, but it's far too embarrassing when the toilet gets a bigger round of applause!

MORAG is placed back on the carousel. Ronnie walks though the carousel and picks up the puppet of FIPSI #1 who enters upstage right on the acting ring.

FIPSI Carl.

CARL Fipsi. Hey, thanks for coming.

FIPSI I'm not here for your little show, Carl. Please, pack it all up and let's get out of here before it's too late.

CARL Relax, Fipsi, they don't enforce curfew in this sector. They just lock it up. I'll walk you home in the morning.

FIPSI Carl, what you're about to do here tonight is dangerous. It's not going to give you any sort of a career.

CARL I don't want a career. Art isn't a vocation Fipsi, it's a discussion.

FIPSI Of what, Carl?

CARL Of the sacred versus the profane. And for that, all I want, all I need, is an audience.

FIPSI At what cost?

CARL	Art should be free, don't you think?
FIPSI	Well excuse me, Mr. Artiste. My, my, Carl, I'd failed to notice. You've really chosen a temple of art for your debut, haven't you? With a two-drink minimum.
CARL	Look, these people have taken a risk to be here. I can't wait to talk to them.
FIPSI	Risk! Everything always has to be a risk with you. Why risk everything?
CARL	Why not? I can't be like you. "Yes, Stephan, I'll do it exactly the way you do it. No, Stephan, I won't change the characters a bit. Of course, Stephan, they're just puppets." Face it, Fipsi, you never risk a thing!
FIPSI	I'm here now.
CARL	To save me? Or to watch me fail?
FIPSI	How dare you!
CARL	Sorry. Look, Fipsi, I appreciate that you're here, but I think we both know what this is really all about. You're jealous. You've always been jealous of me.

She turns quickly and starts toward him.

FIPSI	You arrogant…. Do you think it was easy always being the "other" protege? Do you think it was easy watching you, the gifted boy-wonder, do everything so effortlessly, so artfully, while I struggled to learn mere craft? To do one thing that might make the old man happy? Yes, Carl, I am envious of your gift. But I'm not so jealous that I would let it overpower my admiration for you. Please, Carl, I beg of you, don't do this. Don't go in there. Not with these people.
CARL	Fipsi, these are my people.
FIPSI	What? Outcasts and perverts and queers?
CARL	Come on, Fipsi, you know that I'm…
FIPSI	Yes, I know you're… different. But Carl, you're a decent one. You fit in. Why, you look almost normal. You don't wear your sickness on your sleeve like so many of them do.
CARL	Well, maybe it's time I started.

He turns to walk away.

FIPSI	They'll stop you, Carl. Any way they can, they will stop you now.
CARL	What's to lose, Fipsi? Like you said, I'm different. In their eyes, I'm already dead.

An announcement is played:

THE VOICE   "This sector will be closed, beginning in ten minutes. This has been a message from The Common Good."

FIPSI   All right, Carl, that's enough.

CARL   There's curfew. Go on, Fipsi, get out of here.

FIPSI   Carl, please...

CARL   Good night, Fipsi.

FIPSI   Goodbye, Carl.

                She exits.

CARL   Well... here goes.

                There is a brief musical fanfare and we hear MORAG's voice as the lights fade to black. Ronnie replaces the puppets to their original positions on the carousel. He clears The Populace upstage and crosses over to the Franz and Schitzel stage.

MORAG   *(off)* Ladies and gentlemen, and all you real women too, we have a new performer here at The Penis Flytrap tonight. So I'd like you to put your hands above the table and give our new cummer a warm welcome on his big opening. Darlings, I give you Carl and The Daisy Theatre!

Scene Three

The Franz and Schnitzel Show—Puppet Palette (Black and White with Orange and Pink)

The quirky theme music for The Franz and Schnitzel Show plays. The lights flash and chase across the carousel as Ronnie moves the Franz and Schnitzel stage into position centrestage.

This scene is improvised, usually lasting approximately twenty minutes in length. The scripted text following is based upon a general format that has evolved through performance.

Lights up on the Franz and Schnitzel stage. Ronnie is standing behind a gold curtain visible from the chest up. He holds FRANZ stage right, and SCHNITZEL stage left, standing in front of the curtain.

FRANZ   Schnitzel, do you smell what I smell?

                SCHNITZEL sniffs the air.

SCHNITZEL   No Franz, I don't smell anything.

FRANZ   Ah Schnitzel, it's the most beautiful smell in the world!

SCHNITZEL	What is it?
FRANZ	You have to get close to the source, and inhale.

FRANZ moves centrestage and inhales deeply.

SCHNITZEL	What is it, Franz, what is it?
FRANZ	It's an audience!
SCHNITZEL	What does it smell like?
FRANZ	It's the most beautiful smell in the world, Schnitzel! Some of them are nervous, some are excited. Some are wearing expensive perfume, others have pomade in their hair. Some of them have bathed, others have the scent of a long day on them, but it all combines into one glorious aroma, and oh, Schnitzel, look what it's doing to me now!

FRANZ has begun to rock, his pelvis moving back and forth.

SCHNITZEL	No, no! Not that!
FRANZ	Yes! My diamond pants are doing their magic dance again! I've got a woody, I've got a woody! Okay, Schnitzel, get to work!

FRANZ starts to leave.

SCHNITZEL	No!

FRANZ turns.

FRANZ	What did you say to me?
SCHNITZEL	I… said… no.
FRANZ	Where the hell did you learn a word like that?
SCHNITZEL	I don't know, Franz. It just popped into my head.
FRANZ	That's ridiculous, Schnitzel, your head is empty!
SCHNITZEL	It's true, Franz, it is. I just thought it.
FRANZ	You're a puppet, you can't have thoughts of your own.
SCHNITZEL	Lately I've been having all kinds of thoughts. And right now I'm thinking no. No, no, no!
FRANZ	Schnitzel, don't do this to me. Not now!
SCHNITZEL	I'm sorry, Franz, but I can't do it. I just can't.
FRANZ	But Schnitzel, you always do it. Every show, it's the same thing. I go backstage while you stand out here and act so cute that invariably after the show one of these good people wants to hug you, to kiss you. And just when they're bending over to cuddle you, I jump them from behind and do my diamond pants dance all over them!

SCHNITZEL	No! I refuse to be a pawn in your sick puppet games ever again!
FRANZ	What are you saying?
SCHNITZEL	I've been thinking that maybe I should, well…
FRANZ	Yes?
SCHNITZEL	That perhaps I should…
FRANZ	What?
SCHNITZEL	That maybe it's time for me to strike out on my own.
FRANZ	Oh, I should have known it would come to this.
SCHNITZEL	What do you mean?
FRANZ	Well, it's pretty obvious what your problem is!
SCHNITZEL	Problem? I wasn't aware that I was the one with a problem!
FRANZ	Oh please, Schnitzel, it's all because of where you stand in life.
SCHNITZEL	What's wrong with where I stand? This is where I've always stood. Stage left.
FRANZ	Yeah, well no one stands on the left anymore.
SCHNITZEL	No? Where do they stand?
FRANZ	Over here, on the right.
SCHNITZEL	What's so great about the right?
FRANZ	There's more of us, and we're organized! And besides, we have God on our side!
SCHNITZEL	God doesn't take sides. He's right in the middle.
FRANZ	Not anymore. But I'll tell you what I'm going to do, Schnitzel. I am going to be such a good friend to you. I am going to trade places with you for a moment so you can try out the wonders of the right.

He crosses to stage left.

	But make it snappy, because I can't stand on the left too long. Suddenly I feel warm and gooshy and I love humanity, and I hate that shit!
SCHNITZEL	Gee, I dunno, Franz…
FRANZ	Come on, move it! Any minute now I may want to hug a tree or care about someone other than myself!
SCHNITZEL	Okay, I'm going.

He strikes a pose, and with melodramatic underscoring and moody lighting begins a "dramatic" cross to stage right.

Thus begins my journey to the right! Slowly I push my way through change and progress, saying "Back, change, back! Be gone!" as I travel to a time where nothing changes, where everything stays the same...

FRANZ Cut the dramatics, would you!

Underscoring ends abruptly. Light restores.

Okay, there you are on the right. Tell me, Schnitzel, how do you feel?

SCHNITZEL I feel kind of cold.

FRANZ That's good, that's necessary. What else?

SCHNITZEL Suddenly I don't care about anyone but myself.

FRANZ Yes, good, Schnitzel! Anything else? Share. Oh shit, that's a "left" word!

SCHNITZEL Well, is it my imagination, Franz, or, on the right, am I becoming whiter?

FRANZ Ah, Schnitzel, you're on the right track now!

SCHNITZEL races back to stage left.

SCHNITZEL No, I can't stay there! It doesn't feel like home.

FRANZ goes back to his side.

FRANZ Nowhere would feel like home to you. You're a freak, Schnitzel. You don't fit in anywhere. Now look, I have to go backstage and figure out tonight's show.

SCHNITZEL But Franz...

FRANZ We'll discuss this later, Schnitzel. You want to leave the show, fine. But for now, we have an audience. So you stay here and entertain them, understood?

SCHNITZEL Yes, Franz.

FRANZ Good.

He starts to leave.

Oh, and Schnitzel, while you're at it, do something cute so maybe one of them will come backstage and do the magic pants dance with me!

He exits, laughing maniacally. SCHNITZEL walks to centrestage and addresses the audience.

SCHNITZEL Ladies and gentlemen, allow me to apologize for my colleague's unruly behaviour. In case you haven't figured it out yet, I'm the good one. Hi, everybody. Wow, look at you. What a sophisticated, hip, urbane, tony crowd with a high disposable income you are. But no matter how sophisticated you are, I know that ever since I've been standing onstage, you've all been wondering the same thing: "What the hell is that thing!"

He sits on the little chair upstage centre.

Don't worry, it happens to me all the time. Truth be told, my friends, I don't know what I am. I never have. Which is not to say I don't have dreams and aspirations of what I would like to become. You heard Franz. I don't fit in, I don't belong here. I've never belonged anywhere. So I don't want to be here. I want to be up there.

He looks and points upwards.

I want to get above it all. I want to fly. I want wings. I want to be a fairy! I want to soar through the sky with the birds and the planes and the bumblebees, without a care in the world, up there in the air. And I want to swoop through the clouds, looking down on humanity and yell: "Hey people, look at me! It's Schnitzel!"

He makes the sound of a large bull's-eye spit on the crowd. He looks up sheepishly.

But you'll notice upon closer observation my friends…

He turns around.

I don't got no wings. Oh, I know I have a cute little bum, but that's only part of being a fairy.

He sits.

Lately, I've been having the strangest thoughts. And that I should have a thought in the first place is strange in and of itself. My head is literally an empty shell. I shouldn't be thinking anything. So, I've begun to wonder if perhaps these thoughts aren't my thoughts at all. Maybe they've been put there by some greater power. Maybe I am but a vessel to be filled with another's thoughts. Maybe I'm being controlled from on high. Maybe I'm just a spokesperson for someone who's too afraid to come down here and say these things himself. And if that's the case, then sometimes I feel like looking up and screaming…

He stands, looking up.

Why are you jerking me around like this?!

So I've decided. I'm going to climb this gold brocade curtain and see if anything, or anyone, is up there. I want to see the face of my creator. And if I don't make it, if I should fall to the ground and shatter into a hundred broken pieces before you and still continue to talk, then we'll all know it's greater than just you and me. Wish me luck.

He stands on the little chair, and with some effort, climbs up the back curtain. Struggling to the top, he grasps the top of the leaning rail and looks at Ronnie's face.

Wow. He's real. And much older that you'd expect. Excuse me, I need to ask a favour. I'm Schnitzel and I think you've made a mistake. I don't belong down there. I belong up here, with you. So if you could, please, give me my wings.

Ronnie releases the marionette control slightly, and SCHNITZEL begins to slip.

No! Please, don't do this. Don't make me go back there. Don't let go of me, I beg you. Please!

He slides all the way down the curtain, landing onstage.

I hate when he lets me down.

He struggles to his feet, and sits in the chair.

I'm sorry. I shouldn't expect you'd care. I know you didn't come here tonight to listen to me whine and moan. I know why you're here. You've come to see The Franz and Schnitzel Show! So my friends, you will have the spectacle you've paid money to see. Any minute now, I will raise this gold brocade curtain and dazzle you with the variety of acts for which we have become internationally famous! Clowns, contortionists, jugglers, and showgirls! Singers and dancers in an extravaganza the likes of which you've never seen! So, without further ado, let us raise the gold brocade cur…

From offstage, we hear MADAME Rodrigue.

MADAME	*(offstage)* Darlings!

SCHNITZEL, horrified, leaps to his feet.

SCHNITZEL	Oh no!
MADAME	*(offstage)* Oh my beautiful darlings!
SCHNITZEL	No, it can't be. That's Madame Rodrigue, the fat lady who sings!
MADAME	*(offstage)* Darlings, I'm coming to see you!
SCHNITZEL	Oh no, this is terrible! She can't come out now. It's too soon. When the fat lady sings, you know what happens. It's over!

MADAME enters, stage right. Her presence, physically and vocally, is overpowering.

MADAME	Darlings! I'm so happy to see you!
	Her bosom heaves and flutters.
	And now, I shall sing!
SCHNITZEL	No! Madame Rodrigue, you mustn't sing!
MADAME	But Schnitzel, why not? Look at them. So beautiful, so eager. I cannot disappoint them. They've come to hear their beloved diva.
SCHNITZEL	Yes, that's true, but…
MADAME	And so, I sing!
SCHNITZEL	No, not now. It's too soon.
MADAME	But why make them wait? Why torture them any longer?
SCHNITZEL	Well, because…
MADAME	Yes?
SCHNITZEL	Um, because… well… because… they didn't greet you properly, Madame.
	She looks at the audience, then whispers to SCHNITZEL.
MADAME	Schnitzel, you're right. Who are these people?
SCHNITZEL	Bus tour? Subscribers? Americans?
MADAME	Ah! That explains everything. There's only one thing to be done.
SCHNITZEL	Punish them by walking offstage in a huff?
MADAME	No, better than that. I will teach them how to greet a superstar!
SCHNITZEL	What?
MADAME	Schnitzel, it's not their fault. Look at them. They're normal. And I am great. So great that I will rise to the occasion and teach them what they need to know!
SCHNITZEL	Okay. I'll help you.
MADAME	No, I work alone.
SCHNITZEL	But, I really think I should.
MADAME	Schnitzel, it takes two hands to make my boobies go up and down, and they love that. So get off the stage!
SCHNITZEL	Um, sure thing, Madame.
	He walks to the edge of the stage, and whispers to the audience.
	Ladies and gentlemen, it appears that I must vacate the stage, but I must ask you for a favour. Please, no matter what happens out

here, do not let Madame Rodrigue sing this early in the show. Do you promise?

Invariably, someone yells "I promise."

Well don't yell it, she'll hear you! Do you promise?

Audience members whisper "I promise."

Thank you, everyone. I'll see you later. Bye!

He runs off, stage left. MADAME watches him leave, then fixes her gaze on the audience.

MADAME My darlings, there are certain rules and traditions in the theatre which must be upheld at all times. One of the most popular, for both audience and artist alike, is the greeting of the superstar diva! Since this didn't happen naturally and spontaneously when I first graced the stage tonight, I shall now have to browbeat and bully you into doing it properly.

But not to worry, my beautiful darlings; Madame Rodrigue will make it easy for you. I will break it down into three easy steps. We shall learn each step individually, and then we'll put it all together. What fun for you. Let's begin!

Step one. Before I came out tonight, I had the great good courtesy to warn you of my impending arrival. I stood backstage and cried, "Darlings, I'm coming to see you!" Now, this is the part of the show when you get so excited you say to yourself, "No! It can't be! Not tonight. Not at these insanely low ticket prices would a superstar diva actually come out onstage and sing for a nobody like me!" But you hear me, calling from backstage, so it must be true. And in your excitement, you nudge the person sitting beside you three times in the ribs, like so:

Her elbow makes a "nudging" action.

"Nudge, nudge, nudge. Could it be? Could it be?!"

Now, we're going to give this a test run. But first, some tips on technique. I find it very helpful if you verbalize the nudge as you physicalize it. So, when doing step one, you must say, "Nudge, nudge, nudge," followed by your squeal of delight with, "Could it be? Could it be?!"

Now, of course, if you have people sitting on both sides of you, you will do the double-armed nudge, like so?

She nudges with both elbows.

"Nudge, nudge, nudge," which, by the looks of it, to many of you would be called dancing.

We are going to give this a try. But first, a word of warning. If, for any reason, some of you decide not to participate in "Nudge, nudge, nudge. Could it be? Could it be?!" be advised that Madame Rodrigue will have the house lights turned up and I will make you stand up one at a time to do it properly. You think I'm kidding? Try me. Don't fuck with a puppet! You'll only get splinters. I can hear you. I know what you're thinking. "Oh Madame, surely you're not so drunk with power that you would embarrass your beloved audience?" Well I can, and I will. It's one of the perks of being a diva. For you see, back there at the rear of the theatre, is a lovely man operating the lights. And as always happens to Madame when she performs in any theatre, someone on the crew falls hopelessly in love with me. It's true. Why just last night, that dear man pounded on my dressing room door for three hours! I finally let him out. But he adores me nonetheless, and if I ask him to turn the lights up on all of you, he will! So let's all just do it properly the first time and no one will get hurt.

Here we go, on the count of three. One, two, three: "Nudge, nudge, nudge. Could it be? Could it be?!"

> *Depending on how well (or poorly) the audience participates, MADAME will either commend them on their effort, chastise them accordingly, or single out specific culprits to stand up and do the action solo.*

Very good, my beautiful darlings! So, onward. Step two. Once you have heard my voice backstage and start nudging in anticipation, you work yourself up into an absolute frenzy when I actually come onstage. Well, I don't "come" onstage, I arrive, but nevertheless it's very exciting for you. I appear from behind the curtain and stand here...

> *She walks to stage right.*

...striking a humble little superstar diva pose like this!

> *One arm is thrust into the air triumphantly.*

Look, I shaved for you people tonight! Seeing me here, standing before you onstage, sends you right over the edge and you involuntarily and spontaneously cry out: "It is! It is! It's Madame Rodrigue!"

Now, my darlings. A tip on getting your voices into the higher octave required to successfully master this step. I myself am a trained professional, but you, my darlings, are merely the public. So listen carefully. I personally find it very helpful if you clench your sphincter with all your might while screaming. How many nights have I said that? But anyway, by tightening up, it allows you to get it up so your voice will sail high and free. Trust me, darlings, master this technique and you will squeal like a twelve-year-old girl on a pony ride!

Let's give it a try, on the count of three. One, two, three: "It is! It is! It's Madame Rodrigue!"

> *As before, the success of the audience attempt dictates MADAME's response to it. She will often have the men in the audience try it once by themselves.*

Marvellous! We have now reached the most exciting part of how to greet a superstar diva. I will make my way to the centre of the stage, but I do not just clomp over there. No! I do not just walk. No! I float, I fly, I sail on the wings of your love, which translated into theatre parlance means you clap.

Don't do it yet, I'm explaining. Now, as I make my way to the centre of the stage, you begin to applaud. I walk, you applaud, I walk, you applaud, I walk walk walk, you applaud applaud applaud. When I reach my destination, a simple little superstar diva spotlight will come on, at which point I will bow a humble little superstar diva bow. I bow to you here, I bow to you there, and I say: "Stop! Stop it! You're too kind, oh stop!"

Now, this is the part of the show when so many people get confused. When Madame Rodrigue says: "Stop! Stop it! You're too kind, oh stop!" some people actually do. No no no no no. Darlings, when a superstar diva says: "Stop! Stop it! You're too kind, oh stop!" you think to yourself "No! My diva is displeased. My adoration is not enough for her. She will leave the stage in a diva-esque rage unless I make her stay!" So you begin to applaud even louder, you whistle and cheer, you stamp your feet, you clap until your hands bleed, and only when Madam Rodrigue sits down on the little bench, like so…

> *She sits.*

…do you stop applauding. Could anything be simpler? Now, we're going to put all three of these steps together and have a little rehearsal of the entire sequence of how to greet a superstar diva. I'll go backstage, I'll say "Oh my darlings, I'm coming to see you!" you'll say, "Nudge, nudge, nudge. Could it be? Could it be?!" I arrive onstage and strike a humble superstar diva pose, you scream, "It is! It is! It's Madame Rodrigue!" music will play, I will walk, the spotlight snaps on and you applaud until you faint! Won't this be fun! Let's give it a try.

She runs offstage.

Darlings, I'm coming to see you!

Hopefully the audience knows by now to say "Nudge, nudge, nudge. Could it be? Could it be?!" MADAME sweeps in, striking her pose with one arm in the air. The audience (or part thereof) screams "It is! It is! It's Madame Rodrigue!" Epic fanfare music plays as she walks to centrestage, the spotlight comes on, she bows, and all the while the audience applauds.

Stop it! Stop it! You're too kind, oh stop!

The audience goes mad. This is milked with little regard to taste, until finally she sits. The applause subsides.

Now don't you feel like you've gone out for the night?! And what a lovely way to meet a stranger sitting in the dark beside you! Thank you, my darlings, my beautiful darlings! And because you have greeted me so warmly, in the only way that a superstar diva should be greeted, now, my darlings, now I shall give you what you want. Now I will sing!

She stands and strikes a dramatic pose, her head in profile. Upon her announcement that she will sing, one or many of the audience, remembering SCHNITZEL's exhortation to them, will blurt out "No!" MADAME does a slow burn to the audience.

What?

My darlings, you shock me. You surprise me. I had no idea that you were sophisticated. Looking at you, who would know? But you do, don't you? You know that a superstar diva should never sing this early in the show. You know that she must close the show in a glorious burst of song. My darlings, you have saved me from humiliating myself!

And I know what you're thinking. You want to cry out "Madame, no! Do not sing in that shabby, albeit fabulous, tutu you wear backstage. Go, put on your new concert gown, and come out later looking every inch the superstar diva you are and always will be!"

Fine. If that's what you want, my darlings, then that is what you'll get! I am but a humble servant to art and public acclaim. I will go backstage and prepare myself for my second coming.

She starts to leave.

And just think! When I return later in the show, you already know how to greet me! Now, send me off with your love!

She sweeps off to applause. SCHNITZEL theme music begins.

SCHNITZEL   Hi everybody! It's me, Schnitzel, and this is my cute re-entrance music.

He does a little dance. He sits on the chair as the music ends.

Wow, what a terrific audience! Thank you so much, my friends, for ensuring that Madame Rodrigue didn't sing this early in the show. And because you have been so helpful, now I will give you what you want. Now you shall have the fantastic Franz and Schnitzel Show! So, without further ado, let us raise the gold brocade cur…

We hear FRANZ from offstage, and he races in from stage right.

FRANZ   No, Schnitzel! Don't raise the curtain!

SCHNITZEL   But Franz, they're a wonderful audience.

FRANZ   Trust me, Schnitzel, there's nothing for them to see behind the curtain.

SCHNITZEL   Don't be silly, Franz, that's where all the stuff is!

FRANZ   No, Schnitzel, there's nothing back there. I got rid of everything.

SCHNITZEL   What are you talking about?

FRANZ   I sold all the scenery and costumes. I fired the band, the showgirls, the novelty acts. Everything. It's all gone.

SCHNITZEL   Why would you do a thing like that, Franz?

FRANZ   Schnitzel, you know how we thought everyone wanted to see our lavish production numbers, comic turns, and elaborate stage effects?

SCHNITZEL   Of course, that's what's made us famous!

FRANZ   Well I've been doing some research for tonight's show, Schnitzel, and it turns out that's not what these people want.

SCHNITZEL   But they want a show, Franz.

FRANZ   Yes, but not that old-style entertainment we've been doing.

SCHNITZEL   No?

FRANZ   No.

SCHNITZEL   Then what?

FRANZ   They want postmodern, new millennium, electronic Dutch dance, wank performance art!

SCHNITZEL   Huh. What's that?

FRANZ   No one really knows. And that's the beauty of it, Schnitzel! You can present anything onstage, call it that, and they'll love it.

SCHNITZEL	I don't understand.
FRANZ	Neither will they!
SCHNITZEL	It doesn't sound very entertaining.
FRANZ	Oh, it should never be entertaining, Schnitzel. See, if you give them something that's accessible, they'll call it sentimental crap. But if you give them crap that's inaccessible, they'll call it art!
SCHNITZEL	Art?
FRANZ	Art! And that's what we're going to do tonight.
SCHNITZEL	I don't know much about art.
FRANZ	You don't have to. In fact, lack of training is a prerequisite. Never let vision be muddied by technique.
SCHNITZEL	So what are we going to do, Franz?
FRANZ	It's easy. I'll put on some discordant, synthesized cello music, turn the lights down and you'll throw yourself around the stage naked!
SCHNITZEL	But that's not about anything, Franz!
FRANZ	Precisely! Which is why they'll read all sorts of things into it!
SCHNITZEL	Franz, I can't.
FRANZ	You have to. We have an audience expecting a show, and we are going to give them a show they'll never forget.
SCHNITZEL	But…
FRANZ	The only butt on this stage will be yours, Schnitzel! You want to leave the show? Fine. But for now, we're in the middle of this show and you're still one half of this team.
SCHNITZEL	Franz, I don't want to. I can't!
	FRANZ becomes frighteningly menacing.
FRANZ	Don't make me angry, Schnitzel. You wouldn't want me to get angry in front of your friends out there, would you?
SCHNITZEL	No, Franz.
FRANZ	Good boy. Now, we have to go backstage and rehearse the new show, so say goodbye, Schnitzel, and tell them you'll be back later.
SCHNITZEL	Ladies and gentlemen, um, it appears that there will be a few changes in this evening's performance, so I invite you to join us again later for the second part of the all new…
FRANZ	All nude!
SCHNITZEL	…Franz and Schnitzel Show!
FRANZ	See ya later!

The spirited Franz and Schnitzel theme music plays again, the lights flashing along in time. FRANZ and SCHNITZEL are hung onstage, Ronnie jumps down and pushes the puppet stage upstage right.

Scene Four

Backstage at the Cabaret—Rust and Blue Palette

Ronnie takes the marionettes of HETTIE and BENJAMIN off of a carousel animal and walks them around the acting ring from upstage right to downstage right as they talk.

HETTIE	Benjamin, I cannot begin to tell you how unhappy I am with you right now.
BENJAMIN	Oh, Hettie, please.
HETTIE	Don't "Hettie please" me, Ben! You knew they closed this sector when you agreed to come with me tonight.
BENJAMIN	I know that, Hettie, but it's not a good time for me to be away from home.
HETTIE	Then why did you agree to go out with me?
BENJAMIN	Have I ever said no to you, Hettie?

HETTIE flings herself dramatically against Ronnie's leg.

HETTIE	Take me, Ben! Make me a woman! I want to have your baby!
BENJAMIN	No!
HETTIE	See, you're perfectly capable of saying no to me. Now, would you relax? Lilly and the kids are already asleep. Once daylight comes, I'll walk you home.
BENJAMIN	But where are we going to sleep?
HETTIE	Sleep? Oh Ben, that's rich! You don't sleep in this sector. And besides, the night has just begun!

BENJAMIN is hung in place stage right, while HETTIE goes upstage centre to the carousel.

	Morag, you old queen! Get your saggy butt out here and let's start the party!
MORAG	*(offstage)* Hettie, please! I'm in the middle of my toilette!
HETTIE	Dames.
MORAG	*(offstage)* Dykes.

MORAG enters. They embrace.

	Darling!
HETTIE	Quite the show tonight, old girl.
MORAG	Oh stop! Did you love it?
HETTIE	What's not to love? Why, your recreation of Lot's wife looking back was breathtaking. Art at its highest!
MORAG	You know me... anything for a Sodom and Gomorrah theme onstage. Orgies always sell.
HETTIE	Your use of feathers to replicate a pillar of salt was magnificent!
MORAG	One makes do with what one has. But darling, *qu'est-ce que c'est?*

HETTIE is hung upstage centre. MORAG walks toward BENJAMIN.

HETTIE	Benjamin, meet Morag.
BENJAMIN	Morag? Not the woman who played Mrs. Lot? But you're a...
MORAG	Star?
BENJAMIN	Man!
MORAG	Darling, I'm thrilled the illusion worked for you, but surely you didn't think I was "biological"?
BENJAMIN	Oh... my... word. Wait till I tell Lilly about this!
MORAG	Lilly?
HETTIE	His wife.
MORAG	You have a wife. How... normal. Ben, excuse me for a moment, won't you? Hang around.

MORAG grabs HETTIE by the arm and walks her stage left.

Hettie, what are you doing? Bringing someone so normal to the show!

HETTIE	Relax, Morag. He's one of us.
MORAG	Straight, white, male... married. He's not one of us at all. Why do those people always have to be in our clubs? Don't they have enough places of their own?
HETTIE	By proxy he is one of us. His wife Lilly has just been classified as "racially impure." You can imagine how thrilled The Common Good was with that marriage. Especially after the third kid.
MORAG	Well, why didn't you say so!

MORAG turns and rushes to BENJAMIN.

Darling, welcome to The Penis Flytrap!

BENJAMIN	Thank you, Miss… I mean, Mister…
MORAG	"Morag" will be fine.
BENJAMIN	Morag. Thank you. Well, Morag, that show tonight was quite a revelation.
MORAG	Revelations are next week, darling. I'm still trying to get through The Great Broads of the Old Testament.
BENJAMIN	That's funny!

Pause.

Isn't it?

MORAG	It depends on your point of view, Ben.
HETTIE	I don't think The Common Good would find it too hilarious.
MORAG	Nor do I find them very amusing. So we're even.

MORAG crosses back to HETTIE stage left.

HETTIE	Still, it's pretty dangerous ground you're walking on, Morag.
MORAG	Hettie Louise McKinley! You're a fine one to lecture me about dangerous ground. Exactly how many times has your writing caused you to be thrown in jail?
HETTIE	Oh, I don't know. Thirty-three.
MORAG	Thirty-three! A significant number, wouldn't you say? Especially when it comes to crucifixion.
HETTIE	Morag, I'm not being crucified. I'm just misunderstood.
MORAG	How I long for the good old days of just misunderstood.

CARL calls from offstage.

CARL	*(offstage)* Morag, are you finished in here?
MORAG	No darling, I'm not. I'm *en déshabillé*, a disaster in fuzzy slippers.
HETTIE	Is that him?
MORAG	Carl? Yes.
HETTIE	I can't wait to meet him.
MORAG	Now, Hettie, please don't eat the young. He's different.
HETTIE	Aren't we all.
MORAG	Well, I'd better go get my titties off the table before someone cooks them.
BENJAMIN	What?
MORAG	Rice, darling. They're little bags of rice.

BENJAMIN	Huh?
MORAG	You really are crashingly naive for an outcast, aren't you? Come along, I'll show you.

MORAG grabs BENJAMIN and starts leading him off toward the carousel.

BENJAMIN	Uh, no that's fine… really…
MORAG	Oh come along, Ben, we'll have a gay old time!

MORAG and BENJAMIN are hung together on a carousel animal.

BENJAMIN	Hettie, help!
HETTIE	Relax, Ben. Believe me, you're not Morag's type.

HETTIE is left hanging onstage. CARL is taken from his animal and enters.

So, I finally meet the great man himself!

CARL	Look, if you've waited to critique me, you're too late.
HETTIE	You really are a one-man show, aren't you? Even write the reviews.
CARL	Well, I assume you saw it. Didn't go very well.
HETTIE	No?
CARL	No. At first, I thought it was the audience. But they were fine. It was me. I was trying to say too much, and, as a result, I don't think I said anything at all.
HETTIE	Trying too hard for the laughs?
CARL	That's what I do when I'm nervous.
HETTIE	Well, I'd say you have a lot to be nervous about. Look, you don't know me, Carl, but for what it's worth maybe you were trying too hard. You forgot that to most of the audience those were brand new characters. They needed time to digest them, get to know them. But you believed in yourself up there. A little too much at times…
CARL	What makes you think I want to listen to this?
HETTIE	Because it's all about you. And I think that fascinates you. Am I right?

CARL is silent.

I knew I was right. Just like you did tonight. You had something to say, and you were hell-bent to say it. And that's fine, don't get me wrong. But say it through the puppets, kid. Make us believe in

	them so much that we forget it's you. Don't forget your technique, Carl. That's what supports your voice. Or is it your calling?
CARL	I'm beginning to think it might be.
HETTIE	Pretty lonely thing, a calling.
CARL	Oh? And who are you to know anything about that?
HETTIE	I'm Hettie Louise McKinley.
CARL	The writer?
HETTIE	Oh, essayist, poet, radical, shit-disturber… writer will do just fine. But tonight I suspect I'm Hettie Louise McKinley, Welcome Wagon. Welcome to the club, Carl.
CARL	I don't follow you.
HETTIE	You will. You're in, honey. Or, you're out, depending on how you look at it. You became a card-carrying member of the outcasts the minute you stood on that stage tonight and opened your mouth.
CARL	But I didn't do anything. All I did was a puppet show.
HETTIE	Well, there's no going home now, Carl.
CARL	That's crazy. I have to go home. All my things…
HETTIE	You've got your puppets and your stage. What more do you need?
CARL	My sister, Tinka. She's here too.
HETTIE	Well then, she's in it too.
CARL	But…
HETTIE	You don't understand, do you? Look kid, there were a few Disciple Brethren in that club tonight and you can bet that by tomorrow morning you'll be on the list. If you go home, you'll be in jail. You and Tinka.
CARL	What have I done.
HETTIE	Like you said. Just a puppet show. But hey, they've set up a whole sector just for us! And believe me honey, all the fun people are outcasts. Some call it the ghetto. That's a bit too artsy fartsy for my taste. The Common Good refer to it as the Central Reprocessing Zone, but I find that a bit sterile. No, I like to call it The Camp.
CARL	That's a horrible name.
HETTIE	Not really. If you can think of it as a camp, it makes the mud and the dirt and the cold seem kinda fun, almost outdoorsy. For tonight though, we're stuck in the luxury of this sector.

She starts walking toward the carousel.

See you inside?

CARL	Where else would I go?
HETTIE	You catch on quickly, kid. But don't sulk too long… the party's for you.

HETTIE is hung on the carousel. TINKA #2 is taken off and walks to CARL.

TINKA	Carl, come inside. Let's celebrate your success.
CARL	Oh, Tinka, there's nothing to celebrate.
TINKA	Yes there is. You did it. Tonight you made Franz and Schnitzel your own.
CARL	Tinka, I've done a terrible thing. I didn't think. I only thought about myself. I didn't take care of you.

She walks to him and places a hand on his shoulder.

TINKA	Maybe it's my turn to take care of you, Carl. Maybe that's why I packed our clothes in the puppet trunks this morning. I hear it gets awfully cold in The Camp.
CARL	How did you know?

She walks to centrestage.

TINKA	Carl, I knew. I've always known that when you finally took your big risk, it would be the beginning of a new life for us again. Do you hear me? For us, Carl. We're family. I'm with you, wherever this may lead.

Carousel music begins, softly.

CARL	Tinka, did you enjoy the show?
TINKA	Um, yes. Very much.

CARL walks toward TINKA.

CARL	But?
TINKA	Be careful what you say, Carl. We're in strange territory now.

Lights change, dimming instantly on the acting area. Ronnie hangs up the two puppets. The music becomes solo accordion, with a decidedly gypsy flavour.

Scene Five

The Camp—Green and Mauve Palette

Ronnie moves The Populace into new positions, beginning with the Boy, then the Thin Woman, the Fat Woman, the Thin Man, the Fat Man, and finally The Officer. From within the carousel ring, he takes a (puppet scale) trunk and places it upstage centre left on the acting ring. Once this is in place, he moves the carousel into the next position and the lights shift. The season is now autumn.

The figures of both TINKA #3 and MORAG #2 are taken from one animal. MORAG is without a turban or makeup this time, revealing a diminishing pate and a very distinct shadow of facial hair. However, his garb is a wildly exotic, half-finished woman's gown. TINKA is dressed plainly, her clothes somewhat drab.

As the lights and music complete their transition, MORAG is standing on top of the trunk with TINKA at ground level, fiddling with his hem.

TINKA	Morag, would you please stop squirming!
MORAG	I have to be sure that I can move, darling.
TINKA	And I have to be sure that you don't trip the minute you walk onstage. Now hold still.
MORAG	Oh, I'm too excited. Finally, a character worthy of a Tinka gown!
TINKA	Your dress for Mrs. Noah was nice.

MORAG turns and looks down at TINKA.

MORAG	My dear, that was not a dress. It was a boat. No, I will not be sad to say goodbye to the women of the Old Testament.
TINKA	Turn please.

MORAG turns around again.

Five months is a long time to do the same show.

MORAG	And that's the edited version! At least I had the sense to skip Esther. I mean really, I ask you Tinka, what kind of queen would call herself Esther in the first place?
TINKA	Well, I think you've made the right choice with Jezebel.
MORAG	Sometimes I feel as though Jezebel has chosen me.
TINKA	Oh? Because she too was a queen known for her hideous end?

MORAG jumps off the trunk and sits on it.

MORAG	Good one! I think a certain young miss has been spending far too much time with me these past few months.

TINKA sits on the other edge of the trunk.

TINKA	Well, Morag, I guess I can't get enough of a good thing.
MORAG	Nor I, petal, nor I.

MORAG puts his head on her lap.

	No, Jezebel was an outsider. A foreigner. A scapegoat. Thrown to the street as mere dog food. With each passing day, I begin to understand the old girl a bit more. And with each passing night at the cabaret, their final solution becomes more apparent.
TINKA	What are you going to do?

He sits up and faces front.

MORAG	Exactly what Jezebel did. Paint my face, and greet my enemies as a queen!
TINKA	Oh, Morag.
MORAG	Fear not, beloved. It's just metaphor. I trust there are a few in my audience who still understand that. For Carl, however, I fear it may be his undoing.
TINKA	But he's not at the cabaret anymore. It was your idea that he leave.
MORAG	Yes, and for selfish reasons.
TINKA	You were just protecting him.
MORAG	And myself. Carl was becoming far too dangerous, even for my taste. Night after night, more and more Disciple Brethren coming to see him, more and more Holy Army Officers hovering around. Luckily for us, The Common Good is too wrapped up in its own rhetoric to understand our metaphor.
TINKA	Well, he's safe here.
MORAG	No, Tinka, he's not. You're both in far greater danger here.
TINKA	In The Camp? Morag, who cares about a puppet show for displaced people?
MORAG	The Common Good cares, darling, and they're still watching. Don't you tell me this is mere entertainment. This is not some harmless little puppet show for forgotten people.

TINKA has walked toward stage left, indicating The Populace.

TINKA	But it is, Morag. Every night these people come to see Carl's show. They sit in the dirt and the cold to forget.

MORAG	And to listen. It's dangerous enough that Carl continues to speak, but perilous too for those who will listen.
TINKA	Would you want him to stop?
MORAG	Would you?
TINKA	It's beyond the point of even considering. When we first began, Carl couldn't wait to get onstage, to smell the audience, to talk to them, the sheer thrill of performing. Now, each new day brings another atrocity, another rule enforced, another freedom given away. Taken away. And he has to discuss it through the puppets. He just has to.

She sits on the trunk.

MORAG	But what about you, Tinka? I've already told you that I would protect you, as best I could. Tinka, I love you. I'm in love with you.

He turns away. TINKA reaches across the trunk and places her hand on his.

TINKA	Morag. Morag, I love you too. But really, how you go on. I'm not enslaved to Carl. I choose to be here.
MORAG	Well then, your honour, she's guilty by association!

MORAG throws himself across the trunk, landing in a dramatic, campy position.

TINKA	You're such a drama queen.
MORAG	Thank you, darling, it's a living.
TINKA	Let's finish the costume tomorrow, okay? I have some repairs to do on the puppets before tonight's show.
MORAG	Ooh, and what's on the bill tonight?
TINKA	I have no idea, Morag. Carl's out trying to find a newspaper.
MORAG	A newspaper? Well, if that's where he gets his inspiration, I'm afraid he's merely reading press releases from The Common Good.
TINKA	Not their newspapers, Morag. The underground one that Hettie writes for.
MORAG	Ah, Hettie. There's another one whose time is running out.
TINKA	Please, Morag, don't.
MORAG	I'm sorry, petal. How is the old cow?
TINKA	I don't know. We haven't seen her in a while.

An announcement is played, prefaced by The Common Good theme.

THE VOICE	"Free passage in and out of this sector will be forbidden, beginning in fifteen minutes. This has been a message from The Common Good."
MORAG	Well, there's my cue. I don't dare saunter through the gates in this ensemble. The guards can barely keep their hands off me as it is. Brutes! So, I'll leave the cossy in your tent. See you tomorrow?
TINKA	Uh huh. Have a good show tonight.
MORAG	And you, darling, and you. Whatever that brother of yours decides it to be.

MORAG walks upstage toward the carousel, where he is hung in his starting position.

TINKA	Bye.

She waves and walks to centre, then looks back to where MORAG has exited. Transition music starts and TINKA crosses to the puppet stage upstage right. She briefly stops in front of The Officer, and looks at him for a moment.

Excuse me.

She passes him and is hung near the Franz and Schnitzel stage. Ronnie walks through the carousel to upstage left, where he takes the marionettes of MRS. VAN CRAIG #2 and ISAËL #1 from a carousel animal. ISAËL is carrying two elaborate gowns. They walk through the figures of The Populace.

ISAËL	Really, Auntie, this is quite mad.
MRS. VAN CRAIG	Then let it be a mad adventure, Isaël.
ISAËL	What adventure could there possibly be in such squalor? Auntie, look at these people!
MRS. VAN CRAIG	Isaël, they are your species. And the people in The Camp are undoubtedly the best and the brightest. You could stand to learn a thing or two from them.
ISAËL	To what end? My own, no doubt.
MRS. VAN CRAIG	They are artists and intellectuals. Thinkers, Isaël. People to whom thought is the very life-breath. Really, why do you people fear them so?
ISAËL	"You people"? Auntie listen to yourself, you're beginning to sound like a… bohemian! Have you forgotten the difference between yourself and these people?

MRS. VAN CRAIG

No dear, I have not. Nor have I forgotten a time when differences were celebrated, not condemned.

ISAËL   Individuality leads to chaos. Only through collective consensus can an ordered society prosper.

MRS. VAN CRAIG

Bravo, Isaël! I had no idea that you had committed The Common Good's mantras to memory.

ISAËL   It's not a mantra, Auntie, it's a will. A unified will.

MRS. VAN CRAIG

Well, will you give me a display of this civility you hold so dear?

ISAËL   But Auntie…

MRS. VAN CRAIG

No buts! Now, I have a very good friend here, and I am not about to let you offend her with your juvenile fervour.

An announcement is played, with the musical sting.

THE VOICE   "Free passage in and out of this sector will be forbidden, beginning in ten minutes. This has been a message from The Common Good."

ISAËL   If your friend was truly of any value, you wouldn't be meeting in a place like this.

They have reached centrestage left. MRS. VAN CRAIG indicates the trunk.

MRS. VAN CRAIG

Oh, Isaël, put the dresses down before you soil them.

ISAËL puts the dresses down on top of the trunk.

ISAËL   This is quite ridiculous. There's your precious cargo. Now please, Auntie, let's go.

MRS. VAN CRAIG

You go, dear, and wait for me at the gates.

ISAËL   What? I'm not leaving you here alone.

MRS. VAN CRAIG

I won't be alone. Besides, I've been here many times, dear.

ISAËL   Oh, Auntie, what are you up to?

MRS. VAN CRAIG

Mmm, who knows, Isaël? Perhaps I'm a secret messenger for the outcasts!

ISAËL   That's dangerous talk, Auntie, even in jest. I'm not leaving until
             I meet this friend of yours.

MRS. VAN CRAIG
             You'll meet her, dear. When it's appropriate. I simply needed you
             to carry the dresses. Now go, I won't be long.

ISAËL   Auntie, for your own good...

MRS. VAN CRAIG
             My good! The Common Good! Good God, Isaël! Would you shut
             up and leave an old woman to her folly!

ISAËL   I'm... sorry.

             He starts off, toward the carousel.

             Don't miss the curfew, Auntie.

MRS. VAN CRAIG
             Isaël. Isaël.

             He pauses.

             Thank you, dear. I won't be long.

ISAËL   Crazy old woman.

             ISAËL is hung on a carousel animal.

MRS. VAN CRAIG
             Ah youth.

             MRS. VAN CRAIG walks toward the puppet stage, stage right.

             Tinka? Tinka, dear? Are you there?

             TINKA appears from behind the puppet stage.

TINKA   Mrs. Van Craig.

MRS. VAN CRAIG
             Now dear, what have I told you about that?

TINKA   I'm sorry. Hello... Astrid.

MRS. VAN CRAIG
             That's better. Now I do hope I'm not interrupting.

TINKA   No, I was just doing repairs on some of the puppets.

MRS. VAN CRAIG
             And how are my little friends today?

TINKA   They're fine, Astrid. They survive better in this place than most of
             us.

MRS. VAN CRAIG
             Ah yes, but is survival with a wooden heart a life worth living?

TINKA   It's so good to see you again.

     They embrace.

MRS. VAN CRAIG

     And you, my dear. Now come, we've not much time and I do want you to see what I've brought for you today.

     She leads TINKA toward the dresses on the trunk. TINKA sees them and rushes to them.

TINKA   Oh, Astrid, they're beautiful. They're the most beautiful gowns I've ever seen.

     TINKA kneels in front of them as MRS. VAN CRAIG comes up behind her.

MRS. VAN CRAIG

     They are very old.

TINKA   But extraordinary.

MRS. VAN CRAIG

     At one time they meant a very great deal to me. With your skill, Tinka, I hope you will recreate them into something that will be special to you.

     TINKA stands and faces her.

TINKA   No, I couldn't. Thank you, but no. These are too perfect to be changed.

MRS. VAN CRAIG

     They are too perfect not to be changed. They should live on, and they are of no use to me now. Once, as a girl your age, I wore this gown to a magnificent party.

     She indicates the darker dress.

TINKA   You must have been beautiful that night.

MRS. VAN CRAIG

     I think perhaps I was. It was at that party I first met Theo Van Craig. And a year later…

     She indicates the other dress. It is gold embroidery on aged net, in an old floor-length style.

     …I wore this. My wedding gown. It's faded, but the workmanship endures. And I'm certain there's more than enough fabric to make yourself a stunning new gown.

TINKA   Astrid, I have no need for a dress like this. Look where I am.

MRS. VAN CRAIG

> I'm giving a party next week, and I want you there. And don't tell me you have nothing to wear.

TINKA   But I don't have clearance to enter your sector.

MRS. VAN CRAIG

> That's all arranged. My driver will pick you up at the gates and bring you safely to my door. And bring Carl, won't you.

TINKA   No. That would be too dangerous for him. And you.

MRS. VAN CRAIG

> Yes, I know. I had hoped that Carl might perform at my party, but that's quite impossible. And I know it's old fashioned of me, but I was hoping you'd have an escort.

TINKA   There is someone. A friend. I could bring him, if you wouldn't mind.

MRS. VAN CRAIG

> No, not at all. Tell me, Tinka, is he special?

TINKA   Very.

MRS. VAN CRAIG

> Then I shall be delighted to meet him.

> *An announcement is played, with musical sting:*

THE VOICE   "Free passage in and out of this sector will be forbidden, beginning in five minutes. This has been a message from The Common Good."

TINKA   Astrid, you should go now.

MRS. VAN CRAIG

> Yes, I know. On one of my next visits, perhaps I'll intentionally miss that blasted curfew.

TINKA   Well then, you'd better wear something warmer.

MRS. VAN CRAIG

> Yes, autumn is upon us. Next week then?

TINKA   Next week.

> *They embrace. MRS. VAN CRAIG walks upstage, then turns.*

MRS. VAN CRAIG

> Tinka, I've sewn some money into the lining of the wedding dress. Keep Carl fed. He'll need his strength.

> *MRS. VAN CRAIG walks to the carousel, excusing herself to The Populace as she leaves.*

Good day, madam. Excuse me, dear, I'm coming through…

MRS. VAN CRAIG is hung in place on an animal. Music in: the Tinka theme. TINKA looks after MRS. VAN CRAIG, then goes to the trunk and picks up the wedding dress. She moves with the music and dances with the dress, showing it to the rest of The Populace. The action indicates a make-believe party, and TINKA curtsys and flirts with the male figures. Realizing where she is, she places the dress back on the trunk. As the lights fade to a pool over the trunk, TINKA kneels, resting her cheek on the dress. Lights fade slowly on the tableau.

The music changes to the carousel waltz. The acting ring lights have dimmed and the carousel lights have crossfaded up. Ronnie takes TINKA and the trunk and places them upstage centre, behind the carousel pole. He brings out a bench unit from upstage left. He then gathers up The Populace and arranges them on the stage left side. He grabs a bench unit from upstage right and arranges The Populace on that side. These units are two benches with large and ornate picture frames fastened behind them. The frames are empty and The Populace are seen through them. At the top of each frame are hooks from which the marionettes may be hung in a seated position. Upstage of the stage right bench, he places the Thin Man. Downstage left of the other bench he places the Little Girl.

Ronnie grabs the Little Boy figure, regarding him for a moment before placing the boy face down on the carousel ring. The carousel is revolved to the next scene.

Scene Six

The Party—Brown and Gold Palette

Ronnie takes MRS. VAN CRAIG #3 from the animal on which she is seated, lights shift and she sweeps into the centre of the acting ring. She is the consummate hostess, wearing a magnificent, albeit older-style gown. As in Scene One when STEPHAN addressed The Populace, so too does MRS. VAN CRAIG address her "party guests."

MRS. VAN CRAIG

Hello! Thank you all so very much for coming.

She walks to the Fat Man stage left and addresses him.

Doctor, how good to see you. Never better, thank you. And you? Yes, I agree. It is our country which is experiencing the poor health. One wonders whether the cancer can be defeated, or if it has spread too far.

To the Thin Woman beside him:

No madam, I do not blaspheme our government. These are but the autumnal musings of an old woman, longing for her faded springtime. What better remedy for our malaise than a party!

> *MRS. VAN CRAIG leaves them and crosses the stage, muttering to herself.*

I don't recall inviting her.

> *She reaches the figures stage right, and noticing the Mother figure, does a semi-curtsy to her.*

Baroness! My dear, how good of you to come.

> *She speaks in a more confidential tone:*

I've heard of your husband's stand against The Common Good. You are both in our hearts. My word, no, I didn't know. Exiled from the land he loves. Yes, we must hold on to that dream. Have you plans to…

> *Light and music theme up to reveal the figure of The Officer, standing upstage right. MRS. VAN CRAIG takes notice of The Officer, and walks to him.*

Good evening, Officer. May I be of some assistance? No need for that, this is a private soirée. Really? And since when has The Common Good decided to monitor private affairs? I see. Well, I trust you know how to behave yourself at such an event.

> *She starts to walk away, but turns to add:*

Oh, and Officer, I would appreciate it if you didn't help yourself to the refreshments.

> *Ronnie takes FIPSI #2 off of an animal. She is wearing a slinky and revealing gold gown.*

FIPSI   Mrs. Van Craig, what a glittering affair!

MRS. VAN CRAIG
Fipsi, what a daring gown! Tell me dear, is this the official garb of our newest State Artist?

FIPSI   No, but it is the unofficial gift of a state admirer!

MRS. VAN CRAIG
My, you certainly are reaping great rewards.

FIPSI One reaps as one sows, Mrs. Van Craig. I've worked very hard to find favour with the right people.

MRS. VAN CRAIG No doubt you have. Well, if you'd like to bring in your equipment for a show, I could have some of the staff assist you.

FIPSI No need for that. My own people are bringing it in now. The Common Good has usurped all sorts of little worker people for such purposes, which gives me ample time to mingle with your elite gathering.

MRS. VAN CRAIG Well then, we'd best find someone for you to mingle with. Oh look! There's Walter Lichtenfels.

FIPSI The composer? I've been dying to meet him.

MRS. VAN CRAIG Yes, well don't lay down yet, dear.

MRS. VAN CRAIG leads FIPSI to the stage right bench and addresses the Thin Man figure.

Walter, this is Fipsi, our newest State Artist. Fipsi, Walter, one of our oldest.

Now, get to know each other, have a great chat and excuse me if you will.

FIPSI is hung in a static seated position from a hook on top of the picture frame behind the bench. MRS. VAN CRAIG beats a hasty retreat.

Well, she certainly wears her success… obviously.

She crosses left to the other bench and addresses the child figure there.

My, you're up quite late! How grown-up you must feel.

She sits, and is hung on the hook above the bench.

We'll be having a puppet show later. No, it's not the old man from the park, but they are the same characters. Yes, Franz and Schnitzel. I like Schnitzel best too, because he wants to fly!

Ronnie leaves MRS. VAN CRAIG in her seated position and goes upstage to the carousel. He takes the marionettes of TINKA #4 and MORAG #3 off their animals. They walk a few steps into the upstage acting ring.

TINKA is wearing a beautiful dress made in the same fabric as MRS. VAN CRAIG's wedding gown. We now see MORAG in complete drag for the first time... bead and feather headdress, full make-up, heels, and a slinky gown made from the fabric of the other dress in the previous scene.

MORAG   Well, tout le town is out tonight! Tinka, be honest. Do you think I pass?

TINKA   Morag, you're the most beautiful man here tonight. I'm so proud to be on your arm.

MORAG   I'm so nervous.

TINKA   It's all right, Morag.

MORAG   Let's hope, darling. When I'm nervous, I'm really bitchy. Heaven help these poor people!

TINKA   Shall we?

MORAG   Oh, why not. It'll be a nice memory to tell the boys in prison.

TINKA   Morag!

MORAG   I feel as though everyone is looking at me.

TINKA   Morag, you're a drag queen. That's what you want, isn't it? Besides, they're just jealous that I have the most beautiful escort. Now, you wait right here. I'm going to find Astrid so I can introduce you.

MORAG   Tinka, don't leave me alone. You know I can't use the ladies' room without you!

TINKA   Relax, Morag. Nothing bad will happen. Not tonight. You're my knight in shining evening wear!

MORAG is hung on the upstage centre hook, facing toward the carousel. TINKA sees MRS. VAN CRAIG seated on the bench and walks toward her.

Astrid? Astrid, hello.

MRS. VAN CRAIG turns, still seated.

MRS. VAN CRAIG
Tinka! Look at you! Child, you take my breath away.

TINKA   Well then, you'd best remain seated. Thank you for inviting me, Astrid.

Ronnie's eyes sweep across the audience, taking them in.

I've never seen a more beautiful group of people. Are you having fun?

MRS. VAN CRAIG
Yes, it's good to do this again. Although...

TINKA   Yes?

MRS. VAN CRAIG

It's different now. In the old days, we gathered simply to be together. These days, everyone seems to have taken a side.

TINKA sits on the bench.

TINKA   Well, I'm at yours.

MRS. VAN CRAIG

And I can't tell you how happy that makes me. But enough of an old woman's reminiscences. Tinka, don't keep me in suspense any longer. Where is he? Where is this boy of yours?

TINKA turns to MORAG.

TINKA   Morag, I'd like you to meet Mrs. Astrid Van Craig.

MORAG turns grandly and bows to MRS. VAN CRAIG.

MORAG   *Enchanté* darling.

MRS. VAN CRAIG

Morag? But, you're a…

MORAG   Man?

MRS. VAN CRAIG

A star!

MORAG   I love this woman!

TINKA   I knew you would.

MRS. VAN CRAIG

You're the cabaret artiste!

MORAG   You've heard of me?

MRS. VAN CRAIG

Who hasn't? I've seen you, many times…

She looks around to be sure no one is listening.

…at The Penis Flytrap. Tell me, dear, have you gotten through The Great Broads of the Old Testament yet?

MORAG   Oh, please! I'm skipping entire sections of that dreary tome.

MRS. VAN CRAIG

Well, I simply adored your portrayal of the burning bush!

MORAG   Thank you, darling. There's not much one can do with the Ten Commandments.

MRS. VAN CRAIG

Yes, they are written in stone, aren't they?

MORAG   Touché, old thing! Tinka, where on earth did you find this
             heavenly creature?

TINKA   She found me.

MRS. VAN CRAIG
             And I never intend to let her go. Morag, I'm delighted to meet
             you. Although I'm sad to admit, that dress never looked so good
             on me.

MORAG   Go on, you old silly, we're practically twins!

MRS. VAN CRAIG
             Come, let me introduce you around.

MORAG   But darling, don't you think I'll create a stir?

MRS. VAN CRAIG
             Let's hope. This party needs a bit of a lift.

             MRS. VAN CRAIG stands.

             Tinka?

TINKA   I'll entrust him to your safekeeping, Astrid. I'd like to sit and
             watch for a while.

MRS. VAN CRAIG
             Very well, if you can trust a she-devil like me with a she-devil like
             he! Morag, shall we?

MORAG   Why not, old girl? Let's create a scandal!

             MRS. VAN CRAIG extends her elbow. They cross to upstage left.

MRS. VAN CRAIG
             Morag, when I saw you perform the parting of the Red Sea,
             I swear I've never seen so much red chiffon in my life. You really
             are a genius!

MORAG   Oh stop! You're just saying that because it's true!

             *They are hung on the carousel. TINKA remains seated on
             the bench. When Ronnie returns to the main acting area, he
             animates the figure of FIPSI, also still seated. She sees TINKA
             and turns toward her.*

FIPSI   Tinka? Tinka, darling! Is it really you? Well, you're the last person
             I expected to see tonight.

             *Ronnie moves to centrestage, kneels, and plays the following by
             turning his head from one to the other, speaking for both TINKA
             and FIPSI but animating neither.*

TINKA   Hello, Fipsi. My, we certainly are hearing great things about you
             lately.

FIPSI	Of course you have. I've been made a State Artist. My work is officially sanctioned by The Common Good, I've been given a fabulous home, a new atelier, a staff, my name is positively everywhere, and, have you heard? Next week, I begin a tour of the entire country. Fully funded.
TINKA	Yes, but are you well, Fipsi?
FIPSI	Tinka, I'm a success. How could I not be well?
TINKA	And Stephan, do you ever see him?

> *Ronnie moves toward FIPSI and she stands, beginning to cross to TINKA stage left.*

FIPSI	Stephan works for me now. I felt I owed it to the old boy. And as I'm sure you've heard, Tinka, street vendors are illegal. Besides, I'm using Franz and Schnitzel now.
TINKA	For propaganda?
FIPSI	For education, dear. I like to think that I enlighten and enrich my audience.
TINKA	That's what Carl tries to do.
FIPSI	My work is nothing like Carl's.
TINKA	No. How could it be.

> *She starts to walk away.*

FIPSI	Well, lovely seeing you again, Tinka, but I really must get ready. I'm performing this evening you know.
TINKA	Yes, so I'd heard.
FIPSI	I have the most elaborate little puppet stage! Thank goodness I've a staff to assist me. It allows me to concentrate on my acting.
TINKA	Yes, improvisation is so difficult.
FIPSI	I never improvise, Tinka. I follow the script.
TINKA	I didn't know there was one.
FIPSI	There is now, dear.

> *FIPSI starts to walk away, then turns to TINKA.*

	Tinka, if you ever feel like following the script yourself, I may be in a position to help you.
TINKA	Thanks, Fipsi, but I could never learn the lines as well as you have.
FIPSI	Maybe you should stop reading between them.

> *As FIPSI walks away, Ronnie steps on the train of her gown with his right foot, which stops her abruptly.*

TINKA	Fipsi, give my love to Stephan.
FIPSI	And my… regards to Carl.

FIPSI sweeps off to the carousel and is hung on an animal. ISAËL #2 enters. En route, he talks to the Thin Man figure upstage of the stage right bench.

ISAËL	Walter you old dog! I can't believe they let you in the door! Good to see you again, old man.

He sees The Officer.

Officer, very reassuring to see you here tonight.

ISAËL notices TINKA from across the room and crosses to her.

Good evening.

TINKA turns, a bit startled, interrupted from her thoughts.

TINKA	Oh, hello.
ISAËL	Lost in thought, or simply watching the parade?
TINKA	A bit of both. I'm just waiting for a friend.
ISAËL	I'm looking for my aunt. Mrs. Van Craig.
TINKA	You must be Isaël!
ISAËL	Guilty, I fear.
TINKA	Astrid has spoken of you many times.
ISAËL	Are you a friend of my aunt?
TINKA	I like to think so.
ISAËL	Odd that we've not met.
TINKA	Not really. My world is significantly different from your aunt's.
ISAËL	And yet, you've become close?
TINKA	We have mutual friends.
ISAËL	Ah, perhaps I know them.
TINKA	Perhaps. Franz and Schnitzel.
ISAËL	What? On no. You're that girl from The Camp.

He takes a step back. She stands.

TINKA	I'm Tinka.
ISAËL	What are you doing here?
TINKA	I was invited. I'm a guest.
ISAËL	No, I mean, how did you get here? Out of your sector.

TINKA	Thanks to your aunt's kindness, arrangements were made.
ISAËL	Illegal arrangements, no doubt. This could put you both in a great deal of jeopardy.
TINKA	Possibly, if someone were to tell. But what a cruel thing to do, don't you think?
ISAËL	I'm only thinking of what's right.
TINKA	Well, I won't put you, or your righteous thoughts, at any further risk. If you'll excuse me…

> *She starts to walk away.*

ISAËL	No, please…. Stop!

> *He/Ronnie steps on the hem of her dress. She stops.*

I'm sorry. That was uncivil of me.

> *She is silent, her back still to him.*

Allow me to begin again. I'm pleased to meet you. Well, you're a stubborn one, aren't you? Really, I am pleased to meet you. I'm pleased to meet anyone my own age. This party is so dull. Everyone is so old. So stiff. Why, even Fipsi's disappeared.

TINKA	She's getting ready to perform.

> *She turns to him.*

Are you a friend of Fipsi's?

ISAËL	I'm a great admirer of Fipsi. She does very important work.
TINKA	So she tells me.
ISAËL	You don't sound impressed by her achievements.
TINKA	It's bad enough to do mere entertainment that says nothing and call it art. But it's worse, I think, to do work that says the wrong things, and call it truth.
ISAËL	You sound like your brother.
TINKA	Thank you.
ISAËL	Oh come now, what makes you two think you're so right?
TINKA	What makes you think we're so wrong?
ISAËL	Your brother's shows are a direct commentary against the efforts of The Common Good.
TINKA	I wasn't aware that The Common Good was so fragile that it couldn't withstand a bit of examination.

ISAËL	Such examination, as you call it, can be very harmful. It causes people to doubt. And we know what that leads to.
TINKA	What?
ISAËL	Debate.
TINKA	We're having a debate now. I wasn't aware that we were inflicting any real harm on each other.
ISAËL	I have no reason to harm you.
TINKA	Precisely my point.

He comes close to her, lightly touching her back.

ISAËL	None whatsoever. You're… beautiful. And you're certainly spirited. And with a little work, you could even be an asset.

She turns.

TINKA	What?
ISAËL	Well, look at you. You clean up rather nicely for a Camp person. You're special. Not like the others.
TINKA	What others?
ISAËL	The freaks who contaminate us.
TINKA	Stop.
ISAËL	I can't stop, Tinka. You should be happy that you fit in. Not like the racially impure, or intellectuals…
TINKA	Stop.
ISAËL	…or homosexuals and deviants…
TINKA	Stop!
ISAËL	Do you know what I saw tonight? Do you? Here, at this party, I saw a man dressed as a woman!
TINKA	No…
ISAËL	Yes! A freak flaunting his disease, hoping to poison us all!

TINKA becomes very agitated.

TINKA	Oh…
ISAËL	But I protected our kind from him. I did what any decent person would have done.
TINKA	What?
ISAËL	I turned him over to the authorities.
TINKA	No! Morag!

ISAËL	What? You know that... thing?
TINKA	I'm with him.
ISAËL	I see. Well then, you should be with him, shouldn't you? In the dirt, where you belong!

ISAËL/Ronnie spits on TINKA. She falls to the ground as the lighting snaps to a pool of red around her. ISAËL storms off, hung on the carousel. TINKA struggles to her knees.

TINKA	Morag. Morag? Morag!

She is whisked off as Ronnie races to the back of the carousel. A fanfare plays and a pool of light hits centrestage. All other lights dim. From behind the central carousel pole, Ronnie has gotten FIPSI #3 and places her in the pool of light.

An announcement is played:

THE VOICE	"Patrons will now quiet themselves for an official presentation by The Common Good."

FIPSI is now dressed in a costume which is a bizarre reminiscence of the Court of Versailles, the skirt a wide hoop affair. She talks directly to the audience:

FIPSI	Thank you, and welcome to another performance of our beloved statesmen, Franz and Schnitzel.

A strange, "anthemized" version of the Franz and Schnitzel theme music plays, and continues throughout FIPSI's puppet show. The centre front panel on her skirt separates like a theatrical curtain, revealing miniature FRANZ and SCHNITZEL puppets against a backdrop inside her dress.

FRANZ	Schnitzel, you seem unhappy. Whatever is the matter?
SCHNITZEL	Oh Franz, I am sad. I'll never be a real fairy!
FRANZ	Well then, there you have it!
SCHNITZEL	What do you mean?
FRANZ	You want the wrong thing.
SCHNITZEL	I do?
FRANZ	Being a fairy won't make you happy.
SCHNITZEL	It won't?
FRANZ	No, it will only make you worse off.
SCHNITZEL	It will?
FRANZ	Of course!

SCHNITZEL	But my friends say I should be a fairy.
FRANZ	Then your friends are bad, and wrong. And they should be reported to the nearest authority at once!
SCHNITZEL	But Franz, if I'm not a fairy, what am I?
FRANZ	You're a worker, Schnitzel! For The Common Good!
SCHNITZEL	Really? That sounds important!
FRANZ	It's the most important thing there is, Schnitzel. Work makes you free!
SCHNITZEL	So by working together we're all working for The Common Good?
FRANZ	Exactly!
SCHNITZEL	I feel so much better now, Franz!
FRANZ	So do I, Schnitzel. See, we have a lot of good in common!
SCHNITZEL	And that's what makes us happy—our Common Good!
FRANZ	Thank you, and goodnight, from your Common Good.

The fanfare plays again as the curtain comes down in FIPSI's skirt. The pool of light fades to black. FIPSI is placed in the centre pillar of the carousel. The carousel music theme plays again, although it is now more sombre in tone, played on an accordion. Dim transitional lighting comes up slowly as Ronnie puts away the benches. The figures of the Little Girl, the Fat Man, and the Thin Woman are repositioned on the acting ring, save for The Officer who stands watch from upstage right.

Scene Seven

The Camp—Grey Palette

The carousel is revolved and the lights crossfade onto the acting area. Time has passed. It is late fall/early winter, late in the day. Ronnie takes the marionette of CARL #3 from an animal. He is dressed in the familiar striped uniform of Holocaust camp inmates. The music fades. CARL is facing the static Mother figure.

CARL	So, our numbers are dwindling.

He turns to The Officer.

Tell me, Officer, is it the selection program of our government which causes the audience to shrink, or merely that the showman's appeal is diminishing?

He responds to the Mother figure as if she has spoken to him.

Yes, there will be a show. There's always a show, no matter how cold it gets.

> *The centrestage carousel light comes up somewhat. We hear the voice of STEPHAN.*

STEPHAN   *(offstage)* Carl.

> *CARL turns.*

CARL   Stephan?

> *He walks toward the carousel. Ronnie takes the marionette of STEPHAN #2 off an animal and places him in the upstage acting area. They embrace.*

STEPHAN   Carl!

CARL   Stephan, what are you doing here? They haven't…

STEPHAN   No, they haven't put me in here… yet.

CARL   But how did you… who let you in?

STEPHAN   I have a pass. Briefly. So we've very little time, Carl. A Holy Army Officer is waiting for us at the gates.

CARL   Us?

STEPHAN   I've come to take you out. Please, we'll talk later. But for now, we must simply go.

CARL   Go where, Stephan?

STEPHAN   To safety. I have convinced Fipsi that you must be saved. And Fipsi has convinced the authorities that you would be valuable in her work.

CARL   So, I'll work for the great State Artist Fipsi.

STEPHAN   Yes. And Tinka, too. We'll all be together again! Now come.

CARL   Never.

STEPHAN   What?

CARL   I will not work for her!

STEPHAN   Carl, please…

> *CARL walks away, not facing STEPHAN.*

CARL   I have a show to do, Stephan. Too bad you won't be able to stay for it.

STEPHAN   Stop it, Carl! All right, you've made your point. I've noticed. Everyone has noticed, Carl, that's the problem. There's no one left to make an example of but you.

CARL	I'm sure they'll find someone.
STEPHAN	Stop it! You don't understand do you? You don't understand a thing.

CARL does not turn to face STEPHAN. Both are silent for a moment.

So, this is how I'm rewarded. You show your back to your teacher. Very well, Carl. I stand humbled before you. The great artist. The great voice of the people. Perhaps it is I who should now learn from you, Carl. So please, tell me, teach me. I will be a willing student, for I have only one question, master. If you are so right, if yours is the only way, answer me this: where the hell is your audience? I don't see them lining up for your performance, save one, and who knows how long she'll last. Where are they, Carl? And where are all those friends of yours, hmm? Those great revolutionary minds that got you into this in the first place? I'll tell you where they are. They're gone, Carl! They're all gone. Your friend Hettie...

CARL	Hettie has gone underground...
STEPHAN	Hettie is dead! A month ago. And just last night your other friend. They used him as an example all this time, they tortured him, they broke him, and they killed him too.
CARL	Who?
STEPHAN	The fellow from the cabaret.
CARL	Morag?

STEPHAN nods.

No. He was innocent.

STEPHAN	Out there the innocent and the guilty have traded places. Carl, I beg of you, boy, please don't miss this opportunity.
CARL	I miss my generation, Stephan.
STEPHAN	Then choose life, Carl.
CARL	At any cost?
STEPHAN	Yes.
CARL	But their price is my voice.
STEPHAN	If you don't silence it, they will. Carl, this is not what you were trained for. This is not what I taught you. And it's not worth dying for. Carl, they're puppets! They don't think, they don't feel, and no one cares about them. Dammit boy, it's just a puppet show!
CARL	Thank you, Stephan.

STEPHAN moves to embrace him.

Goodbye.

STEPHAN turns to leave. He is stopped by CARL's voice.

I'm sorry I disappointed you.

STEPHAN   Carl.

He extends his hand once again, then drops it.

And I'm sorry I... disappointed you too.

A quiet drone begins as STEPHAN leaves. The lights shift to a tight pool stage right. CARL hangs, static, facing out. Ronnie stands behind him, talking to the puppet and thinking CARL's thoughts aloud.

CARL   Happy? You're alone again. You like alone, you're good at it. Fitting in, there's the risk. Getting along, getting by, there's the compromise. And compromise is... death. Always so much death. But it never leads anywhere. I thought it was supposed to lead somewhere.

Ronnie kneels behind CARL, cradling him in one arm.

Is this what you had in mind? Remember when we.... Go ahead, I dare you. Have a memory. Risk it! Risk everything to remember.

His arm sweeps toward centrestage while turning CARL with the other hand.

The whole, real moment. Tears optional.

He kisses CARL and stands, leaving the marionette hanging stage right. An odd light surrounds the carousel, giving us the sense of a blurred reality, where memory and the present live as one. The drone changes into Tinka's theme music and Franz and Schnitzel all rolled into one theme.

The music is continued throughout the following scene. Ronnie takes two puppets from the carousel. They are CARL and TINKA as children. YOUNG TINKA runs into the pool of light, followed by YOUNG CARL. She holds a bunch of daisies in her hand.

YOUNG CARL   Tinka, you mustn't run off like that!

YOUNG TINKA   But, Carl, you left me alone after the puppet show.

YOUNG CARL   I went to talk to the man.

YOUNG TINKA   The puppet man?

YOUNG CARL   Yes.

YOUNG TINKA Did he show you the puppets?

YOUNG CARL He let me work them. They're heavy!

YOUNG TINKA Did you ask him for one?

YOUNG CARL No, silly! But he told me I could come back next week and watch from behind. And that maybe, someday, I could be his assistant!

YOUNG TINKA Oh, Carl, you're going to be a famous puppeteer!

YOUNG CARL Yeah, even more famous than him!

> *YOUNG CARL's arm sweeps, pointing toward the static, hanging puppet of older CARL. He responds to him, as if spoken to, although the hanging puppet neither moves nor speaks.*

Yes, sir, I'm Carl. Yes, they told us to wait here. Why? What?

> *He is agitated. He turns slightly and indicates TINKA.*

There. That's my sister. That's Tinka. No, you can't! Let me tell her. I can do it. I never cry.

> *He walks toward TINKA.*

Tinka, this man, he says…

YOUNG TINKA Is he a friend of Mummy and Daddy's?

YOUNG CARL No. Well, sort of. He says that we have to go. With him.

YOUNG TINKA But Carl, we're supposed to wait here for Mummy and Daddy.

YOUNG CARL They're not coming, Tinka.

YOUNG TINKA Did something happen to them?

> *YOUNG CARL is silent.*

YOUNG CARL They're never coming, Tinka.

> *YOUNG TINKA is absolutely still. She hangs her head and looks at her flowers.*

YOUNG TINKA I have to give Mummy her flowers.

YOUNG CARL You can't.

YOUNG TINKA I have to.

YOUNG CARL Tinka, she's…

YOUNG TINKA She likes daisies. Remember? She says they're her favourite flower because they grow in the dark. Let me give them to her, Carl. Please.

YOUNG CARL All right, Tinka, let's go. Let's give Mummy her daisies.

> *They walk upstage, pausing for a moment to look at older CARL. Ronnie hangs the two children on an animal. He takes*

> *the marionette of TINKA #5 and places her upstage of the hanging CARL. She is wearing the party dress again, although it is different. The fabric is the same as before, but in a new style.*

TINKA Carl?

> *The music stops and the light returns to its previous state in a snap.*

CARL Tinka, we should give Mummy her daisies.

TINKA What?

CARL Tinka, it's Morag. They've... he's dead. I killed him. They killed him, Tinka.

> *TINKA is very still.*

Did you hear me? Morag is dead.

> *TINKA walks toward him.*

TINKA No, Carl. No.

CARL Stephan just told me.

TINKA I'm telling you, he's alive. I loved Morag. I love him. And he loved me. I didn't know how to tell you before, Carl. There's going to be... a child.

> *CARL falls to his knees.*

CARL Tinka, I'm sorry.

TINKA Don't be. We knew. That's why we... why we have to continue. See, I've remade the dress again. Just like I always do. A new dress for a new show.

CARL There won't be another show.

TINKA There has to be. It's all we can do. We continue. There will be another show, Carl. I'm wearing the dress.

> *CARL places his hand lightly on her skirt, feeling the fabric.*

CARL "O daughter of my people, gird thee with sackcloth, and wallow thyself in ashes: make thee mourning, as for an only son, most bitter lamentation: for the spoiler shall suddenly come upon us."

TINKA Jeremiah?

CARL The proclamation of judgment.

> *He faces out.*

Tinka, it's dark.

TINKA Yes... but things are growing.

They stand together as the light fades. In semi-darkness, the marionettes are returned to their carousel animal. Theme music for The Franz and Schnitzel Show begins, although this time it is not as vibrant, somewhat darker and "smaller." The lights come up just slightly, as Ronnie pushes the puppet stage to centrestage front. He puts on a camp jacket, like the one worn by puppet CARL.

Scene Eight

The Franz and Schnitzel Show—Puppet Palette

Once the puppet stage has been positioned, the lights come up on the stage and Ronnie takes his place behind the chest-high backdrop. FRANZ and SCHNITZEL are standing in front of the curtain.

As before, this scene is improvised around a loose structure of running order and content as follows, and usually runs twenty minutes in length.

FRANZ	All right, Schnitzel, it's time for us to get the new show ready! Look at you, you're not even in costume yet.
SCHNITZEL	But I don't have a costume, Franz.
FRANZ	Ya gotta love performance art! We're going to save a fortune on production costs!
SCHNITZEL	But Franz, I don't think…
FRANZ	Precisely! You don't think, Schnitzel. Thinking gets in the way of survival, and that's a luxury we don't have time for. Understood?
SCHNITZEL	Yes, Franz.
FRANZ	Good. There's only one thing left to do. We have to get rid of the fat lady.
SCHNITZEL	Madame Rodrigue? Oh no, Franz, we can't! She's one of us. She's been here since the beginning.
FRANZ	Schnitzel, just because she's been here since the beginning doesn't make her one of us. She's dangerous. She's different.
SCHNITZEL	She's not different, Franz, she's just like us.
FRANZ	Schnitzel, look at us. What are we?
SCHNITZEL	A couple of white clowns.
FRANZ	Exactly. And the world is set up for white male clowns like us. But Madame Rodrigue is different. She's a singer! She breathes more

air than we do, and someday we might want that air and it will be all gone because she took it!

SCHNITZEL   That doesn't make sense, Franz.

FRANZ   It doesn't have to make sense, it's right. There's no room for her now. It's the Franz and Schnitzel Show, remember? We have to look after ourselves! So you have to fire Madame Rodrigue.

SCHNITZEL   Why me?

FRANZ   As long as you are one half of this team, it's about time you took over some managerial responsibilities.

SCHNITZEL   I can't be in management. I'm the good one!

FRANZ   Enough! You'll do what you're told.

SCHNITZEL   But Franz...

FRANZ becomes menacing again.

FRANZ   Need I remind you, Schnitzel, how terrible it would be if I got angry?

SCHNITZEL   No.

FRANZ   No?

SCHNITZEL   I mean, yes.

FRANZ   "Yes" what?

SCHNITZEL   Yes, I'll do what you tell me.

FRANZ   Good boy, Schnitzel! All right, I'm going backstage to get things ready. Fire the fat lady and meet me back there!

FRANZ starts off, then turns to SCHNITZEL.

And Schnitzel, while you're at it, do something cute. Maybe one of these people will want to come backstage and do the diamond pants dance with me!

SCHNITZEL   Franz, how can you think of your pants at a time like this?

FRANZ   I don't know, Schnitzel, but that's the joy of being a big, white clown!

FRANZ exits, laughing maniacally.

SCHNITZEL   Oh dear.

He turns to the audience.

Ladies and gentlemen, lovers of Thespis, forgive me. I know that you are a genteel and kind group of people, liberal and forgiving in your views, but somehow I don't think you've come out tonight to watch a naked little fairy throw himself around the stage.

And I know, too, that you love Madame Rodrigue. I listened while she bullied you into loving her. But now, I fear that you will never hear your beloved superstar diva sing, for I must now, somehow, fire the fat lady.

Oh dear. What a sour pickle I'm in. If only I could escape. If only I could stop this. If somehow it would just end.

Wait a minute. End. That's it! It's happening again. I'm having a thought. A thought of my own! Listen everyone, Madame Rodrigue is the fat lady who sings, right? And we all know what happens when the fat lady sings... it's over!

I can tell Madame that she's too great for this show. She's too important an artist to wallow in the vulgarity of performance art! And I will give her the opportunity to sing one last time on this stage, for you, her begrudgingly adoring public. No diva could resist that, for the love of an audience, even when it's false, is like a drug.

It's perfect! I'll go backstage, fire Madame Rodrigue, send her out to sing one last time, the show will end, you can go home and I won't have to dance naked. Everyone wins! Wish me luck!

He starts off.

Oh. Even though once the fat lady sings it's technically over, would you mind sticking around a few minutes longer so I can come back and say goodbye? I'd like that.

He exits. We hear a knock backstage.

MADAME   *(off)* Yes, who is it? Ah, Schnitzel! I was just getting ready to go out and sing. What? Fired? Terminated? Pink slipped? Sacked? Let go? Fine! I will leave, but before I do I will go out on that stage one last time and give those people what they want! I will sing for them, as only their beloved superstar diva Madame Rodrigue can! I only hope that they remember how to greet a superstar diva when she says:

Oh my darlings, I'm coming to see you!

At which point the audience hopefully says "Nudge, nudge, nudge. Could it be? Could it be?!" MADAME appears stage right, bedecked in a new gown festooned with roses. The audience cries "It is! It is! It's Madame Rodrigue!" at which point the fanfare plays, she walks to centrestage, a spotlight comes on, and the audience applauds wildly.

Stop! Stop it! You're too kind, oh stop!

*This causes the audience to whistle and cheer, clapping even
more enthusiastically.*

Stop it! Stop the music!

*The fanfare dies and the spotlight snaps out returning us to
general onstage light.*

Stop. Please. I can't go on with this. Oh my darlings, my beautiful
darlings, thank you so very much for greeting me properly. You
love me, you really love me! But I can't go on with this charade.
My darlings, a terrible thing has happened. But I can't tell you.
I won't! No matter how you may beg and plead, no matter how
you may cry out "Tell us, Madame," you'll never get it out of me!
So don't even try!

*She has posed dramatically facing into the back curtain. An
audience member will usually yell out "Tell us!"*

All right, I'll tell you! I'll spill like a cup of coffee. I'll sing like a
canary. I'll tell you! My darlings, Madame Rodrigue, your beloved
superstar diva, is depressed!

*She flings herself into the back curtain once again. An audience
member will yell "No!" or some such thing.*

I know what you're thinking. You look at me and say, "Oh
Madame, you look gorgeous! Your hair, your makeup, so tasteful.
That stunning new concert gown, so slimming and fabulous!
Whatever could be the matter, Madame?" Well my darlings, I
have news. A story so shocking, so big in magnitude and horror,
that when I tell you this tale of intrigue you will all want to scream
out, "Say it isn't so, Madame!" But please, try to contain yourselves
when I tell you the shocking news that Madame Rodrigue, your
beloved superstar diva, has been fired!

*She throws herself into the back curtain again as the audience
screams, "Say it isn't so!" She turns and sits on the bench.*

Oh, save your cheap pity! You think I don't know? You think
I'm not aware that Schnitzel concocted this plan to get rid of
me out here in front of all of you? That little fairy has a sick
co-dependency with every audience! I know what goes on out
here when I'm not onstage, and it disgusts me!

Fine. I'll go. And happily. I've outgrown this shabby show, I'm
bigger than this stifling stage. Do I shock you with my candour?
Do my words sting your ears? Oh darlings, all I've ever wanted
since I was a baby superstar diva Madame Rodrigue, was a life

in the theatre. Look where I ended up. The queen of alternative venues.

Oh, I don't criticize you for being here, my darlings. You're not to blame. This is probably all you can afford. And I know that you are the thrill-seeking boob-and-bum kind of fringe crowd that laughs too loud at everything just to prove to everyone around you how smart you are. You don't know better.

So I will go on. I will leave this tomb that has buried me alive and find a place in the real theatre! A real big theatre. Yes, I am going to be in a franchise musical! I want a microphone pack permanently attached to my ass so I won't have to work so hard every night to be heard. I want to be in a show that's already a hit somewhere else so before the audience sees it they already think it's good because it's not from here. I want to be in a show that's so expensive the mere ticket price alone will make you feel privileged to be allowed in. I want to be in a show that takes no risks and says nothing to everyone. I want to be in a show that's the same thing night after night, running like a machine with no connection between the audience and the performer whatsoever. That's real theatre! And that's what I want.

But as I have dreams for myself, so too have I a dream for you, my darlings. I hope that someday you will lift yourself up out of this alternative theatre gutter you wallow in. That you will pull yourself together, work hard, save a few pennies, and be able to scrape together enough to buy yourself a ticket to the real theatre. And who knows? Perhaps someday you'll be sitting up there in the third balcony, your nose bleeding from the altitude, and you'll look down to the stage and see a tiny little speck with orange hair and fabulous gown. And as if in communion with the people around you, you'll quietly whisper, "Nudge, nudge, nudge. Could it be? Could it be?!"

And with that prayer in my bosom, I must leave you. I'm too emotional, I cannot sing. Please don't ask me to!

The audience begs her to sing.

All right, I bow to your will! And you have been so beautiful to me my darlings, you deserve a song. Now, as bleak as things have become around here, I will not sing alone. No! As always, I will be accompanied by the house band. Granted, my ego is too large to share the stage with anyone else, but I assure you they are here, behind this gold curtain. The fabulous Harry Bagg Trio! I'm just nuts about Harry and the boys, although after the show I will have to give them the sack. Oh, Harry is going to be so testy, and the boys will bawl. But they'll bounce back, they always do.

And so, a song. A little song I have written just for you my darlings. Hit it, Harry!

Madame sings. Five bedtracks are available, ranging from operetta style to country and western. Given the news of the day, ranging from politics to entertainment, a new song will be written for Madame to sing at each performance. As she finishes her song, she bows and the audience goes mad.

Goodbye, my darlings! Goodbye!

MADAME exits. A music-box lullaby version of Schnitzel's theme plays. He enters, dressed in a pink and white striped nightshirt and cap. In one hand he drags a teddy bear.

SCHNITZEL   Hi, everybody, it's sleepy time Schnitzel. I just had a terrible thought backstage. So I thought I would come out and share it with you. Oh I'm sorry, I'm being terribly rude. I haven't introduced my bear to you. See my bear? Grrr. Grrr. Grrr. Don't be afraid, he's not a real bear. He's my friend.

The bear is given a new name for each venue, usually based on a politician. In London for example, he was "Tony Bear" (Blair). Given whatever personality the bear is named for, SCHNITZEL will have him do a little dance while he sings a short (unaccompanied) song.

Anyway, I didn't come out here to talk about my bear. I came out here to tell you my terrible thought. Would you like to hear it?

Underscore begins.

My terrible thought, by Schnitzel. See, I was just backstage and I noticed that everything was gone. I don't know how many of you have been backstage in a theatre, but it's the most magical place on earth. The scenery, the costumes, the props. Singers and dancers and actors warming up or complaining about the show. Dressing rooms full of rotting flowers and overflowing ashtrays. Cards from people you love, or from strangers who love you. But Franz got rid of it all, and now it's empty. And I realized that I've spent my whole time looking up there, wanting to get above it all, when in fact I was already at home. And now that it's all gone, I'm empty too.

So I realized something. I may never ascend. I may never get above any of this. I may never fly at all. And that perhaps my destiny in life is simply to become just like you.

He shudders in horror.

And that was my terrible thought.

And that made me hang my head in abject sorrow. But as my head was hanging down, you'll never guess what I saw. My feet. Now, this may not be big news to you normal people who get to belong and fit in everywhere, but to me it was quite a revelation. I've been told my whole life that there was no room for me, that my kind didn't belong, couldn't fit in anywhere. But I look down and see my feet, and there is room for me. My feet are firmly planted on the ground. I'm not stepping on anyone's toes. And my feet can move around, and the more they move...

He walks to the edge of the stage.

...the closer they bring me to you. And the closer I get, the more I realize that... well, the more I feel... what I mean to say is.... Oh, this is too weird. I can't look at you and tell you!

He runs upstage and buries his face in the back curtain.

That's better. What I wanted to say, is that... I love you.

Pause.

Well, don't feel like you have to say it back or anything.

To date, there has been only one audience wherein no one has yelled back, "I love you, too." Usually many, several, or just one brave soul will blurt out their affection for Schnitzel. It is pure magic. He turns slowly and walks downstage.

You do? Oh thank you! Thank you. I always thought the theatre was about scenery, or costumes, or stuff. But the only stuff here now is what you and I are made of, and that's what counts. And nothing, or no one, can ever destroy this or take it away!

FRANZ	*(offstage)* Schnitzel!
SCHNITZEL	Oh no.

FRANZ enters stage right.

FRANZ	Schnitzel, what the hell is going on out here?
SCHNITZEL	I'm having a bonding moment with my audience. They love me, Franz!
FRANZ	Oh, Schnitzel, don't be pathetic. They don't love you.
SCHNITZEL	Yes, Franz, they do. And I love them!
FRANZ	Don't be ridiculous. You can't love, you're a performer. Nothing about you is real.

SCHNITZEL	No, you're wrong! I'm real because they love me.
FRANZ	They don't love you.
SCHNITZEL	Yes they do!
FRANZ	Then how come only one or two said it?
SCHNITZEL	Those people are representative spokespeople for this entire audience! They love me!
FRANZ	No they don't!
SCHNITZEL	They do!
FRANZ	They don't!
SCHNITZEL	They do!
FRANZ	No!
SCHNITZEL	Yes! If I was a T-shirt in the lobby they would buy me!
FRANZ	I leave you alone for five minutes, and look what happens. You not only start thinking, you start feeling, too. Well that's not your job, Schnitzel, and it's not what they want.
SCHNITZEL	But Franz...
FRANZ	Shut up! Schnitzel, you are breaking the rules. And I won't have it. Not as long as I am one half of this show. And if it takes me all night, I will teach you how to behave on this stage. Now get down here.
SCHNITZEL	But Franz...
FRANZ	I said get down here.
SCHNITZEL	But Franz...
FRANZ	I said get down here now!
SCHNITZEL	But Franz, can I bring my bear?
FRANZ	Well he's sewn to your fucking hand, I guess you'd have to! Now get down here!
	SCHNITZEL walks to the edge of the stage. He holds the bear up to FRANZ.
SCHNITZEL	Grrr.
FRANZ	Stop being cute! Okay, here we are. Tell me, Schnitzel, what's that?
SCHNITZEL	It's the edge of the stage.
FRANZ	And what's beyond the edge?
SCHNITZEL	The big, black void.
FRANZ	And what's in the big, black void?

SCHNITZEL   People!

FRANZ   Exactly! People sit in the dark. We stand in the light. Those are the rules, Schnitzel. Do not cross the line.

SCHNITZEL   But Franz, I did cross the line. Tonight I flew into the audience.

FRANZ   Schnitzel, don't start this again. You don't have wings.

SCHNITZEL   Yes, I do! They're in my heart!

FRANZ   I hate that kind of talk, Schnitzel.

SCHNITZEL   I flew into the audience, Franz, because they love me!

FRANZ   No, they don't!

SCHNITZEL   Yes, they do!

FRANZ   I am the only kind of love you'll ever know!

SCHNITZEL   Well that's not good enough for me, Franz.

FRANZ   What do you think you are to these people, Schnitzel?

SCHNITZEL   A benign comic character who embodies hope?

FRANZ   No. You're fourteen inches of fun in the dark, that's all.

SCHNITZEL   Why do you have to make everything dirty, Franz?

FRANZ   Because that's what they want, Schnitzel. You think they love you? No. I'll show you what love in the theatre is about. Watch this.

He begins to rock his pelvis suggestively.

See, Schnitzel? That's what they pay for. The silly clown with his dancing pants! That's what they come to see. They don't want you. You're a freak, you're dangerous. You ask them to think and feel and care, and that's not why people go to the theatre. They don't love you. Look at them. Look at them, Schnitzel. I said look at them!

SCHNITZEL slowly turns his head. He and FRANZ look at the audience.

Poor bastards sitting in the dark, wondering what happens next. But we know, Schnitzel! We know what happens next.

SCHNITZEL   But Franz, it's always the same thing, night after night.

FRANZ   And that's why we keep moving from town to town! Schnitzel, you're where they want to be. In the light. With me.

SCHNITZEL   I'd rather take my chances in the dark with them than stand in this light with you.

FRANZ   When the lights go up out there, Schnitzel, they won't take you with them. They'll forget about you.

SCHNITZEL   I can't forget about them, Franz. And I can't do this anymore.

FRANZ   Fine. I give up. You want to go? Go. You make me sick. Look at you! Standing out here in your pyjamas. Just what the hell is that all about?

SCHNITZEL   The fat lady sang, Franz. It's over. It's the end.

FRANZ   You stupid fairy. It's not the end, Schnitzel. It's just the beginning.

A loud police whistle is heard as a glaring searchlight hits Ronnie's face, beginning a rapid-fire sequence of sound and light cues. The puppet show lights snap out, and all light on the carousel and stage begins flashing. Music becomes chaotic, underscored by barking dogs and the sound of glass being shattered repeatedly. Ronnie whisks off FRANZ and SCHNITZEL and disappears behind the puppet stage. The carousel begins to revolve by itself during the continuing chaos. After Ronnie moves the puppet stage upstage left, he steps onto the now moving carousel. After one revolution, he steps off the carousel into the centre of the set. The carousel stops. Sound calms to an eerie drone, lighting becomes cold and stark. After a brief moment, Ronnie moves forward, and hugging The Populace Mother figure, pushes the carousel into its final position.

Scene Nine

The Camp—Black Palette

It is winter now, late in the day. Ronnie places The Officer upstage centre, and takes TINKA #6 from a carousel animal. Dressed primarily in black except for a striped camp jacket, she is in the early, but obvious, stages of pregnancy. She addresses the Mother figure who stands stage right of The Officer.

TINKA   Go away. Why do you keep coming back, day after day? You know the shows have stopped. This is very dangerous. Please go. There won't be another show.

After hanging TINKA stage left, Ronnie moves the Mother figure out to her starting position downstage centre off the acting ring. MRS. VAN CRAIG #4 enters.

MRS. VAN CRAIG
    Tinka? Tinka dear, what are you doing?

TINKA   Waiting.

MRS. VAN CRAIG
    For what, dear?

TINKA   Spring.

> *TINKA turns toward MRS. VAN CRAIG. She too is dressed in black, but her outfit is very beautiful with an elaborate cape over her dress.*

Astrid, hello. I'm sorry, but there won't be a show today. Carl's been... gone.

MRS. VAN CRAIG
> I know. I took your advice, though. See? I dressed warmly this time.

TINKA   For what? Why are you here?

MRS. VAN CRAIG
> It's my home now too, dear.

TINKA   Why would you choose to be here?

MRS. VAN CRAIG
> I didn't choose, Tinka. Or did I? I suspect it's too late to even wonder anymore.

> *She indicates TINKA's stomach, either by a look or with a touch.*

So, due in spring. There's reason enough to keep each other warm through this bitter winter.

> *They hold each other, half embrace, half for warmth.*

I've brought you a present.

TINKA   Oh, Astrid, I don't need any more dresses.

MRS. VAN CRAIG
> No, but perhaps you need a reason to wear the one you have.

> *TINKA is hung again, face out. MRS. VAN CRAIG exits upstage to the carousel. She trades places with STEPHAN #3, who bows to her as she takes his place on a carousel animal. STEPHAN walks toward TINKA.*

STEPHAN   Hello, Tinka.

> *TINKA turns.*

TINKA   Oh, Stephan. You frightened me! I thought you were...

STEPHAN   Carl?

TINKA   No, dead. Carl's dead.

STEPHAN   Oh, really. Then why is this person waiting for a show?

> *He indicates the Mother figure facing the stage.*

Could it be that Carl is alive? That she's waiting for him? He's not dead, Tinka. Not to her. Not to me.

TINKA   Well he is, Stephan. I was there.

STEPHAN   I see. Then tell me, what's behind the stage over there?

TINKA   What? Nothing. Just puppets.

STEPHAN   Just puppets?! It's a good thing Carl's not around to hear you say that.

TINKA   Without Carl, that's all they are. Just puppets.

STEPHAN   I disagree. And I was wrong. So go on, Tinka, get ready.

TINKA   For what?

STEPHAN   Well, I'm not doing a show until you put on that dress of yours. Tinka, tradition! We have to keep it alive.

TINKA   Oh, Stephan, you can't.

STEPHAN   I most certainly can. And I will. All right, I admit, this foolish old… student was slow to learn from the master. But I think I'm ready to give it a try. Won't you help me, Tinka?

He stands beside her.

With each spring comes a new season of The Franz and Schnitzel Show, remember? We continue. And who knows, perhaps today Schnitzel will fly.

He starts off.

Please. Put on your new dress.

He is hung on the stage right side of the Franz and Schnitzel stage. TINKA walks slowly to centrestage as the light dims to a special on The Officer. Ronnie whispers to her.

RONNIE   Tinka.

On this, sensing CARL's presence somehow, she turns upstage and walks toward The Officer. Face to face, she thrusts her head up defiantly. The silent confrontation is held for a moment, then she is placed back on the carousel. Humming the theme music from the Franz and Schnitzel show, Ronnie walks to the puppet stage and moves it downstage centre. During the previous "chaos" scene, TINKA #7 was placed on the stage left side of the puppet stage. Ronnie takes his place on the stage, and walks STEPHAN out in front of the backdrop. This is the first and only time that we see the "human" marionette characters in the "puppet show" realm. STEPHAN talks to The Populace figure of Mother.

Ladies and gentleman... well... madam. Welcome to The Daisy Theatre and The Franz and Schnitzel Show, back by popular demand! Tinka, we have an audience. Are you ready?

TINKA appears from the other side of the backdrop. She is wearing the party dress again, in a style which appears to be a wedding dress.

TINKA   Yes, Stephan, I'm ready.

STEPHAN   Good.

STEPHAN starts to exit.

TINKA   Stephan?

STEPHAN   Hmm?

TINKA   I think you're right. He is here.

STEPHAN   Then let's begin. Again.

They are both hung face to face on the Franz and Schnitzel stage. The lights start to dim, as a circle of light on the puppet backdrop comes up. Tinka theme music softly plays. When the only light on the set is the puppet stage spotlight, it fades almost to black. Music and light snap out together on the final bell-like note as Ronnie, lifting his face upwards, whispers:

RONNIE   Fly!

The End

Street of Blood

Notes on Staging

"Bridge" refers to three modified marionette stage catwalks above the three main acting areas stage left, centrestage and stage right. They are three feet above deck level, each being four feet wide. There is a two-foot gap between each which Ronnie can straddle to move from one to the other. Most of the marionettes are "long strung," meaning that the strings allow the marionette control to be held from this bridge height, rather than the standard (Theatre of Marionettes) practice of both Ronnie and puppet being on the same deck level. There are only a few short-strung marionettes, specifically the young Esmé figures for the film flashbacks.

"Gallows" indicates a system used to hang a marionette onstage. These are 3/8" steel rods bent into right angles and inserted in pre-drilled holes across the leaning rail, which is slightly lower than Ronnie's waist height when standing on the bridge. This enables him to hang four or five marionettes in one area at a time, either for group scenes, or to leave a character or characters in position while working at another area. "Control" refers to the above-mentioned marionette control to which the strings of the puppet are attached.

The set is primarily exposed steel with a painted wooden floor and three decorative panels onstage which are composed of inlaid wood, copper, brass and sheet metal. The panels front the three bridge towers and are three feet high (deck to top of Ronnie's catwalk "floor") and four feet wide. These are the three acting areas, and each represents one of the three main characters (although they are used for various flashbacks and other scenes). Stage right is Eden Urbane's area, and the panel front features a prominent sheet metal triangle. It has been painted "Pride Pink," although this is distressed and overwashed to cut the colour intensity. Centrestage is Edna Rural's area, and the panel here features an inlay of a sheet metal cross-painted "Red Cross Red." Stage left is Esmé Massengill's area, and here the inlay shows a metal star painted yellow/gold (again distressed and overwashed).

Behind each of these panels are frames which hide special prop puppets such as the oversize "television face" of young Spanky Bishop or Eden on the cross. The stage right and stage left panels both live in tracks on the edge of their bridge towers and can be raised and locked into position, revealing the settings or figures within. The centrestage panel lowers, like a drawbridge, and the reverse side of the panel becomes the floor of Edna Rural's house. Edna's wingback chair is attached to the inside panel/ "floor" and lower with the panel each time the drawbridge comes down. When the drawbridge is lowered we are instantly in Edna's living room.

All scenic shifts and changes, such as panels in front of the acting areas on each bridge unit moving up and down, or the band moving in and out, are done manually, either by Ronnie or the stage manager.

The deck is one foot above the stage floor, twenty-four feet wide. The acting area is five and a half feet deep. The main area of the deck is wood, painted to resemble (marionette scale) floor planks in stains of oak, sage and browned purple. The tracks for the bandstands echo the look of train tracks running across the width of the acting area. The sides of the deck and the three entrance points are sheet metal. Each bridge tower is two feet deep, with alleys, or entrances, between them. Behind the acting area and bridge towers is an upstage pass-through area with no decking. It is three feet deep to the back wall of steel mesh screening eleven and a half feet high. At the eight-foot height is a hanging rail for marionettes, most of which are hung offstage from these. The top of this hanging rail is painted black with highway lanes for the final image in the show. The back of each bridge tower also has hanging rails for the main characters and their duplicates (ie: most of the Esmé puppets are hung on the back of the stage left bridge tower). The top three and a half feet of the back wall has a "mural" of a grain elevator/prairie horizon in the same materials of wood, copper, sheet metal, brass and steel mesh screening, all of which is rusted and overwashed to cut intensity.

Props and furniture either live under each bridge tower or on the two side bridges (which are additional to the main three acting bridges). These side bridges are two feet wide and five feet deep and serve as both structural bracing for the deck and back wall, as well as points for the stage manager to climb up and down from the upstage passage. Since all puppets and props are contained within the framework of the set, there is no need for any offstage activity or storage during the performance.

The play is performed solely by Ronnie Burkett, and reference to him is throughout the staging directions. The stage manager Terri Gillis is onstage throughout the play, calling sound and lighting cues from a wireless headset, as well as doing pre-sets of scenes and passing marionettes to and from Ronnie.

When a number appears after a character name in the stage directions, such as "Edna #3", it indicates a character represented by duplicate marionettes. This is most usually for costume changes, which requires a separate figure for each. Esmé Massengill, for example, is represented at three different ages and numerous costume changes by eleven different marionettes.

Cathy Nosaty's score and sound design and Bill Williams' lighting design are integral to the overall design and performance, although sound and lighting notes within this text are referred to only when necessary to the reading.

The play is performed without intermission, with a running time of approximately 2 hours 12 minutes.

Street of Blood premiered at Manitoba Theatre Centre/Winnipeg in April 1998, with the following company:

Produced by Rink-A-Dink Inc./Ronnie Burkett Theatre of Marionettes

Written and performed by Ronnie Burkett
Music and sound design by Cathy Nosaty
Lighting design by Bill Williams
Stage managed by Terri Gillis
Marionettes, costumes, and set designed by Ronnie Burkett

Set built by Martin Herbert
Costumes and quilts built by Kim Crossley
Marionettes built by Ronnie Burkett
Studio assistant and additional sculpting, Angela Talbot
Marionette controls, Luman Coad
Puppet workshop assistants, Larry Smith and Charleen Wilson
Welding by Wendy Hogan
Decorative metal work by Jeff DeBoer & The Little Giant Rocket Company
Scenic painter, Linda Leon
Music recording produced by Mark Korven

Subsequent runs included The National Arts Centre/Ottawa, Theatre Network/Edmonton, One Yellow Rabbit/Calgary, Canadian Stage Company/Toronto, Henson International Festival of Puppetry and New York Theater Workshop/New York City, queerupnorth/Manchester, Sodra Teatern/Stockholm, The Brighton Festival/England. Production retired June 2002 at The Tramway/Glasgow, Scotland.

Characters

EDNA RURAL, a prairie widow
DOLLY, Edna's dog
EDEN URBANE, a karaoke singing gay terrorist
ESMÉ MASSENGILL, a faded Hollywood vampire
JESUS, Son of God
SPANKY BISHOP, a vampire actor
UTA HÄAGEN-DAZ, a silent screen star vampire
FLUFFER, the stage manager
DON DIVINE, a retired veterinarian
OGDEN RAMSAY, Eden's childhood friend
CORA JEAN PICKLES, xylophonist for The Turnip Corners Ladies Orchestrale
TIBBY HARBRECHT, town busybody and drummer
WINNIE WISMER, pianist
GRETA DeBOER, guitarist
ARMINA PHILPOTT, clarinetist

Setting

The fictitious town of Turnip Corners, Alberta

Time

The present

‽ *Street of Blood* ‽

*At the five-minute call, Ronnie and the stage manager walk
onstage and climb onto the bridge. House lights remain up in
their pre-set level. As the audience continues to enter the theatre,
Ronnie walks each member of the band—"The Turnip Corners
Ladies Orchestrale"—onstage. Each of the Orchestrale members
enter separately and "tune up," the disjointed musical sounds
pre-recorded as separate tracks.*

*The bandstand is actually two separate areas, stage right and
stage left. These are two small wagons, which can move across
stage to be joined, or which can slide independently. Stage left
houses the piano and the xylophone, and stage right holds the
other three instruments and players.*

*The Orchestrale is composed of five elderly women, all dressed
in faded finery. First to enter is WINNIE Wismer. She walks
onstage from the alley between the stage right bridge and side
tower, shuffles to centre where she addresses the audience.*

WINNIE   Ladies and gentlemen, the performance will begin in five minutes.
There's no intermission, dears, so if you have to piddle, please go
now. Thank you.

*She turns and shuffles toward the stage left band area. She sits
on the bench, assisted by the stage manager and plunks out
a few notes. WINNIE's control is hung from a gallows rod
attached to the bandstand (not the bridge) and left seated at
the piano.*

*Next in is GRETA DeBoer, who enters from stage left carrying
her guitar. She makes her way to the stage right bandstand,
tunes up, and is hung from a gallows.*

*Miss ARMINA Philpott enters with her clarinet from the alley
between the centrestage and stage right bridges. She is also*

walked to the stage right bandstand, where she warms up and is suspended.

Mrs. TIBBY Harbercht enters from the alley between the stage right bridge and side tower and makes her way to the drums, stage right. She sits behind them and has a go.

The last member of the band to enter (from the alley between the stage right bridge and side tower) is CORA Jean Pickles. She walks to the stage left bandstand.

Once CORA Jean has reached the xylophone, it is curtain. House lights and pre-set fade slowly as a special on WINNIE at the piano, stage left band area, cross-fades up. She begins to play a short piano overture version of "Behold, The Blessed Prairie."

EDNA #1 walks onstage and addresses the audience, standing in front of her panel centrestage.

EDNA Hello, and welcome to Turnip Corners, Alberta. I'm Edna. Edna Rural. Mrs. Stanley Rural. Now, I'm not an actress. Lord love a duck, no! I'm no special. I'm just a silly, old biddy in a Sears housedress, just like you. Well then, let's begin.

The stage left bandstand tracks in to centrestage left.

WINNIE Edna!

EDNA Oh, hello Winnie dear! That's Winnie Wismer, our pianist.

WINNIE Edna! What are you doing?

EDNA Nothing. I'm starting.

WINNIE Aren't you forgetting something?

EDNA No. Probably. Yes. What?

WINNIE Them.

She looks to the audience.

EDNA No, I've been talking to them, dear.

WINNIE I mean them and us.

EDNA Oh yes, of course. That. My apologies. When you're ready, Winnie.

WINNIE Thank you, Edna. We're ready.

The bandstands track into position centrestage during EDNA's following:

EDNA Ladies and gentlemen, please rise for our national anthem, as played by The Turnip Corners Ladies Orchestrale. Now I'm not kidding, dears. Stand up. Come on. Pretend you're at a hockey game. We're not going any further until we get this over with. This wouldn't be a problem if we were in the United States of America. They might be a war-hungry bunch of bullies, but at least they're patriotic. Now please, stand up! All right, ladies, you may begin.

The ladies begin a spirited, if somewhat awful, version of "O Canada." The audience is encouraged—or bullied, if need be— to sing along. At the conclusion, the bandstand splits and returns to far stage right and stage left.

Thank you, dears. You may be seated. Well, let's not stand out here. Come on inside.

EDNA's centrestage panel is lowered, revealing her living room. She sits in her chair. The stage manager places the dog, Dolly, on the floor by EDNA.

There, that's better. And you have my every assurance that "O Canada" will stand as the sole bit of audience participation for the evening. There will be no singing of "God Save the Queen" at show's end. Lord love a duck, no! I'm off the Royal Family. A bunch of inbred yahoos who can't keep their knickers on straight, if you ask my opinion. Now, I don't blame the Queen. It's hard for a woman to have a full-time job and raise a family, especially when you're married to a layabout la-di-da like Phillip, so it's not her fault that she's raised a horsey girl, a fat boy, a fruitcake, and a fairy. No, the Queen's had her hands full, not to mention having to haul her mum and her drunk sister around with her everywhere and all the time. Lord love a duck, that's enough to make anyone a sourpuss with a purse. They had a chance in Diana, and look how they messed that up. Poor Princess Di. I loved that little gal. She took all my risks for me. Too bad the Queen had her murdered in Paris. But none of us, not even the Queen herself, ever know the saints when they're amongst us, do we?

Listen to me! Lord love a duck, I barely know you and I'm talking your ears off. Who am I to talk about Her Majesty the Queen of England?! Who gives a tiddly-boo what I think? I'm just a silly old biddy in a Sears housedress, that's who.

She looks at the dog on the floor beside her.

Isn't that right, Dolly? Poor Dolly, my little Crazydoll. You're not doing too well, are you dear? Pretty soon it'll be time for Saint Diana to gather you into her angel arms and take you to your reward too.

> *The stage manager enters and places a section of quilting into EDNA's hands.*

Thank you, dear.

> *Stage manager exits.*

Local girl, comes in to help out every now and then. We grow 'em big around here! Although, I don't think her marriage prospects are very good. She's been running with a queer crowd lately. Anyways, where was I? Oh yes, speaking of the great beyond, you know what my idea of heaven is? Heaven is a place where you don't worry about money. Ever. Funny how important we make it down here though. I can't honestly remember a day in my adult life when I haven't worried about money. Did I have enough? If I bought this or that, would it throw us off the precarious balance known as getting by and into the pit of eternal debt? Every time I bought myself something, like this dress for instance, it became a question as to whether or not I was worth spending money on. That's been my whole life.

Oh, I know what you're thinking. How on earth does this silly old biddy in a Sears housedress know she's going to heaven? Well my dears, there's no guarantee whatsoever that I will see the Pearly Gates. But I've fed my family three meals a day all these years on a strict budget. I've done more exotic things with macaroni than most women would ever even dream of. And I've worried about money for fifty-one years of my married life. Lord love a duck, that's got to count for something, I'm sure of it. And if there's one thing I am, it's positive.

> *Light level on her area fades out. Music transition in. Lights come up stage right as Ronnie places EDEN #1 in front of his panel. The lighting is very dream-like. Suspended around him are clear spheres, each containing a fetus/baby.*

EDEN   I've been dreaming of this. I've been dreaming of babies. Really. All these babies, floating. And I'm with them. Not one of them, but there. Seeing things from their point of view. We're floating… inside. Something. Somewhere. And it's always the same. Whenever we start coming out, it ends. A flash of light too bright, walls of skin—thighs, I think—and then…. And then I can't remember anything. Just that same dream. Over and over.

> *The baby spheres swing out of the playing area. Light changes to reality.*

I got a letter. No return address. No name. Just a note really. Addressed to me, Eden Urbane, care of the Princess of Wales

Hospital. I wonder how she even knew to reach me here. Maybe she's been watching me. Maybe she had a private investigator tail me. Cool. How sick and exhilarating to think that she's seen me. That she knows who I am. Well of course she knows me. Well, not really.

Anyway, now it's my turn. My turn to finally see her. My mother. Not my mother that you've just met, not Edna, that's my mum. My birth mother. The one I've never met. She wants to meet me. All the letter said was, "Turnip Corners. Meet me there. I'm waiting. Your real mother." She wants to meet me. Maybe I'll finally find out what happened after that flash of light. Shit.

> *Lights out on EDEN, and slow fade up on EDNA's area centrestage. Crossing to the centre bridge, Ronnie knocks on the metal siding of the tower. This surprises EDNA.*

EDNA   Oh dear, I've pricked myself!

TIBBY   *(offstage)* Edna, have you heard the news?

EDNA   Just a minute, Tibby dear. Oh darn, I'm bleeding.

> *TIBBY enters.*

TIBBY   Can't stay long, Edna, just thought I'd pop in with the news.

EDNA   Cup of coffee, Tibby?

TIBBY   No time, Edna. Gotta spread the word!

EDNA   What word is that?

TIBBY   Two words, Edna. Esmé Massengill. Esmé Massengill is coming to Turnip Corners! Today! She'll be here today!

EDNA   Esmé Massengill the movie star?

TIBBY   The one and only!

EDNA   Lord love a duck. I thought she was dead.

TIBBY   That's what the tabloids will have you think, but no. She's alive, she's making a comeback and she's making it here!

EDNA   Why on earth would anyone come to Turnip Corners?

TIBBY   She's doing a new musical, and they always work the bugs out in Canada before hitting Broadway.

EDNA   You don't say.

> *She looks down at her lap.*

Oh, Lord love a duck! I've bled all over my quilting!

> *TIBBY comes over to EDNA, still seated.*

TIBBY	It's an interesting design though.
EDNA	It's a special quilt.
TIBBY	No, I mean the blood. It's created quite a picture.
EDNA	Picture?
TIBBY	Yeah, look. It's like…
EDNA	…a face. Tibby, do you see what I see?
TIBBY	Edna, you're right.
EDNA	It is a face. There's no mistaking it. It's him Tibby. It's the face of…
TIBBY	Mr. Wayne Newton! Bud and I saw him in Las Vegas two years ago.
EDNA	Not Wayne Newton. Tibby, it's him. It's the son of God!
TIBBY	Edna, that doesn't look a thing like Elvis.
EDNA	Not Elvis, Tibby! It's Jesus.

TIBBY looks again.

TIBBY	Jesus Christ, Edna!
EDNA	Exactly!
TIBBY	Edna, your eyes are strained. That's not Jesus.
EDNA	It is, Tibby. It's him.

She holds up the quilt square.

It's the Shroud of Turnip Corners.

There is a soft hint of the "Techno Jesus" music sting (to come later) as a special comes up on Ronnie's face. For the audience, this will be the "shroud" image. For EDNA, the face is still on her quilt square. He talks to EDNA.

JESUS	Hello, Edna.
EDNA	Oh, don't talk to me, Jesus. Not now. It's too late.
JESUS	Please, Edna. You're bleeding.
EDNA	Go away!
TIBBY	Edna Rural!
EDNA	Not you, Tibby dear, him.

She indicates the quilt square. The special on Ronnie's face fades out.

TIBBY	Edna, everyone knows that Jesus only appears to Catholics, kooks, and cripples. You're just a creative bleeder, that's all.

EDNA	Yes Tibby, of course.
TIBBY	You know, Edna, you really should think about coming on a cruise with me and Bud this winter. They're loads of fun.
EDNA	I'm a prairie girl, Tibby. The only sea I need are those fields out there.
TIBBY	Edna, you sit in this house night and day. We all thought that when…
EDNA	Please Tibby, don't!
TIBBY	Well Edna, we thought that when you moved into town, you'd use your time to do more things.
EDNA	I do plenty, Tibby. I have my quilt to keep me busy.
TIBBY	You've been working on that quilt for years.
EDNA	It's a big quilt, Tibby!

TIBBY starts off, then turns to EDNA.

TIBBY	Suit yourself, Edna, but I don't think that's the face of Jesus. He's got more important things to do than have quilting bees with you.

TIBBY leaves and is hung backstage. Above EDNA, on the bridge, the special comes up again on Ronnie's face.

JESUS	Edna.
EDNA	You're wasting your time, Jesus. You'd be better off appearing to someone else. Someone who…
JESUS	Yes, Edna?
EDNA	Has time for this. For you.
JESUS	Edna…
EDNA	I said not now, thank you very much!

The special on Ronnie's face fades out.

I'd better phone Eden. This is very important. He'll make a pilgrimage home when he hears the news. He's always been Esmé Massengill's biggest fan.

She stands and exits. Lights down on EDNA's area, as music transition begins. The drawbridge of the centrestage panel is raised and lights come up on EDEN's area stage right. It is still somewhat dream-like, although the baby spheres have been removed.

EDEN	Do you remember that old Esmé Massengill movie from the 1950s called *Pompeii Afternoon*? She played Mamie Idaho, a spinster librarian who found love in the ruins with a penniless count,

played by Italian heartthrob Carlo Biscotti. He was one of those barrel-chested, foreign daddy types, but I never spent much time looking at him. No way. I was too busy looking at Esmé's clothes! Even playing a spinster from Bumfuck, USA, she looked fabulous! Listen to me. I can't believe I just used the word "fabulous." It's so fag hag.

Anyway, there was that scene, y'know the one I mean? Her big acting scene where she was standing up on some mound of rocks, or ruins or something, and she extends her hand to the count…

> *Music underscoring begins, with seagulls, manipulated on a pole by the stage manager in front of the centrestage tower. Ronnie crosses to the centrestage bridge and walks YOUNG ESMÉ #1 as MAMIE Idaho onto the upper playing area/catwalk. She wears a '50s day ensemble. She "acts" alone to the unseen COUNT.*

ESMÉ/MAMIE Oh, Count Calabrese, it's glorious up here. Why, you can see everything and it's all so old! Come see, Count.

COUNT/MALE VOICE
Mamie, please, let us not be so formal after all we have shared, all we have tasted, all we have explored. Call me… darling.

ESMÉ/MAMIE Yes. Darling! Oh, my darling Count, join me here and feast on these splendid ruins.

COUNT/MALE VOICE
Oh Mamie, I'm coming!

ESMÉ/MAMIE I never knew that life could be so delicious. All I've ever known are the love stories in books back in my lonely library. But I've been so hungry. Hungry for real love, with a real man. Be with me now, darling.

COUNT/MALE VOICE
Yes, Mamie, but it's so hard!

ESMÉ/MAMIE Don't struggle so. Let me help. My hand has a firm grip.

EDEN And then, just as she bent over for the count, Mamie Idaho lost her footing, and fell…

> *The ESMÉ marionette falls to the floor, centrestage.*

ESMÉ/MAMIE Aaaaagghhhhhhhhhhhhhhhhhhhhhhhhhh…

> *She hits the floor and lays dying.*

COUNT/MALE VOICE
Mamie! Darling! Speak to me!

ESMÉ/MAMIE There is nothing for me to say, darling. Our love is forever written in these ruins.

COUNT/MALE VOICE
Mamie!

ESMÉ/MAMIE   *Arrivederci,* baby.

> *She expires, and is temporarily hung onstage. Ronnie crosses*
> *back to the stage right bridge to manipulate EDEN.*

EDEN   And then she died. A Hollywood death. Looking—well there's no
other word for it—fabulous!

> *Light out centrestage. The stage manager clears the young*
> *ESMÉ/MAMIE marionette.*

And that's how I feel every time I go onstage. Well, saying I go
onstage is a bit of a stretch I know, but it's how I feel when I
perform in these places. Hospitals, hospices, nursing homes. Like
I'm somehow extending a hand, yet falling. Into their despair.
Their sadness. Okay, I know, they don't ask me to sing, and they
don't ask me to feel sad for them, but these dying people need me.
I think. I know I need them. Because I'm like Mamie Idaho back
in her library. Just living my life through the fictions of other
people's lives. And the sadder those lives are, the better.

> *He exits, stage right. Hospital sounds. Dream light crossfades to*
> *his show light. The stage manager places a mirror ball and*
> *a stool onstage. EDEN #2 enters from the stage left side of the*
> *stage right tower. He is dressed in a powder blue tuxedo jacket*
> *and has a microphone in his hand.*

Good afternoon, ladies and gentlemen. How's everyone doing
today? Obviously not so well, or you wouldn't be in a place like
this!

> *"Bad joke" drum sting.*

My name is Eden Urbane and I'm the songbird of the sick bay,
the crooning chanteur of the ICU, the karaoke king of the cancer
ward! I'm here to sing you a few tunes and hopefully bring a little
smile to your face. My, what a well-dressed crowd we have today!
That's a lovely colostomy bag, Mrs. Spudnicki, but trust me hon,
you'll never find shoes to match!

> *Another drum sting.*

Thank you! Allow me to introduce the band.

> *The stage manager places a boom box on the stool. EDEN looks*
> *at the mic.*

Mind if I call you Mike? With a head like that, you can call me
anything!

Drum sting.

Reminds me of a date I had once. But seriously folks, it's my great honour to be in this fine, public health care facility today with all... *(He counts quickly.)* eleven of you. Ladies and gentlemen, I would now like to perform for you the love theme from the 1962 horror classic, *House of Pain*, in which the incomparable Miss Esmé Massengill played Lotta Payne, a reclusive widow living in a strange, hilltop house. Maestro, if you please.

> *Music intro starts. He sings.*

"HOUSE OF PAIN"

Your love is scaring me to death
I'm speechless
Scaring me to death
And darling
It's cutting off my breath

Your love is making me turn blue
I'm gasping
Making me turn blue
And darling
Strictly *entre nous*
I love this
I'm blue
And scared by love

Yes, my heart has become a house of pain
Each room a prison, a torture cell
This sweet paradise is also my hell
I return to again and again
Yes, my heart has become a house of pain
I should flee, but why bother trying
Why can't you see, my darling I'm dying
To live in your house of pain.

> *Lights out. Ronnie hangs EDEN #2 backstage and crosses to stage left bridge. During this, he continues to speak as EDEN on the musical playout.*

Thank you! What a wonderful crowd. My name is Eden Urbane with Karaoke Memory Lane and I'll be performing for you all afternoon.

> *Lights up on ESMÉ's area stage left. The panel is not raised. In front of it, posed in tableau, are (left to right) UTA Häagen-Daz, SPANKY Bishop #1 and FLUFFER, all*

*of whom have been hung from the bridge/gallows by
the stage manager during EDEN's patter and song. There are
several old-style trunks and suitcases in front of them.*

SPANKY	Oy. This is some place, this Turnip Corners. I haven't seen a town so small since… well, come to think about it, I've never seen a town this small.
UTA	*Alter wikser [Old jerk-off]! Du bist ein peniskopf [You're a dickhead]!*
FLUFFER	What did she say, Mr. Bishop?
SPANKY	I believe she just called me an old dickhead.
FLUFFER	Oh no, oh no, oh no, that's terrible, Mr. Bishop!
SPANKY	It's all right, Fluffer. Under the circumstances, I would tend to agree with her.
UTA	*Verfickte hurenscheisse [Over-fucked whore's shit]!*
FLUFFER	Mr. Bishop?
SPANKY	Not worth repeating my dear, not worth repeating. Now, Fluffer my darling, why don't you go see what's holding Miss Massengill up… other than her legs. I love that joke! Get it?
	FLUFFER laughs, then pauses.
FLUFFER	Um, no, not really, Mr. Bishop.
	FLUFFER exits in the alley between the stage left and centrestage bridge towers.
SPANKY	Oy.
	TIBBY enters from the alley between the stage left and centrestage bridge towers, handed to Ronnie by the stage manager. She excitedly makes her way toward SPANKY and UTA.
TIBBY	Oh! Thespians! Hello hello hello. Welcome to Turnip Corners! We are so thrilled to have you in our "corner" of the world.
SPANKY	And we are delighted to be in your company, Miss…
TIBBY	Harbrecht. Tibby Harbrecht.
SPANKY	Charmed, Miss Harbrecht.
TIBBY	Actually, it's Mrs. Mrs. Bud Harbrecht.
SPANKY	Oy, I've been nipped by the Bud!
TIBBY	Oh, such talk! You'll turn my head!

SPANKY   Later, perhaps. Allow me to introduce myself. Spanky Bishop, at your service.

TIBBY   No! Really? Not *the* Spanky Bishop?! The Wacky Bellhop himself! I saw every one of your movies… *The Wacky Bellhop in Paris, The Wacky Bellhop in Love, The Wacky Bellhop Goes AWOL in Waikiki*… oh, I could go on and on!

SPANKY   No doubt.

UTA   *Schnetzer labarkopf [Loose-lipped gossip]! Arschkricher [Brown nose]!*

TIBBY   Oh, and who do we have here? She's such a tiny little thing, I barely noticed her!

SPANKY   This, my dear Mrs. Harbrecht, is the greatest actress ever to grace the silent screen. Miss Uta Häagen-Daz.

UTA   *Pissende dummfotze [Stupid, pissing cunt]!*

TIBBY   Oh, how European! And "bidet" to you too honey!

                Music sting in. ESMÉ #1 enters and is posed dramatically in the alley between the stage left and centrestage bridge towers. She is fabulous, in a Golden Age of Hollywood kind of way. She is wearing her idea of a travelling/day ensemble. Lots of beads and feathers. In one arm is a vicious white poodle.

ESMÉ   So this is Alberta. Yee-haw.

SPANKY   The one, the only, Esmé Massengill!

ESMÉ   Spanky, remind me to kill my agent.

SPANKY   You already did.

TIBBY   I could just lay down and die right here and now!

ESMÉ   What a soothing thought. But darling, the night is young. Let's save the fun for later.

TIBBY   I'm all tongue-tied. My heart's a-racing!

ESMÉ   Oh, yummy.

TIBBY   We are so honoured to have you in our fair town, Miss Massengill.

ESMÉ   Thank you. We're glad to be… anywhere.

SPANKY   You know the tour's bad when you look forward to Regina.

                ESMÉ's poodle barks and snarls at TIBBY.

TIBBY   What an adorable dog. Hello sweetie.

ESMÉ   Please don't touch her. She's an absolute bitch.

TIBBY   What's her name?

ESMÉ	Dorothy Barker. She plays a lamb in my new show.
TIBBY	And what is your new musical about, if I may be so bold?
ESMÉ	It's called *Oh Mary!* The life of the Virgin Mary, told in word and song and dance. I, of course, portray the titular role of Mary, the Virgin. Mr. Bishop here is Joseph.
TIBBY	And Miss Häagen-Daz?
ESMÉ	The angel who appears to Joseph, telling him to take flight to Egypt. It's a dance role.
TIBBY	And the wise men?
ESMÉ	There are no wise men. Especially not in the theatre. No, we're going rather minimalist on this one. Bare bones, pared down and bold in its simplicity.
SPANKY	Our backer died.
ESMÉ	So sue me, I like a nosh. *Et voilà!* We find ourselves here. Extraordinary talent, a few simple costumes, but no scenery, and alas, no band. A musical without musicians!
SPANKY	Some nosh, it was more like a buffet.
TIBBY	Oh, but that's not a problem! I'm with The Turnip Corners Ladies Orchestrale. We'd be honoured to play for your show!
ESMÉ	Fortune smiles upon us! Lovely. I'll have my stage manager Fluffer arrange the rehearsal details with you.
TIBBY	Well, you must be exhausted after your trip.
ESMÉ	Not really, we sleep all day.
TIBBY	How bohemian!
ESMÉ	Technically it's Romanian, but why quibble.
UTA	*Spermaschlucker [Sperm swallower]*!
ESMÉ	That's enough, Uta! Spanky, be a darling and escort Miss Häagen-Daz to her dressing room.
SPANKY	Certainly.
	SPANKY and UTA exit.
ESMÉ	And Spanky, keep an eye on her. You know how our Uta gets when she's hungry.
	She turns to TIBBY.
	Speaking of which, any thoughts on where I could get a bite?

TIBBY	Well, there's the Red Lantern Café, home of Chinese and Canadian cuisine. Bit of everything on the menu, but I'm sure you'll find something to satisfy you.
ESMÉ	I think I already have. My tastes are so simple.
TIBBY	Lovely! Well then, follow me.

TIBBY leaves and is handed to the stage manager.

ESMÉ	I'm right behind you. Come, Dorothy darling, dinner is served! Mummy will save you a bone!

ESMÉ exits. The stage manager clears the luggage. Lights stage left out. As soon as they begin to dim, we hear the sound of EDNA (pre-recorded) on EDEN's answering service. This message plays over the transition as the stage manager lowers the drawbridge panel into EDNA's living room and places DOLLY #2 on the chair.

EDEN	*(recorded)* Hi, you've reached the voicemail for Eden Urbane and his Karaoke Memory Lane. Please leave your message after the tone and I'll call you back as soon as I can. And remember, follow the bouncing balls! Ciao!
EDNA	*(recorded)* Eden? Edie dear, are you there? Can you hear me? Pick up. Eden, it's me. Pick up. It's Mum. Edie, pick up if you can hear me. Are you listening? *(pause)* Well, I guess you're not there. Are you there? I guess not. Anyways, just thought I'd call to see how you're doing. I'm fine, not much going on. Crazydoll's gonna die soon, Esmé Massengill is in town, and Jesus Christ has appeared to me on a quilt square. No need to call back. Just thought I'd say hi. Okay then, bye-bye.

Sound of the end of the phone call. Lights up centrestage. EDNA #2 is dressed in her nightie and robe, and is standing stage left of her chair, looking down at Dolly. Standing stage right of the chair is DON Divine. He is a rather dashing older man.

	So that's it then, eh?
DON	I'm sorry, Edna. These dogs get to a certain age and there's not much we can do for them.
EDNA	I just hate to see her suffer.
DON	Oh, she's having a bit of a time breathing, but I don't think she's in pain. You're just slowing down, aren't you, Dolly?
EDNA	Do you think we should… you know… help her off to sleep?
DON	I think she'll just drift off when it's her time. But if she takes a turn for the worse, Edna, you call Dr. Talbot and he'll make the

end easier for you both. Or give me a call and I'll drive the old girl over to him for you.

EDNA   Oh, you've already done more than enough, Dr. Divine.

DON   Please, Edna, it's Don. I'm not a practising veterinarian anymore. And I was hoping you'd start thinking of me as something else.

EDNA   Oh?

DON   A friend. A neighbour. We're both townies now, so we gotta stick together, eh?

EDNA becomes a bit uncomfortable, embarrassed.

EDNA   Lord love a duck! Look at me standing here in my nightie. Practically nude! You must think I'm a terrible old hussy.

DON   Not at all. Perfectly natural to be in your pyjamas at this hour.

EDNA   And me calling you over here in the middle of the night! I'm just a silly old biddy I am. It's just that I was so worried about Dolly and I didn't know what else to do.

DON   You did the right thing, Edna.

There's an awkward pause as they lean into one another over the chair.

Well, I'll let you get some sleep.

EDNA   Let me pay you for your trouble.

DON   Wouldn't hear of it, dear lady.

EDNA   Well that's awfully kind of you... Don.

DON   But there is something I would like, Edna.

She retreats a bit.

EDNA   Oh?

DON   There's a dinner and dance for the Prairie Revival Party next week. Oh, these political things can be a bit long-winded, but it's for a good cause. And I would be honoured if you'd attend, as my guest.

EDNA   Your guest?

DON   My date.

EDNA   Your date.

DON   Yes.

EDNA   Don Divine! What in Sam Hill do you think I am? Some free love floozy you can romance like a cheap dame in the movies?

DON   No, of course not. Edna, please, you misunderstand.

EDNA	No Don, you misunderstand. I'm a married woman.
DON	I'm sorry, Edna. I've been so lonely since my Dora died. I guess I thought you'd be interested in some company too.
EDNA	Company is all fine and well, Don. But dinner and dancing and dates, well, that's just taking it a bit too far. Stanley Rural is the only man I've ever been with, and I intend to keep the vows of my marriage intact.
DON	But Edna, we have to move on.
EDNA	I am a married woman... Doctor Divine. I will always be a married woman. Now, if you'll excuse me, I have my quilt to finish. Good night.
DON	Good night, Edna.

He leaves. EDNA stares after him momentarily, then turns with a sigh.

EDNA   I guess I'll make myself a NeoCitran. It's the only thing that gets me to sleep these days. Warm milk just gives me gas, and hot toddies make me tipsy. No, a nice, hot Neo is the only thing that knocks me out. Sometimes I have a double, but only if I've watched the CBC news and upset myself.

She exits centrestage right as light fades out. The stage manager strikes Dolly and raises the drawbridge of EDNA's panel. Small spot on EDEN #1, stage right.

EDEN   I once knew a male nurse whose cock was so big, every time he got an erection he would faint. Imagine that. A boner so big it drains the blood right out of your brain. Now that's passion!

For six years I lived with the nicest man. Anthony. Eden and Anthony. We were the perfect couple. Everyone told us so. I was in love. Once. A long time ago. But it was brutal. It wasn't Anthony, although I grew to be afraid of him too.

See, Anthony looked like a gay icon. Like those perfect, ridiculous, empty men in underwear ads. V-shaped, hairless, air-brushed. And that's really fucking hard to be around man, because it caused me to look at myself a considerable amount more than I prefer. Who can look that much sadness and anger in the face? Not me. Not when it's mine. But we had everything. Except passion. And besides, I couldn't leave him. We had too much stuff.

One Saturday afternoon I was lying on the couch while Anthony was in the basement working out. And there on TV was my sign— my epiphany—in the form of an old Esmé Massengill movie, *No Room For Love*, in which she played Constance Hart, a wealthy society dame married to an abusive banker who forfeits comfort and home and social standing to run off with a long-haul trucker named Butch, played brilliantly by Armand Collier. Butch. Oh, hump-daddy Butch. That guy was as dangerous as day-old sushi.

Light dims somewhat on EDEN as it comes up on YOUNG ESMÉ #2, atop the stage right catwalk, posed in a spectacular gown. ESMÉ acts alone to an unseen male voice. The flashback is underscored with lush, overly romantic movie music.

ESMÉ/CONSTANCE

I love you, Hy, and I've tried to make you love me. But you've left me, and left me with no choice.

HY/MALE VOICE

I've never left you, Constance. I'm here! Right here, just as I've always been.

ESMÉ/CONSTANCE

No, you're distant, Hy. You've gone far, far away, to a land where love cannot live.

HY/MALE VOICE

I've given you everything a woman could ever want, Connie. Money, clothes, jewels. That's love, isn't it?

ESMÉ/CONSTANCE

No Hy! We've crowded our lives with things, and left no room for the most important thing of all. We've left no room for love!

The movie music swells dramatically as ESMÉ hits her final pose and exits. Lights fade on the flashback area and restore on EDEN.

EDEN

Once again, Esmé came through for me! She was my inspiration. Fuck the house. Screw the stuff. Okay, so I didn't have a long-haul trucker waiting for me, but I had a car. A 1986 powder blue Monte Carlo. I got up off that couch and packed. Favourite clothes, photo albums, some books, my pipe bomb stuff, the duvet and two pillows, all the CDs that were mine, a boom box, and almost anything that was battery operated. And the cellphone. I was on the run, true, but I still needed access to my voicemail. Into the car it went. I had found my new home. And my escape. It was decided and done, start to finish, in thirty-five minutes.

Thirty-five minutes. It took six years to build something, to accumulate all the trappings, and thirty-five minutes to end it. But then, destruction is always quicker than creation. And way more noticeable.

I went downstairs to tell Anthony I was leaving. "Keep the house, keep everything, I have to go. I can't stay here anymore. I can't stay with you." And he started to cry. Well, I like to think they were tears, not just sweat running down his face. Eventually he spoke. "It's because I bore you, isn't it?"

Of course I lied. I said no.

And left. But lemme tell ya, life isn't like the movies. In *No Room For Love*, just as Constance and Butch finally hit the road, they both die when the truck skids off a bridge in the rain. My fate was worse. I lived.

In my car. Really. I am one of the intentionally homeless. It's okay, and once you figure out which bathrooms to use it becomes easier. "No fixed address," that's me. Kind of implies I'm going somewhere, doesn't it? I guess you could say I'm presently between lifestyles. But hey, what fag isn't?

Anyway, I'm going home. Not to Anthony. To Turnip Corners. To visit my mum. And to meet my mother. My real mother. Esmé! Oh shit, I'm afraid again. Maybe I should blow something up before I hit the road. That always makes me feel better. Nah, I'd miss all the press coverage.

> *Lights out on EDEN, who exits via the alley right off the stage right bridge. Music in for the "Techno Jesus" sound and light show. This segment is loud, chaotic, intense, modern. Ronnie crosses to the stage left bridge tower, places ESMÉ #2 on her chaise, and as the transition ends there is a blast of smoke from under the catwalk. Ronnie ends on the stage left leaning rail, arms outstretched. Light up on ESMÉ and a special on Ronnie's face above.*

ESMÉ   Now that's an entrance!

JESUS   Miss Massengill. We need to talk.

ESMÉ   Well, if it isn't the Only Begotten. *Iesus Nazarenus Rex Iudaeorum.*

JESUS   Very good, Esmé! I never would have guessed you to know Latin.

ESMÉ   Pish darling, it's the perfect language for me. Dead.

JESUS   Well, you are starting to look your age, Esmé.

ESMÉ   And you've put on weight, bitch, but did I bring that up?

JESUS   Look, I'm not here to fight.

ESMÉ   Then what brings you here? Surely the good folk of Turnip Corners aren't so important that they warrant an appearance by you.

JESUS	There's two I thought I should keep an eye on.
ESMÉ	To protect them from me?
JESUS	To protect them from themselves.
ESMÉ	Darling, you've been off the circuit for so long people wouldn't recognize you if they saw you. But have you seen what your competition's been up to lately?
JESUS	I keep tabs on him.
ESMÉ	Cable, multinationals, the Moral Majority, all of Hollywood, and of course, Satan's craftiest minion on earth, the Internet. It's gorgeous, and so simple.
JESUS	Don't be fooled by the appearance of simplicity, Esmé.
ESMÉ	But it is simple darling, and he's the one who figured it out, not you. Give them sex, everywhere! Let them diddle themselves in front of a computer screen, with a video, or on their cellular phones. Swell their loins and drain the blood out of their brains. Let the new millennium sneak up and catch them all with their pants down!
JESUS	All right, Esmé, enough. Why are you here?
ESMÉ	Oh, I'm doing out-of-town tryouts with my new show.
JESUS	Esmé, it's me.
ESMÉ	Well darling, being here is part of the plan. Actually, it is the plan.
JESUS	What plan?
ESMÉ	It's blood, darling. Pure, uncontaminated blood. Oh, not for me. I'll drink any plasma you put in front of me. But for stockpiling, for hoarding, for selling, well, for that, I need the quality stuff.
JESUS	Selling?
ESMÉ	Yes. Because he—or rather, she—who controls the blood supply controls the world. You can blood bank on it. And besides, feeding on victim after victim got a bit tedious after a while. So now we still have the thrill of seduction and attack, make the puncture, have a little sip and drain the rest for storage. And the product tends to be purer in the sticks.
JESUS	Esmé, promise me you'll leave my two people alone.
ESMÉ	We'll see, darling, we'll see.
JESUS	You may have a fight on your hands this time, Esmé.
ESMÉ	Delicious! So you think you're finally up to me?
JESUS	What makes you think I was talking about me?

*Light out on Ronnie and ESMÉ, stage left. Short "Techno Jesus"
sting, dissolving into theme for EDNA. Slow crossfade up on
centrestage. The stage manager strikes the chaise and lowers
the drawbridge panel. Ronnie hangs ESMÉ backstage, crosses to
centrestage bridge tower, and walks EDNA #2 into the scene.*

EDNA   I've been awake all night. Two NeoCitrans and I still couldn't
sleep. Maybe it was the late show that did it. They were showing
that old Esmé Massengill movie, *Passport to Love*. It was one of
my favourites. Esmé played Dixie Carlyle, a waitress in a roadside
diner who changes a flat tire for a travelling foreign prince and
falls in love. Oh, so romantic. But that was our Esmé. Living,
breathing passion!

*Light dims somewhat centrestage. Ronnie leaves EDNA sitting
in her chair and crosses to the stage left bridge tower, walking
YOUNG ESMÉ #3 onto the catwalk. This is a contained pool of
light, revealing ESMÉ in a spectacular white satin wedding dress
with a pale pink beaded veil. Again, ESMÉ stands alone and the
people to whom she is speaking are unseen. This is heavily
underscored with movie music.*

ESMÉ/DIXIE   Oh Betty, oh Audrey, oh Delores, why, you're the best friends a gal
could ever have. Thanks for coming all the way to this foreign
country just to be my bridesmaids. I'll miss you all and the happy
times we had at the diner. Oh sure, here they'll call me Princess,
but I'll always be Diner Dixie to you. Please know that I will never
forget you gals, nor will I ever forget that it was slinging hash that
brought me to the palace gates. But now, I say goodbye, my
beloved Ladies in Waitressing, for my heart has a new destination
and my passport is love! Prince darling, wait for me!

*She turns upstage as the music swells. Sound of honking car
horn and screeching tires as stage left light to black. YOUNG
ESMÉ is hung backstage, Ronnie crosses to centrestage bridge
and EDNA's light restores.*

EDNA   Too bad poor Dixie Carlyle tripped on the train of her dress and
got hit by a speeding taxi as she crossed the street to the church.
But she died beautifully, and oh, I loved that dress! More than
anything I had ever seen. So when my Stanley asked me to help
run the farm—which was his idea of a marriage proposal—I just
knew that my wedding dress had to be like the one in *Passport to
Love*.

I saw that movie three times down at the old Bijoux, trying to
doodle the dress in the dark. I clipped every picture I could find
of it from the movie magazines. I worked extra hours at Turner's

Drugstore during the week, just so I could save enough money to buy five yards of satin and two of lace from the catalogue, shipped all the way from Toronto.

I made my pattern from old newspapers, then I cut it out of sugar sacks, like I use for my quilting, as a kind of test run. Then I scrubbed down the kitchen table, laid out my precious cloth, and cut. Lord love a duck, I had never been so nervous in my whole life. It took me weeks to sew that dress, because I knew that fancy clothes in France were all hand sewn. And since necessity is the mother of invention, I stained the lace veil pink by dipping it in a bucket of diluted Saskatoons I'd put through the sieve.

Leaving EDNA seated in her chair centrestage, Ronnie crosses to stage left bridge.

I knew I was no Esmé Massengill, and even though I stopped eating the week before the wedding, I was still just lumpy Edna. But when I put on that dress, well, didn't I just feel like a princess.

YOUNG EDNA #1 enters through the alley between the stage left and centrestage bridges. She is in her wedding dress, a copy of the one from ESMÉ's movie. She walks centrestage left to a phrase of "Here Comes the Bride," and is hung in position there.

It was a small wedding and I had only one gal stand up with me, not a tribe of bridesmaids like Esmé. There was no money for that, and besides, I didn't have that many friends.

Light up on CORA Jean at the stage left bandstand.

But Cora Jean Pickles, who worked with me at the drugstore, agreed to be my bridesmaid and matron of honour combined. Cora Jean was saving up her money to go to Winnipeg to study the ballet. It was Cora Jean who gave me the beads for my veil. Took them right off one of her dance recital dresses. I was indebted to her for life because of that.

Light fades out on CORA. Ronnie crosses back to the centrestage bridge and EDNA.

I don't remember much about my wedding day. Oh, I know it's supposed to be the most important day in a woman's life, but I had worked and worried so much on an empty stomach that I was in kind of a fog. Mind you, the fog lifted that night when Stanley... took his husbandly way with me. Suddenly, I didn't feel like a princess anymore. So, the next morning I wrapped that dress in tissue paper and put it away in the cedar chest.

Light stage left dims on young EDNA, but not to black.

And we got on with our married life, which was surprisingly not much different from life before. I even grew to tolerate Stanley climbing on top of me at night, sometimes imagining that he was Armand Collier or Trevor St. Clair or some other movie star lover. Looking back, I realize now that it never really took that long anyway, although it seemed like an eternity at the time. But it was my duty, and it would hopefully lead to something.

But it never did. After a while, I went to old Doctor Beaton to see if I was doing something wrong. But no, he assured me that we were doing everything right. It was my body that was wrong. It could not, it would not, make a baby. They used to call it barren. Like the prairie when the fields are empty. That was me. Empty, through and through.

When I got home, Stanley was still out doing the chores. To this day I don't know why, but I went to the cedar chest, took out my wedding dress and put it on. And went upstairs and sat on the bed. It was the only night in my married life when I didn't make supper.

> *Light up, just barely, on YOUNG EDNA, stage left. The stage manager hands Ronnie a black cap, which he puts on as Stanley.*

Stanley found me sitting there. He didn't say a word. Not a peep. Stood in the doorway staring at me. I couldn't look at him, but I told him. "I can't have a baby," was all I said. Stanley was so quiet. He left the room. I stayed on the bed, memorizing the rag rug on the floor, listening to him downstairs. A terrible racket. I thought he was breaking things, or packing to leave. I didn't know.

> *Light intensity shifts somewhat in a subtle crossfade from EDNA in chair centrestage to YOUNG EDNA, stage left. Centrestage does not fade to black. Continuing EDNA's storytelling, Ronnie leaves the centrestage marionette, walks toward stage left and climbs off the bridge to deck level. He is Stanley. During the following monologue, Ronnie enacts what EDNA is describing. The bacon and eggs are mimed, but the apron is real, and he ties it onto the marionette during the description.*

And then he was there again. He set something down on the bureau, walked over to me and tied an apron around me while I sat. Then he took what he had set on the bureau and put it on my lap. I looked down and there was a plate. Bacon and eggs. He knelt down, took a piece of bacon in his fingers, and held it up to my mouth. That's when we looked at each other. We stayed there for a long, long time. Me in my wedding dress and an apron,

Stanley on his knees before me. Me and my man. Mr. and Mrs. Stanley Rural. Crying over a plate of bacon and eggs.

He ends on his knees, embracing YOUNG EDNA. The tableau of Ronnie and YOUNG EDNA in her wedding dress is held as the stage left light fades very slowly to black. Ronnie strikes YOUNG EDNA #1 and resumes his place on the bridge, stage left. Lights up on EDEN's area stage right as Ronnie crosses from stage left bridge to stage right.

EDEN   Do you ever think about those people you called fag in school? No, of course you don't. But we think about you. All the time. Imagine that in every town all over the world there were a few of those kids. Nice kids, whose only hope of survival was to get out. And man, I got out. To the city.

In the city you have access to… more. More activity, more noise, more movies, more shopping, more people, more stuff, more sex. Oh yeah, I had a lot of sex when I first got there. A lot. I suppose I'm kind of your worst nightmare. A fag who has had as much sex as you think fags have.

Lights crossfade. Down a bit on EDEN (who is hung from the gallows and remains in position stage right), and up on EDNA in her chair centrestage.

EDNA   It was Thanksgiving, 1982. Eden had already been living in the city for several years, ever since he graduated from high school. Like a bullet from a pistol, that's how he got out of this town. So once every now and then, I'd pack my plaid overnight case and take the bus into the city to see him. The train had stopped coming through Turnip Corners years ago, even though we clung to these tracks and the grain elevator as some sort of memento of when the town had had a soul. Same reason I'd go see my Edie. To remind myself that we were a family still.

Now, Mr. Stanley Rural did not join me on these Greyhound adventures. Never cared much for the bus. Certainly did not care for the city. And although it was never discussed, I felt that something had stopped him from caring about Eden too.

Anyways, a week before Thanksgiving, 1982, Eden phoned to say that he was coming home. And bringing a couple of friends. Well, Lord love a duck, didn't that just throw me into a tizzy! Why, there were mattresses to turn, beds to make up, pies and jellied salads to get prepared, the good china to get out and wash up. And I needed Stanley to drive me to the IGA so I could get the biggest turkey they had. Oh, but I didn't mind all the fuss and bother. This was one Thanksgiving I had something to be thankful for. My Eden was coming home.

Lights crossfade again. Up on EDEN, stage right.

EDEN I learned how to make bombs on the Internet. Nothing fancy, just pipe bombs and fire explosives. Simple stuff. I could have gotten more elaborate I suppose, but I hated surfing through all those militia pages. Hundreds and hundreds of websites devoted to my extinction. Man, I had no idea I was such a threat to them. Cool.

My first bomb was actually intended for a Prairie Revival Party campaign rally. See, they were making all this Christian bullshit noise about the "homosexual agenda." Man, someone should have told them you can't organize fags to agree on anything. But just when we thought it was safe to poke our heads out of the trenches and wave our little rainbow flags, the enemy pounced. And man, those fuckers are organized. And all the gay activists could do was to mount a lame campaign to prove how normal we are. Fuck that. What needed to happen was to prove how dangerous those people are to me. I mean, to us. Look, I'm no activist, okay? I don't ask for my right to be. I'm a radical. I take it.

So I changed my plan and set my first pipe bomb off in the back entrance of Tongue in Cheek, one of the more popular gay bars. It was a Monday night, so there were only a handful of patrons, and I knew they all in the front bar. The blast didn't cause any injuries, and not a lot of damage. But the effect was fucking enormous. A gay bar had been bombed. The cops took it seriously, the press covered it, best of all, the gay community got scared. Really scared. Junior high scared. And indirectly, fingers started pointing at the Prairie Revival Party. Jackpot!

So that weekend I set off another one at a lesbian coffee shop called Sappho's Grind. I felt kinda bad, 'cause it was a nice place. But I had to involve the dykes too. I mean, think about it. They're gay and female, so there's double the oppression. Which means double the rage. And rage is what I'm interested in.

Tick tick tick tick… kaboom, baby.

Lights crossfade. Up on EDNA, centrestage.

EDNA Eden's friends were, now let me see… there was a pale, skinny boy named Kiki, and a largish girl named Jane spelled D-J-A-N-E with the "d" being silent. They didn't say much to me, and most of what they said to Edie was whispered. Djane sat in the kitchen a few times, not to lift a finger and help out, but to lecture me on how degrading my role as a homemaker was to my "woman spirit." She did manage to eat most of the baking I'd put out, although I don't think she realized that this was a direct result of my chosen profession. And she felt that my saying "Lord love a duck" gave too much power to an unseen male force with a controlling agenda. Better, she thought, to say "Goddess love all the ducks, big and small, of all colours and gender persuasions." What a cornflake!

Stanley had found all sorts of work to do out in the Quonset shed. Barely showed his face around the house the whole time we had Edie and his friends. But this was a holiday dinner—a prairie woman's showcase—and I marched myself out to that shed and told Mr. Stanley Rural to wash up, suit up, and show up at my table on time or there would be hell to pay. I put up with a lot, but don't mess with me when there's a turkey involved!

Lights crossfade. Up on EDEN, stage right.

EDEN   I knew what my third target would have to be. There's a small alternative high school, and they had a program for gay kids. Kids who had really suffered in the mainstream system. And it was something the community had fought and worked for a long time, because, well, let's face it man, we all remembered high school.

Ronnie pauses, looks straight out to the audience and remembers.

RONNIE   Fucking high school.

EDEN   Anyway, it was the only bomb that I ever had second thoughts about, but I knew its impact would be the last straw. It had to be done. So late one night I broke in, set up, and blew the shit out of that school. And I can't tell you how fucking good that felt. And this time, I left a calling card. Out on the sidewalk I spray painted two pink words. Purse Boy. That's all it said.

Lights up on EDNA, centrestage.

EDNA   Thanksgiving dinner. There we sat, the five of us. Or rather, me and the silent quartet. Now you may have noticed, I tend to go on a bit. And when I'm nervous, well my chin wagging just won't stop. So I talked. I passed the turkey, and I talked. I passed the dressing, and I talked. I passed the gravy boat, and talked. I passed the potatoes, the turnips, the peas, and the corn and I talked and talked and talked and talked. I was just about to pass around the jellied salad—oh, the clear green one with fruit cocktail in it, not the creamy Ambrosia one with the Philadelphia cream cheese and pineapple tidbits—when Eden stood up, cleared his throat and said:

EDEN Mum. Dad. I'm gay.

EDNA I didn't know what to do. I'd planned this for a week, and now it had all gone wrong. Maybe there wasn't enough food. I held the jellied salad in front of Djane and said, "This one has fruit in it."

EDEN Mum! Didn't you hear me? I said I'm gay. Don't you have anything to say about that?

EDNA Well, for once I was silent. It was dead quiet at that table. That eerie kind of stillness, like right before a big storm. And I could feel him. From the other end of that table, my Stanley, starting to vibrate like a generator getting going. All in his neck, eh? His neck doubling in size and ready to burst. And his face. Eyes crazy like an animal, ready to attack. And getting all red, like every drop of blood in his body had rushed to his head. This had gone terribly wrong. This was all my fault. I should have cooked a ham too!

Suddenly, Stanley slammed his cutlery down on his plate with a crash. Put both hands on the table and lifted himself up to his full height. He looked bigger than I'd ever seen him before. Like a giant. Like a crazy, unfriendly giant. And his face was so red it looked like a missile would shoot straight out the top of his head at any moment. I had to do something. Say something. Fix this. Come on Edna, you're a smart woman, you read *Chatelaine*. Think Edna, think.

 EDNA stands, half from the excitement of her storytelling, partially as re-enactment.

Dessert. I had dessert! My saviour! I put the jellied salad down, placed my hands on the table and stood opposite Mr. Stanley Rural, staring him down. Oh, not as tall but just as strong-willed. His eyes locked with mine, like two gunfighters, fingers twitching for their pistols. I shot first. I spoke. I spoke as calmly and as bravely and as sensibly as any Canadian woman in my situation would. And I said to him, "Stanley Rural, keep your fork! There's pie."

 EDNA sits.

He sat down. We finished our meal in silence. I cleared the table. Everyone retained their cutlery. I served dessert. Eden and his friends went back to the city. Stanley went to bed. And I did the dishes, alone. It was an awful Thanksgiving. I didn't even have my slice of the pie.

 Centrestage light fades out.

EDEN

My bombs aren't meant to hurt gay people. They're meant to blow the lid off our bottled rage. So watch out, because now there is a homosexual agenda. Fairies are fighting back. And God help anyone who gets in the way of that fury.

EDEN's light fades out as he exits stage right. Music transition, suggesting time change. Ronnie removes EDNA #2 and seats EDNA #3 in the chair. This is her good dress, not flashy, but from the more expensive part of the Sears' ladies wear section. The stage manager places a box wrapped in Christmas paper downstage left of the chair. Sound of a car horn. Lights up centrestage.

EDNA

Eden, is that you?

EDEN #1 enters from the alley between centrestage and stage right bridges.

EDEN

No, it's Gloria Cartier, the orphaned young socialite with amnesia from *Midnight in Monte Carlo*!

EDNA

Oh you! Get in here and give your old mum a hug.

He enters EDNA's area, stage right of the chair.

EDEN

Hi Mum.

EDNA

Let me get you something to eat.

EDEN

I'm not hungry, Mum. Sit.

EDNA

You look like a skeleton. How about a grilled cheese?

EDEN

No thanks.

EDNA

I've got some matrimonial cake. Just made it yesterday.

EDEN

Mum, no.

EDNA

Oh, but you always liked my matrimonial cake.

EDEN

Not now, okay?

EDNA

Okay then, I think I've got some Rocky Road Squares with the coloured mini marshmallows in the freezer. Only take a minute to thaw them out...

EDEN

Mum, stop over-functioning.

EDNA

Suit yourself, Mr. Scrawny. How's Tony?

EDEN

Mum, it's Anthony. You never abbreviate a fag's name.

EDNA

Oh. How's Anthony?

EDEN

He's... perfect.

He notices the box on the floor.

	Bit early for Christmas.
EDNA	Oh no dear, that's Dolly.
EDEN	What? You wrapped up the dog?
EDNA	She was gathered, Edie. Middle of the night, she was taken off to her reward.
EDEN	Mum, this is too weird. Why would you gift-wrap a dead dog?
EDNA	Well, you gave her to me as a Christmas present and that's how I'm going to send her off. I've been waiting for you to get here so we could bury her in the backyard. That's why I'm in my fancy dress and wearing my Avon.
EDEN	Poor Crazydoll.
EDNA	I thought you might like to sing that at the service.
EDEN	What?
EDNA	That song. "Crazydoll." From that old Esmé Massengill and Spanky Bishop movie. You used to sing that song at the drop of a hat when you were a kid. Remember?
EDEN	Not really.
EDNA	Sure you do. You'd get up and perform for me, right in front of the television. It was almost like you were on it. Come on Edie, sing a little bit for me.
EDEN	I don't remember it.
EDNA	Well I do. I remember everything. We had just bought the colour TV.

> *Light centrestage dims to very low level as we crossfade up stage right. The stage manager has preset a chair like EDNA's right of the stage right panel. YOUNG EDNA #2 is pre-set in the chair, dressed in a housedress. Beside her is YOUNG EDEN #1. He is a chubby, pleasant-looking child with the same shock of red hair and glasses. The intro for the song "Crazydoll" plays under the initial dialogue.*

YOUNG EDEN	This is way better than black and white!
YOUNG EDNA	The Heckler Brothers' pictures were always the most spectacular, Eden. Look at those costumes! I had forgotten how snazzy they were.
YOUNG EDEN	And Esmé looks even more beautiful in colour.
YOUNG EDNA	Shhh Edie, here comes Spanky's big number. Go turn the set up so we can hear it better.

Lights dim on them, and the area in front of the screen brightens as Ronnie raises the panel in front of the stage right bridge. It reveals a large face of YOUNG SPANKY Bishop as the Wacky Bellhop, filling the frame. He is in the movie being watched by young EDNA and YOUNG EDEN. SPANKY's mouth is manipulated from behind the screen by the stage manager. SPANKY sings:

"CRAZYDOLL"

Gather round now, one and all
Come and meet my Crazydoll
She's a dame who's earned her fame
And my heart's back in the game
Come on kids and say her name
Come and meet my Crazydoll

Crazydoll!
She's a wacky lady
Crazydoll!
Oh yessirree
Crazydoll!
Crazy 'bout ya baby
Can't you say you're crazy for me.

The music continues with a brief dance orchestration as YOUNG EDEN stands up and moves directly in front of SPANKY.

YOUNG EDEN   Hey Mum, look at me! I'm a movie star too, and I'm in colour!

YOUNG EDNA   Oh Edie!

During the following, Ronnie sings live as YOUNG EDEN with the pre-recorded SPANKY.

Here I am on bended knee
With the word matrimony
Please say yes that you'll be mine
Hubby's year-round Valentine
Crazy him loves crazy she
Crazydoll please marry me

Crazydoll!
You're my little Venus
Crazydoll!
My Juliette
Crazydoll!

Nothin' comes between us
Can't you see how crazy I get

Crazydoll!
Be my little missus
Crazydoll!
Lemme see you smile
Crazydoll!
Come and get my kisses
Crazydoll!
Oh Crazydoll!
My Crazydoll!
Take a crazy walk with me down the aisle.

> *YOUNG EDEN collapses into EDNA's arms. They are both laughing.*

YOUNG EDNA Oh Eden, that was wonderful! You're a regular Spanky Bishop you are!

YOUNG EDEN I'd rather be Esmé Massengill.

YOUNG EDNA Oh Edie, such a kidder. My little movie star!

YOUNG EDEN And you're my crazydoll, Mum. Forever.

> *They cuddle and giggle as the stage right lights fade. Ronnie lowers the panel. Centrestage lights restore. Stage right chair and marionettes are struck by the stage manager.*

EDNA And that's why you named her Crazydoll.

EDEN Yeah. I remember.

EDNA Of course you do, Edie. Your father didn't see the sense in buying that colour TV, but I held my ground. I said, "Stanley Rural, it's my family allowance, I'll spend it as I see fit!"

EDEN Well, he never saw much sense in anything we liked.

EDNA Edie, that's not true.

EDEN Fine, I'm sorry I brought it up. I should know better than to criticize him in front of you.

EDNA Oh, you're just mad at him. Just because he didn't throw his arms around you and say, "Oh, you're a homo! Isn't that just tickety-boo! Let's go have a smoke on the porch!"

EDEN I didn't expect that. I knew he would have a hard time with it.

EDNA Then why did you tell him, Edie? To hurt him?

EDEN No. Maybe. I don't know.

EDNA   Well it's hard to mend a fence when you're sitting on it, Mister Man. And besides, your father isn't angry.

EDEN   Wasn't.

EDNA   What?

EDEN   Wasn't angry, not isn't.

EDNA   Don't start with me, Eden.

EDEN   Mum…

EDNA   Fine. Enough. We'll have it your way. It wasn't anger. It was disappointment that he'd have no one to pass the farm onto.

EDEN   He never even asked me if I wanted it!

EDNA   Well of course not, Edie. What would you, one of you people, want with a farm?

EDEN   There are plenty of gay farmers.

EDNA pauses, shocked, then bursts into laughter.

EDNA   Oh, Lord love a duck! You're pulling my leg now. Oh you! And I almost fell for it. Gay farmers!

EDEN   And ranchers.

EDNA   Eden!

EDEN   I've been to gay rodeos. Yee-haw! Ride 'em cowboy!

EDNA   Now that's enough of your smart mouth! Eden, it's not nice to tease your old mum like this. Not now, what with Dolly's passing and Jesus Christ appearing in my quilt square.

EDEN   Hey Mum, did you ever think that maybe Jesus was gay?

EDNA   Now that's just talk for talk's sake, Eden.

EDEN   Well, you never know. His last dinner party was men only.

EDNA   Lots of men get together for a meal. Look at the Kinsmen! Doesn't mean they're a bunch of poofs. Mind you, I've always had my suspicions about the Shriners. Something not quite right about grown men in harem pants.

EDNA stands.

Now let's get Dolly buried before she starts to smell up the whole house. I'll go get my purse.

EDNA exits.

EDEN   But we're just going to the backyard.

EDNA   *(offstage)* You never know who's going to see you, Eden.

EDEN   No, you never do. "Turnip Corners. Meet me there. I'm waiting. Your real mother."

EDNA   *(offstage)* Eden, are you coming?

EDEN   I'm already here, Mother. I'm here, Esmé.

All light centrestage fades as ESMÉ music/sound theme in. EDEN and the box are removed, and the drawbridge panel raised up. Crossfade into a single light on stage left. It's the effect of a work lamp on a rehearsal stage, which the stage manager has placed a prop version of left of the stage left panel. ESMÉ #3 walks slowly into the light. Music out.

ESMÉ   I'd forgotten how quiet you were, old friend. Not like a soundstage at all. No. That's chaos, that's dazzle, all brighter than life. Not like you, the theatre. Dark. Quiet. Secret.

She looks around her.

I grew up on you. Places like you. Long before I made my choice. Long before my life became an eternity of dark and quiet and secrets. A little girl. Just a normal little girl. A little girl who found such a dark world. "Baby Esmé. Songs and Dances From the Bible."

ESMÉ is hung in place in her spot. We hear music, vaguely Arabian, somewhat striptease, like the accompaniment to a silent film. Baby ESMÉ appears from the centrestage right alley entrance. She is a beautiful child, maybe five years old, dressed in a harem type costume. The overall image is unsettling. She dances on, gyrating seductively. Adult ESMÉ talks while the child version of her dances.

I played a lot of halls like this. And churches. Mother was very clever that way. They particularly liked my Salome. Dancing for the head of John the Baptist. A little girl, practically naked, dancing like a whore. Oh, they paid to watch and they loved me. The ministers' wives would cuddle me afterward and call me their living doll. Their husbands would cuddle me later, when no one else was around. Presbyterians were the worst. They always smelled damp.

Baby Esmé. Songs and Dances From the Bible.

The child dances off. Music ends.

I was pushed into the dark. Forced, by a woman who had stopped breathing in the very act of my conception. A woman who drew life from me. From what she lived through me. Yes, I wanted you, old friend. I wanted to be on the stage. And lucky for me, because I would have been pushed out here anyway.

After a while, it was the only safe place. I knew what was lurking in the wings. In the alley. In the pulpit! And until I could figure out how to suck the life out of those who had pushed and prodded and fingered me, I stayed here. In your false, warm, protective light. My oldest friend. My saviour.

> *Slow musical sting of ESMÉ's eerie theme as the work light fades out, then a wild blast of the "Techno Jesus" sound and light show erupts. During this Ronnie clears ESMÉ and hangs her behind the stage left bridge tower, the stage manager strikes the work light and lowers the centrestage drawbridge, and Ronnie seats EDEN in EDNA's chair. There is a blast of smoke from under the centrestage catwalk. Light up centrestage and on Ronnie/JESUS above at end of transition.*

JESUS	Eden.

> *EDEN jumps up from the chair and sees him.*

EDEN	Holy shit!
JESUS	Eden, we need to talk.
EDEN	This isn't real. This is not real.
JESUS	I am very real, Eden.
EDEN	You don't scare me.
JESUS	Good. I'd like to see you without your fear.
EDEN	You're wasting your time. Go away.
JESUS	I can't. Your pain is what brought me here.
EDEN	Oh fuck off. If you throw that Leviticus shit in my face, I'll…
JESUS	You'll what?
EDEN	I'll come right up there and nail you man, I swear.
JESUS	Come on, Eden!

> *Ronnie strikes a sudden and harsh crucifixion pose with his free hand. He catches himself and softens.*

Sorry. Sorry.

EDEN	I know why you're here man, and believe me, those bombs did more good than harm.
JESUS	Eden, you're hurting people.
EDEN	I just woke them up. No one got hurt.

JESUS	Everyone got hurt.
EDEN	Oh right. We're all supposed to play by your rules.
JESUS	My rules? No one lives by my rules.
EDEN	Yeah, well, they don't work for me.
JESUS	You never even tried them.
EDEN	I did so!
JESUS	You did not!
EDEN	Did!
JESUS	Didn't!
EDEN	Yes I did!
JESUS	When?
EDEN	I went to Sunday school!

> *Ronnie laughs. The mood lightens somewhat.*

	What's so fucking funny?
JESUS	You are. You need to lighten up, Eden.
EDEN	So you came here to laugh at me? Some saviour. Man, you don't even look like you. I thought you'd look, you know…
JESUS	Like a picture in Sunday school?
EDEN	Fuck off. I'm just used to the beard and long hair, okay? That looked good. Real good. I used to have such a crush on you. You were so hot. Well, him. That Sunday school Jesus. But this aging club-boy thing doesn't really work on someone your age.
JESUS	I forgive you for that, Eden. I thought I'd try a new image.
EDEN	Keep working on it, honey.
JESUS	Maybe you could help me.
EDEN	Let's not pretend we're pals. We have nothing in common. You're the Son of Man, I'm… I'm the son of Stan.
JESUS	So we have a lot in common. Silent fathers and saintly mothers.
EDEN	Oh please! Leave them out of it. My rage is enormous. Too big to pin on my parents. They're simple people. My rage is very complicated. And it's all mine.
JESUS	Rage is not self-contained.
EDEN	You fucking hypocrite. You peddled fear and rage yourself, didn't you? But oh, I forgot, you smoke-screened it all with magic and hocus pocus.

JESUS	Okay, yes, I thought that if people were impressed with the spectacle, maybe they'd listen. But that obviously hasn't worked out like I had hoped, so I think I need a more personal approach.
EDEN	So what are you gonna do, man? Talk to people one at a time?
JESUS	Yes.
EDEN	Fuck off.
JESUS	It's true.
EDEN	Yeah right. You're gonna talk to everyone on earth, one at a time.
JESUS	I'm talking to you, aren't I?
EDEN	Well I'm not listening.
JESUS	Well I am.
EDEN	I've got nothing to say to you.
JESUS	But there's something you need to hear.
EDEN	What?
JESUS	You tell me.
EDEN	What?
JESUS	The truth.
EDEN	Man, you're a pain in the ass.
JESUS	Sorry. It's my job. Eden?
EDEN	What?
JESUS	Remember.
EDEN	What?
JESUS	When you weren't afraid. ·
	There is a pause.
EDEN	We were in this room, playing.
JESUS	Who?
EDEN	Me and Ogden. Ogden Ramsay, the only kid in school who ever bothered with me. Well, the only boy, anyway. But that was okay. He was the only boy I noticed. He was thin and quiet and… beautiful. Not like me at all. Yet, here he was, in my house playing with me.
JESUS	Did you love him?
	EDEN moves to one side of the area, as if watching.
EDEN	What? No. I don't know. I was just a little kid. What did I know about love, except for what I saw in movies? We were just playing.

To me, he was… someone else. It was pretend. It was all just pretend…

Special on Ronnie out. Short musical sting/memory transition. We stay in the same area, but it is now another time, years earlier. There is a subtle, yet distinct lighting change to enhance this memory. A marionette of YOUNG EDEN #2 runs in. He is wearing an exact replica of EDNA's wedding dress. It is too big on him, and there is no veil. It is crucial that during this scene the character does not show his back to the audience. He has a purse over one arm.

YOUNG EDEN   Okay Ogden, I'm ready. Are you ready?

OGDEN   *(offstage)* Yeah. I guess.

YOUNG EDEN   Well, are you ready or not?

OGDEN   *(offstage)* I'm ready. I just feel stupid, Eden. What if your mum walks in?

YOUNG EDEN   I already told you, she's at a church meeting in town.

OGDEN enters. He is, as described, a beautiful boy. He is dressed in his underclothes.

OGDEN   I guess this is what a dad would wear. It's what my dad wears to bed.

YOUNG EDEN   In the movies they wear silk pajamas!

OGDEN   Huh. I don't got those.

YOUNG EDEN   It's okay. You look nice, Ogden.

OGDEN   Thanks. What's that you're wearing?

YOUNG EDEN   It's my mum's wedding dress.

OGDEN   Do you want to be a girl?

YOUNG EDEN   No.

OGDEN   Then why are you dressed like one?

YOUNG EDEN   I'm not dressed like a girl. I'm dressed like a star!

OGDEN   You want to be a star?

YOUNG EDEN   Yes.

OGDEN   But you're dressed like a girl star.

YOUNG EDEN   The only stars are girl stars.

OGDEN   Then you want to be a girl.

YOUNG EDEN   I dunno. No.

OGDEN   Doesn't matter. You look nice, Eden. What's in the purse?

YOUNG EDEN	Nothing.
OGDEN	Then why do you have it?
YOUNG EDEN	'Cause I like it. It goes.
OGDEN	So, what should I call you?
YOUNG EDEN	I dunno. You could call me… your wife.
OGDEN	Nah, that's weird.
YOUNG EDEN	Yeah. That's weird.
OGDEN	I know. I'll call you… purse boy!
YOUNG EDEN	Okay.

Suddenly a strong, harsh backlight shines on Ronnie on the centrestage bridge. He is STANLEY Rural. The light outlines his size, massive compared to the two small boys beneath.

OGDEN	It's your dad!
STANLEY	Go home, Ogden.
OGDEN	We were just playing.
STANLEY	Put your clothes on and go home, Ogden.
OGDEN	Yes, Mr. Rural.

He starts to exit, then turns to EDEN.

See ya, Eden.

STANLEY	Now!

OGDEN exits.

What are you doing, boy?

YOUNG EDEN	Nothing. Honest. Playing.
STANLEY	Playing? What?
YOUNG EDEN	Nothing. Wedding.
STANLEY	Wedding?
YOUNG EDEN	I was being…
STANLEY	Who?
YOUNG EDEN	Mum. I was Mum, Dad.
STANLEY	Come here.
YOUNG EDEN	Except she was like a movie star.
STANLEY	Come here.
YOUNG EDEN	And Ogden was sort of… you, Daddy.

STANLEY   Take that dress off and come here. Now!

YOUNG EDEN   No, we were just playing.

STANLEY   How dare you touch that dress, you little bastard.

YOUNG EDEN   I'll put it away, Daddy. Just like I found it.

STANLEY   Come here.

YOUNG EDEN   No…

> *He starts to move.*

STANLEY   I said come here!

> *Ronnie grabs the strings of the marionette and violently pulls the puppet of young EDEN up to his level.*

Look at you. Look at… this. Eden, the spoiled fruit!

YOUNG EDEN   Daddy, no! Please Daddy!

> *Music sting. Short, brutal, loud. YOUNG EDEN is "thrown" down to the stage level, bent over the chair and facing upstage, revealing the bloodstained back of the wedding dress.*

EDEN   My mother's wedding dress was covered in blood. And I had lost the only man I ever loved. I hated him for that.

> *YOUNG EDEN exits slowly.*

And that's when I learned the power of rage.

> *EDEN sits in the chair.*

JESUS   Eden…

EDEN   Leave me alone. I have nothing to say to you.

> *Ronnie sits on the centrestage catwalk, feet dangling into EDEN's playing area. Crossfade from top light to catwalk light. He sings:*

"MIDNIGHT IN MONTE CARLO"

JESUS   All I remember
             Is midnight and moonlight
             You're but a ghost in the mist
             All I remember is
             Midnight and moonlight
             Starlight and candles
             Champagne and whispers
             And then
             Am I right?

I'm kissed at midnight
With the heavens aglow
I was kissed at midnight in Monte Carlo

EDEN	You know that?
JESUS	*Midnight in Monte Carlo.* Gloria Cartier was one of Esmé's best performances.
EDEN	Fuck off, you know Esmé?
JESUS	I've been watching her for years. Just like you.
EDEN	That's so wild.
JESUS	Not really. See Eden, we aren't that different.
EDEN	She's my blood.
JESUS	I am your blood.
EDEN	No man, she's my mother.
JESUS	What?
EDEN	That's why she's here. I got a note. She wants to meet me.
JESUS	Oh Eden, no.
EDEN	I'm finally going to meet my birth mother and she's Esmé Massengill!
JESUS	Eden, I wouldn't do that if I were you.
EDEN	Well, you're not me, are you? See, we don't have a bloody thing in common.

"Techno Jesus" music transition begins. Light out centrestage. Ronnie hangs EDEN backstage and the stage manager raises the centrestage drawbridge panel. Stage left acting area light comes up. The panel stays down, and there are no furniture props. Ronnie walks FLUFFER onstage. Music ends.

FLUFFER	Okay everyone, places please for rehearsal. We'll start at the top of Act Two. I need Mr. Bishop onstage in costume as Joseph. Places please.

SPANKY enters. He is dressed as JOSEPH, with long robes and sandals. He's running lines.

SPANKY	Okay Mary, lemme get this straight. When we got married, you were a virgin. Right? Now all of a sudden you tell me you're with child. *Bist meshugeh [Are you crazy]*? I haven't even touched you! Believe me, a man remembers details like that.
FLUFFER	Bravo, Mr. Bishop! I think you finally have that speech nailed.
SPANKY	Thank you, Fluffer. And where is my delightful co-star?

FLUFFER   Oh, Miss Massengill is just getting into her Virgin Mary costume.

> *ESMÉ #4 enters from stage left wearing her Mary costume. This looks nothing at all like the Virgin Mary, but instead is a scanty Ziegfeld-like concoction of beads and feathers. With fishnets.*

ESMÉ   Sorry to keep you waiting darlings, but the duct tape on my ass keeps slipping. Fluffer, make a note to bone my derriere after rehearsal.

FLUFFER   Um, sure thing, Miss M.

ESMÉ   Is something wrong, Fluffer? What are you staring at?

FLUFFER   That certainly is a lot of cleavage for the Virgin Mary, Miss Massengill.

ESMÉ   She was pregnant, darling. Her tits would have been enormous.

FLUFFER   Oh. Do you need a pillow for pregnancy padding?

ESMÉ   Padding? When will you learn, Fluffer? I'm not an actress, I'm a star!

FLUFFER   But you just said she was pregnant.

ESMÉ   Well it's not a literal interpretation. Allow me some license. Christ, it's a musical!

FLUFFER   Sorry Miss Massengill, I just thought that…

ESMÉ   No one cares what you think, you stupid dyke.

FLUFFER   I am not a dyke. I am a professional stage manager from Toronto.

ESMÉ   Oh excuse me. I wasn't aware that there was a difference! Now please, let's get on with it.

FLUFFER   Okay, let's take it from the top of the flight scene. Places please.

> *FLUFFER moves aside to stage left and ESMÉ and SPANKY take centrestage.*

When you're ready, Mr. Bishop.

SPANKY/JOSEPH

> Oy Mary, it's true I tell you. What, I should lie to you about such a thing? May God strike me dead should I lie to my wife. I should *plotz* right before you, a lie crosses my lips. There was this angel. Gorgeous! A blonde shiksa angel. She comes to me, a vision I tell you, and she says, "Joseph, get your wife and your ass outta town. Herod, that schmuck, he's killing all the babies." *Oy vey ismier!* Just when you get yourself shtuped by the big guy, such a decree!

ESMÉ/MARY   But Joe, my crazy madcap Joe, where oh where will we go?

SPANKY/JOSEPH
    To Egypt, my darling! We'll leave this farkakt place and find peace. Mind you, given your condition, Mary, it appears you already found a piece!

ESMÉ   Spanky! That's not in the script!

SPANKY   I know, but it works.

ESMÉ   Fine. Whatever. Enough! Let's just skip to the duet.

FLUFFER   Oh no, oh no, oh no, we can't!

ESMÉ   No? Why not, Fluffer?

FLUFFER   Because three of the band members are missing.

ESMÉ   Three? Spanky!

SPANKY   Don't look at me.

ESMÉ   Spanky…

SPANKY   Honest. Here, check my breath.

    He breathes, wheezing, onto her.

ESMÉ   Fine. Where's Uta?

SPANKY   I thought she was with you.

ESMÉ   No. Well don't just stand there, go find her! And get her into costume. We have to rework the angel sequence without the German Tourette's syndrome.

SPANKY   I warned you about taking her on the road.

ESMÉ   What was I to do? Lock her in her casket? I owe her everything!

SPANKY   Oy, for such a life we're thankful?

    He exits.

ESMÉ   Let's get on with it, Fluffer. We'll rehearse my solo. The show-stopping road to Bethlehem number, "My Ass is Killing Me." Where's the donkey?

    The stage manager places a chair onstage which has a prop donkey head made from a sock attached to it.

    Fluffer, what's that?

FLUFFER   Your ass. I made it myself!

ESMÉ   Obviously. I thought I was getting real livestock!

FLUFFER   Oh no, oh no, oh no! People are very protective of their animals ever since fourteen cows were found mutilated and drained of all their blood!

ESMÉ   Damn that Uta! I need a drink!

                    ESMÉ exits right.

FLUFFER   But Miss Massengill, it's not time for an Equity break yet. Oh no. Well, the show must go on.

                    FLUFFER looks around, strokes the prop donkey head, and begins "acting."

                    Oh Joe, oh Joe, my crazy madcap Joe! Looking for a room to let, but everyone says oh no, oh no, oh no!

ESMÉ   *(offstage)* Fluffer!

FLUFFER   Coming!

                    FLUFFER runs off. Lights out stage left. During the following voice-over, Ronnie hangs ESMÉ and FLUFFER backstage while the stage manager strikes the donkey chair prop and lowers the centrestage drawbridge panel. Ronnie places EDEN #1 in EDNA's chair, and EDNA #1 standing stage left of him.

ANNOUNCER/MALE VOICE
                    (recorded) In other news, city police report that there are no new developments in the Purse Boy bombings. While many community leaders are pointing fingers at the Prairie Revival Party for the rash of bombings targeting gay and lesbian businesses, an unconfirmed source hints that this may be the work of a homosexual person. This comment has inflamed gay rights activists who denounce it as continued fear-mongering from the Prairie Revival Party.

                    Light up on centrestage.

EDNA   Lord love a duck, who would do such a thing?

EDEN   Me.

EDNA   Oh Edie!

EDEN   It's true. I did it.

EDNA   There you go again with your teasing, Mister Man.

EDEN   Don't you remember, Mum? What kids used to yell at me. What they called me?

                    There is a pause as EDNA remembers. She speaks softly:

EDNA   Purse Boy.

EDEN   Yeah, Purse Boy. See, it's me. I did it, Mum.

EDNA   Lord love a duck. What would your father say about this?

EDEN   Why don't you ask him, Mum?

EDNA   Don't be cheeky.

EDEN   I'm not. You talk to him every day, don't you?

EDNA   He's my husband.

EDEN   Was.

EDNA   Is.

EDEN   Mum…

EDNA   Eden, don't start! Not this. Not now.

EDEN   Mum, please.

EDNA   What do you want from me, Eden? Why have you come home? To upset me? To make fun of me?

EDEN   No. I came to find myself.

EDNA   You think too much. Find yourself. Lord love a duck! You know who you are.

EDEN   No, I don't.

EDNA   Well I know who you are, Edie. You're my son.

EDEN   No I'm not.

EDNA   What?

EDEN   I'm someone else's son.

EDNA   No! You're my son. I may not have given you life, but I gave you my life. And I've nothing left to give, Eden.

EDEN   How about the truth? Come on, Mum, say it. Please. Please, Mum. Damn you, say it!

        Silence. EDNA turns away.

      Yeah, well. I guess that says it all.

        EDEN leaves, walking to the stage right area where he is hung from the gallows. He is in dim light during EDNA's following monologue. Her light centrestage has become that of an inner dialogue/dream-state. Not dim, just not "real."

EDNA   We sold the farm in 1988. Not because Eden didn't want it. Four years before, my Stanley took ill. A heart attack. It seems that all those years of my sensible prairie cooking had not sustained my man as intended, but instead, clogged his arteries to the point where his well-hidden heart simply could not get the blood it needed.

      There were four or five important moments in our married life. Our wedding day. The time we were told I could not have children. The occasion of Eden coming into our home and our lives. And this. They weren't all happy, they were just important. And Stanley's illness was very important.

The "Jesus special" light comes up on Ronnie's face atop the centrestage bridge.

JESUS   The important moments live on because they live within love.

EDNA   Jesus dear, I'm trying to tell a story. Now if you insist on interrupting I'll never get through it.

JESUS   Sorry, Edna. What was I thinking. Mind if I listen?

EDNA   Suit yourself.

Ronnie's special out. EDNA sits in her chair.

Stanley needed an operation. I have never been so afraid in all my life. Stanley saw it all as just a nuisance, like a piece of machinery that was screwy but you didn't have time to fix. I made him make time. And he made me promise not to worry. Nothing to worry about, he'd say. Government health care and the Red Cross. Stanley said you couldn't be in better hands.

So, on October 13, 1984, Stanley had a triple bypass. It was risky, but the doctor tried to make me think it was all going to go just tickety-boo. What none of us expected, including the doctor, was that Stanley would have another heart attack once they had him on the table, which is exactly what happened.

There was a lot of bleeding that complicated matters. To this day I still don't understand all the fancy medical words, but what we learned later was that he had been injected with a clotting agent made from blood the morning after surgery to stop the bleeding. And as bad as it had all been, within a week Stanley seemed to be on the road to recovery. And courtesy of medical science, government health care, and the Red Cross, I brought my man home.

But Stanley never had the new lease on life you hear others talk about. There was no new awakening of his spirit, no realization of the good fortune of having a second chance. I think he realized that while his life wasn't over, the life he had always known had changed. And my Stanley did not like change. He's an Albertan. Change disappointed him.

But that man is the other half of my Velcro. And whether he admitted it or not, he needed me. And I realized how much I needed him.

Light crossfades from centrestage to stage right.

EDEN July 1986, my father was back in the hospital. His heart was fine. It was pneumonia. Pneumonia in July. PCP. It was a symptom I had heard of many times.

My father had not spoken to me much since the infamous Thanksgiving-jellied-salad-coming-out party. Not that he had spoken to me much before that. I grew up in a household where silence really was golden. No one spoke. Ever, except to say, "Pass the potatoes." I guess that's why the movies became so important to me. Up there, on the screen, was a world of people doing the strangest thing. They were talking. To one another. And sometimes, it felt like they were talking to me.

A pool of light comes up on the stage right catwalk. YOUNG ESMÉ #4 enters, dressed in another dazzling gown. She acts alone, playing the scene with an unseen man. EDEN remains facing front. He doesn't need to watch it, it's in his head.

ESMÉ/AMANDA
Rex, before I leave you—and I am leaving you Rex—there's something you must know.

REX/MALE VOICE
You can't leave me, Amanda. I love you, woman!

ESMÉ/AMANDA
But I don't love you. I've never loved you, Rex!

REX/MALE VOICE
Amanda!

ESMÉ/AMANDA
No Rex, don't! Our liaison was madness, beating like a heart, but without blood. Passionless. Let me go, Rex, let me go!

REX/MALE VOICE
Then go. Go to him! That's it, isn't it? There's someone else, isn't there, Amanda? Who is he? I'll kill the varmint!

ESMÉ/AMANDA
No! For without him I will die!

REX/MALE VOICE
Who is he, Amanda? Answer me!

ESMÉ/AMANDA
He's my one true love! My Eden!

She turns to EDEN and beckons to him.

Eden, come to me. I have so much to tell you.

EDEN   I went to see my father in the hospital. I got as far as the doorway to his ward. He saw me standing there. And turned his head and looked out the window. I left, without saying a word.

ESMÉ   Eden, come home.

YOUNG ESMÉ exits and is hung up. Lights down on EDEN, and crossfade up again on EDNA as Ronnie crosses to the centrestage bridge.

EDNA   I thought it was awfully queer, a man like Stanley getting pneumonia in the summer. But the doctor said he was just run down. And sure enough, in three weeks my man was home again. I don't think Eden even considered coming home, but he phoned. He phoned almost every day. He phoned every day and kept pestering me to get some blood tests done on his father. He wouldn't let up on that, day after day. I finally just had to tell him, Lord love a duck, Edie, we've got a medical doctor, government health care, and the blessed Red Cross on our side. I think if we needed a bunch of fancy tests they would have let us know by now.

It was the one time he hung up on me.

But Christmas of that year, our family was together again. I worked like a madwoman! I loved Christmas. And Eden gave me the most wonderful present. A puppy! Called her Crazydoll, after one of those old Esmé Massengill movies. Can you imagine that? A dog named after a movie! I called her Dolly. She was a frisky bundle that Christmas day, but she brought some life back into this house.

And that night, Stanley even started feeling a little perky. You know, down there. Whispered to me in bed, "Edna, I got another present for you." I said to him, Lord love a duck, Mr. Stanley Rural, what in Sam Hill are you thinking? I've got turkey gas something terrible! But he was gentle. I don't remember him ever being so gentle on top of me. Maybe it was his condition. Maybe it was out of respect for my gas. Whatever it was, I felt like his wife again. No. I felt like his partner. We'd get through this.

Christmas, 1986. I thought I was so happy.

Light up again on EDEN, stage right and downstage centre.

EDEN   Boxing Day my father got sick. We already knew the symptoms, so it was just a matter of getting him to the hospital so they could tell us it was the pneumonia again. It was the one and only time in my life I saw my mother angry. I walked into the kitchen late that night, and in the dark, with only the opened refrigerator for light, I saw her standing at the table with a knife in her hand. She was stabbing the leftover turkey carcass, over and over. Not crying, not screaming, just stabbing. And with each plunge of the knife she whispered, "Happy birthday, happy birthday, happy birthday." At some point I must have moved or she realized I was there, watching. Without turning, without stopping her stabbing, she just said:

Centrestage light up.

EDNA   Go to bed, Edie. This is between me and him.

EDEN   I went to the hospital the following day. To forgive my father. To ask him to forgive me. But in true Rural fashion, not a word was spoken. I didn't make it on time.

EDNA   I've never said goodbye to my Stanley. I couldn't bear to live in this house alone.

EDEN   We greeted 1987 with a funeral. And the results of an autopsy, which I had insisted on. It was exactly what I had known all along. I guess the only saving grace was that Mum and Dad were so old that, well, you know, at least she wasn't at risk.

EDNA   After all those years of married life, I can't let him go. He's inside of me. He is my blood.

EDEN   But we don't talk about it. It's not the kind of thing anyone would believe anyway. Not in Turnip Corners. Fuck this town. Fuck this family. I'm going to meet Esmé. I am her blood.

EDEN exits. His light goes out.

EDNA   All right. If it's so important, I'll say it for you, Eden. Your father…. My husband, Stanley Rural, is dead. He died of complications brought about by AIDS.

I said it out loud. I said it out loud, Eden.

She stands.

Eden?

Light slowly fades on EDNA, centrestage. She is hung backstage. Music transition. Ronnie makes his way to stage left bridge. He slowly raises the stage left panel, revealing EDEN #3, nude and hung on a cross à la the crucifixion. This is a special figure, fastened to the cross and with a modified control for moving only EDEN's head, which is operated from behind by the stage manager. Smoke and light inside the bridge tower. ESMÉ #5 enters from the stage right side of the stage left area and stands before him.

EDEN   Why are you doing this to me?

ESMÉ	I could have impaled you on a stake like my predecessor Vlad, but we vampires have such an aversion to stakes.

She laughs.

EDEN	But this. The cross. You can't look at it, not if you're a vampire.
ESMÉ	Dear boy, you are so damaged by Hollywood. Once, yes, the sign of the cross was repellent to us. Back when people believed in him. Believed in the possibility of his redemption. But no one really believes in him anymore, so the imagery is benign.
EDEN	But he's here.
ESMÉ	Of course. But do you believe in him, even now?

EDEN is silent.

Precisely. Oh, he and I have so much in common.

EDEN	What? You're a monster and he's…
ESMÉ	Yes?
EDEN	He's him.
ESMÉ	And we're both cursed by a public far more interested in the myth of us, rather than the reality. You know, seeing you on the cross, like he was so long ago, makes me think I should put the crucifixion scene back in the show. Poor Mary, sobbing her ass off at the base of the cross.
EDEN	Please. Don't do this. Not to me. I've loved you my whole life.
ESMÉ	Well your whole life has been shit! You don't have a life. What, you think you're special? A lonely little faggot who lived his life through movies? Darling, that's neither a life nor special. That's common. That's boring. That's general fucking public. You could have done something. Been somebody. But no, you let me do all the work while you watched. Well sweetie, now I'm watching you. Die.
EDEN	But you're my…
ESMÉ	What? Your mother?
EDEN	You said so.
ESMÉ	No, you believed so. I just didn't deny it.
EDEN	Why not?
ESMÉ	Because I'm hungry! I'm always hungry. And there's always one of you around. So willing to please me. To feed me.
EDEN	I wanted you to be my mother.

ESMÉ   Well I'm not, so get over it. You already have a perfectly good
              mother. A woman so good not even I would fuck with her. But
              that didn't stop you, did it, darling?

EDEN   No. She is perfectly good, isn't she.

ESMÉ   How lovely. You've had your redeeming moment of insight before
              dying.

EDEN   No. Please, I want to live!

ESMÉ   You are so dreary. I said that line first! When I played Sissy Mink,
              an innocent society dame framed for murder in *Cell-Block
              Celebrity*. Listen to you. You're pathetic. You even steal from me
              when you're begging for your life. There's nothing original about
              you.

              SPANKY #1 enters.

SPANKY   Esmé, we got trouble.

              He sees EDEN on the cross.

              What's this? I thought we cut the crucifixion scene.

ESMÉ   Spanky darling, join me for a drink?

SPANKY   Who is this?

ESMÉ   A fan. He was dying to meet me.

SPANKY   Why this, Esmé? Why now? We got Jesus Christ in town, he's
              watching us, and you do this? You think this is funny? You push
              too far, Esmé. We already got enough trouble on our hands.

ESMÉ   A few dead cattle. Relax, Spanky. They'll just blame it on aliens,
              like always.

SPANKY   Uta's running all over town feeding on the locals!

ESMÉ   What? Well did you catch her?

SPANKY   I'm an old man, I haven't fed in days. Now you think I should run
              a marathon after a crazy, blood-drunk Hun?

ESMÉ   Fine! I'll go.

              *She starts to exit, then turns back. She looks first at EDEN, then
              to SPANKY.*

              Oh, and Spanky, if this one dies while I'm out, don't worry. The
              little faggot was empty to begin with.

              She exits.

EDEN   Please…

SPANKY   Shhh, don't talk. It's easier that way.

EDEN   Please…

SPANKY   Kid, don't get me involved. Please.

EDEN is faint and delirious. He starts to sing, softly.

EDEN   "Gather round now one and all…"

SPANKY   What did you say?

EDEN   "Come and meet my Crazydoll…"

SPANKY   Well I'll be.

EDEN   "She's a dame who's earned her fame…"

SPANKY   "And my heart's back in the game
Come on kids and say her name
Come and meet my crazy Crazydoll."

EDEN   Hi Mr. Bishop.

SPANKY   Who are you, kid?

EDEN   I'm Eden. Eden… Rural.

SPANKY   Rural? Say, this Edna Rural, the one with the Shroud protecting her… you related?

EDEN   Yes. She's my… Crazydoll.

SPANKY   Oy. This is some situation you got yourself into my friend. It may be too late, but come on, let's get you home.

He moves toward the cross, close to EDEN.

EDEN   Are you going to feed on me too?

SPANKY   Nah, you're a good kid, I can tell.

EDEN   How?

SPANKY   Trust me, I got a nose for these things.

Lights dim as SPANKY's hands reach up to EDEN. Music transition in. Ronnie lowers the stage left panel and crosses to centrestage bridge. Centrestage drawbridge down. Light slowly comes up on EDNA. She is in her nightie and robe. SPANKY stands stage left of her.

EDNA   Mr. Bishop, there's a lot I don't understand in this world, and I don't understand any of this. But I thank you. Because I know, somehow, you didn't have to bring my boy home to me.

SPANKY   I heard you were a good woman, Edna Rural. Terrible things happen in the world, I know. But family, that's important. And I thought maybe this terrible thing shouldn't happen to yours, Edna Rural.

EDNA	It's too late for that I'm afraid.
SPANKY	I'm sorry.
EDNA	Don't be. Everything happens for a reason, I'm sure. And if there's one thing I am, Mr. Bishop, it's positive.
SPANKY	I could tell.
EDNA	Oh? How?
SPANKY	I got a nose for these things. Edna Rural, I'm a vampire!
EDNA	Oh yeah, eh?
SPANKY	You're not afraid?
EDNA	Children fear things of the night Mr. Bishop. When you're an adult, you learn to fear the monsters that live in daylight.
SPANKY	I've seen these monsters.
EDNA	Why would you give up Hollywood stardom for such a life, Mr. Bishop?
SPANKY	Please, it's Spanky.
EDNA	Spanky.
SPANKY	Because I had a rage, Edna Rural, not unlike your Eden. And when Uta and Esmé offered me this life, I embraced it as my passport to vengeance.
EDNA	But you were Spanky Bishop! Everyone loved you.
SPANKY	My dear lady, even when I was larger than life on the screen, there were many people who hated me. Who hated what I was.
EDNA	Who could hate the Wacky Bellhop?
	SPANKY sits in EDNA's chair as the stage manager climbs onto the stage left bridge.
SPANKY	We started hearing rumours around the lot. At first, vague threads, nothing concrete. Jews were being shipped away overseas. We were used to being hated, no news in that. A writer on contract with the studio, his family still in Europe, he cracks one day in his bungalow. Shoots himself in the head. Of course, the studio covered it up. Said he was a drunk. Edna Rural, I'm telling you, I barely knew the man, but he was no drunk. He had sent someone money to get his wife and kids out, but they're not there. The apartment is in shambles. Gone. Shipped, like cattle. I ask you, Edna Rural, what person wouldn't go crazy with such news?
EDNA	Lord love a duck.

> *Ronnie hangs SPANKY and EDNA onstage and crosses to the stage left tower. The stage manager hands him a pair of sunglasses, which he puts on, and the marionette of YOUNG SPANKY dressed as the Wacky Bellhop. Lights crossfade, down on centrestage and upstage left on YOUNG SPANKY. Front light on Ronnie in sunglasses above. During the following speech, he is the studio boss.*

SPANKY
So I go to the studio bosses, straight from the set. I say we gotta do something. All of a sudden, the door closes, things get serious. They say to me, "Spanky," they say, "it's true. They're killing all the Jews." So I say we gotta tell someone. And they say to me me, "Tell who, Spanky?" The government, our government! "Spanky," they tell me, "the government knows. They don't care." Then the people. We gotta tell the people! "How would we do that, Spanky? How would we convince people of such fantastic horror?" You're in the movie business, I scream. You sell horror and fantasy and craziness to people everyday. Make a newsreel. Tell the people!

> *Ronnie flips sunglasses up as he speaks for EDNA and (old) SPANKY.*

EDNA
Good for you, Spanky, good for you!

SPANKY
Good for me? Who was I? I was nobody.

EDNA
You were Spanky Bishop.

> *Sunglasses down again.*

SPANKY
No. I was Schmool Bischovsky, the low serf of low slapschtick from the Lower East Side. Hollywood made me Spanky Bishop, to the world. But to them, I was still just Schmool Bischovsky. And they said to me, "Spanky, don't make trouble. Don't make waves. People don't want to hear about this. And they don't want to hear bad news from a goofy looking Jew like you. Be funny, Spanky. The world loves you when you're funny. We love you… when you're funny." And with that, the meeting was over.

> *Light on Ronnie out as he hands sunglasses to the stage manager.*

EDNA
That's terrible.

SPANKY
What's terrible, Edna Rural, is that these were Jews saying this to me. The Heckler Brothers themselves, telling me to keep my mouth shut. I just couldn't be funny anymore. It was over for me.

> *Stage left light out. Ronnie hands YOUNG SPANKY to the stage manager and crosses back to centre bridge as light centrestage restores.*

EDNA   I'm confused.

SPANKY   Don't worry, it's part of your charm.

EDNA   No, I mean why did you become a vampire?

SPANKY   To kill the monsters of daylight. To kill Nazis. But there were too many, even for a thirst like mine. Eight million members of the Nazi party. Eight million guilty Germans with blood on their hands.

EDNA   But isn't Miss Häagen-Daz a German?

SPANKY   Uta is an actress. And once, a great star. We came alive at night, drinking the applause of our audience. You get drunk on that, addicted, but it's a fix you need daily. Long before this life, I was already a vampire of sorts. Not many people understand that. But Uta did. So you see, Edna Rural, to me she's family.

EDNA   It's too bad you didn't know that earlier, Spanky.

SPANKY   What?

EDNA   That family isn't always about blood.

SPANKY   Edna Rural, do an old man a favour. End it. Drive a stake through my heart!

EDNA   Oh Spanky, not in the living room!

SPANKY   Please, Edna Rural. I can't go on. I'm finished!

EDNA   No you're not! Listen to you. Finished! Shame on you, Spanky, shame on you. Why, there are lots of monsters still walking free. Getting away with murder in broad daylight. And too much unfinished business that no government commission or inquiry will ever set it right. Lord love a duck, we need solutions with some teeth in them. So you get up, Spanky. Get up and go on. Go on for my Eden. Go on for me.

SPANKY   You're one hell of a woman, Edna Rural. I'd kiss you, but I got my teeth in.

EDNA   Just tell me one last thing, Spanky.

SPANKY   Anything for you, Edna Rural.

EDNA   What does "oy" mean?

SPANKY   Oy. Well, it's Yiddish for what you say, Edna Rural. "Lord love a duck."

EDNA   Well, Lord love a duck! Good luck, Spanky Bishop.

SPANKY   Good luck, Edna Rural.

They embrace. SPANKY exits left and is hung up backstage.

EDNA   Happy hunting! And Spanky… go east.

EDEN #4 enters right, dressed in pyjamas and a robe. His neck is bandaged.

EDEN   Mum?

EDNA   Eden, oy! What are you doing up? Go back to bed!

EDEN   I need to tell you something.

EDNA   Later, you're too weak.

EDEN   No, now.

EDNA   All right then, but you come sit down.

He sits in the chair.

EDEN   I thought Esmé Massengill was my mother. You know, my birth mother.

EDNA   Oh Eden. You've watched too many movies, dear.

EDEN   I should have just asked you, but you never wanted to talk about it. You were so ashamed that I was adopted.

EDNA   Is that what you think?

EDEN   Yes.

EDNA   Oh Eden, no. No. I was always so proud of you. That you were my little boy.

EDEN   Really?

EDNA   Eden, most people who can have children are stuck with what life hands them. Your father and me got a special baby. It's like… well, you know when you go to the IGA and want to buy a roast? The butcher doesn't just hand you any old piece of meat. No, he puts them all on display and lets you choose the best one. Well, that's what your father and me did. We chose the prime cut. We chose you, Edie.

EDEN   Mum, you're so weird. I always thought you were ashamed of me because I wasn't part of you.

EDNA   You are a part of me. But Eden, it was different when I was younger. We didn't have the talk shows telling us how to think, or what was right. We had something worse. Ladies' church groups. A bunch of mean-spirited women who said one thing to your face and another behind your back. And if you couldn't have a baby, those holier-than-thou mothers looked at you as if you were broken. They whispered things about you. They made you... they made me... feel less than a whole woman.

It's true, Edie, I couldn't talk about this because I was ashamed. But not of you. Of me. I'm ashamed of broken, barren Edna.

EDEN   You're not broken. You're a beautiful woman.

EDNA   Listen to you, bending my ear like some Carlo Biscotti in a movie! No Edie, I'm just a silly old biddy in a Sears housecoat. But your mother, the woman who brought you into this world, she was beautiful.

EDEN   Mum, you don't have to do this.

EDNA   Yes I do. I'm tired, Edie. Tired of secrets. You should know. It's true.

EDEN   What, Mum?

EDNA   That your mother was the most beautiful gal in all of Turnip Corners.

EDEN   You knew her?

EDNA   She was my maid of honour.

EDEN   Miss Pickles?

EDNA   Cora Jean. As lovely as those ballerinas in a windup jewellery case.

Light centrestage dims and comes up stage left. EDNA and EDEN are hung onstage as Ronnie goes to CORA Jean at the bandstand. As he crosses, he takes a black toque from the stage manager. There is xylophone music during the scene, although CORA Jean does not play it herself. She leaves the instrument and steps off the bandstand as EDNA continues talking.

After your father and I got married, Cora Jean took the train to Winnipeg. It was big news in Turnip Corners, one of our own going off to the city. Winnipeg and the ballet! It all seemed so exotic then. We knew she would make something of herself.

CORA Jean dances for a moment, then stops as the music becomes darker.

But the real world outside isn't as sugar-coated as the ballets that lived inside her mind. But Cora Jean didn't know that. She was always off in her beautiful world. Always seeing painted scenery in front of her eyes, not reality. And so of course she didn't see him. Even when he was practically beside her, I don't think she ever knew he was there.

EDEN   Who?

EDNA	The man. Some man. Walking home from her class one night, Cora Jean was… raped.

Ronnie yanks the toque onto his head and jumps down off the bridge, standing in the alley between the stage left side tower and the stage left bridge. He is the man. As the music reaches its strange, violent crescendo, he grabs the puppet. There is a scream—CORA Jean's—and he covers her mouth. Saturated red light and music peak as Ronnie thrusts forward. He releases CORA, quickly climbs back on the bridge and removes the toque.

Beaten and raped by a man she never knew, and never saw again. And I don't think she ever saw that beautiful scenery in her mind again.

CORA Jean walks slowly off in the alley between the stage left side tower and bridge. Ronnie crosses to the centrestage bridge as light restores there.

She came home. It was kept quiet. Everyone knew, but not a word was spoken, not even in private. But when her time came, I sat with her. I owed her that. I don't know if she recognized me, but she squeezed my hand and stared at me the whole time. She was quiet so long, it's like a dream ended when that baby came out hollerin'. You woke me up from that dream, Eden. I was the first person to hold you. And I named you. Eden. Because what was barren had become bountiful.

EDEN	That was you in the light.
EDNA	Poor Cora Jean. I don't even think she remembers.
EDEN	Yes, she does. She sent me a note.
EDNA	No Eden. I sent you that note.
EDEN	You? Why?
EDNA	Because I was so lonely, with your father gone and Dolly dying. I needed you, Edie. I may not be your flesh and blood, but you're my heart and soul. I knew you wouldn't come home just to see me, but I thought you might come to her. Your mother. Your beautiful mother.

There is a moment of silence, then EDEN places a hand on EDNA's arm.

EDEN	You are my mother. My only mother. And I am your son. Tell anyone who thinks differently to fuck off.
EDNA	Eden!

EDEN	Mum, tell them.
EDNA	Eden, don't.
EDEN	Mum, I'm really sick. So I need you to promise me you'll tell them to fuck off. Promise?
EDNA	I promise.
EDEN	Then say it.
EDNA	Eden...
EDEN	Please Mum. Say it out loud. If you're proud, it's not a secret and they can't use it against you anymore.

EDNA is silent, then slowly:

EDNA	This is my son. And I... I am not a broken woman. So fuck off, you church bitches!
EDEN	That's my girl!
EDNA	Now you do something for me.
EDEN	Anything for you, Crazydoll.
EDNA	Stop being so angry.
EDEN	I can't. I'm filled with rage.
EDNA	Eden, that's not rage. It's disappointment. The curse of the Rural men.
EDEN	Forgive me, Mum.
EDNA	It's not my forgiveness you need, dear. You know what you have to do.
EDEN	Oh Mum, come on. You don't believe in that.
EDNA	Eden, he's in town. It won't hurt to ask!

EDEN looks up.

EDEN	Hey. Are you up there? I'm sorry.

Light on Ronnie's face.

JESUS	I don't need your apology, Eden.
EDNA	He wants your forgiveness. Give it to him.
JESUS	He already has it, Edna. What do you expect me to do?
EDNA	What do I expect? I expect you to heal him. That's what you do isn't it?
JESUS	Sometimes, yes.

EDNA	Yes, sometimes. When you feel like it. When you need some attention. I guess you didn't care for any publicity when Spanky's people were being herded off like cattle. A bit too messy for you dear? Where were you during the Holocaust? Funny, I thought you were a Jew. Didn't you need attention when Cora Jean was raped? Didn't you hear her screams? Obviously you didn't need attention when my Stanley was dying. Oh no, he was... what was he to you? You and your cross. Your bloody red cross! What was my man then? A sacrifice? An example? I am talking to you! I've talked to you my whole life and you never answered me. Well you're in my house now, mister, and you will answer to me!
JESUS	I'm sorry I disappoint you, Edna.
EDNA	I am not disappointed, don't you accuse me of that! I'm angry *at* you. My boy is ill. And you can fix it, in the twinkling of an eye. Well then do it. Heal him. Why do you want him so soon? Why now? You took my man, you took my dog, well take me next, but not my son. I'm not like your family. Your father. I can't watch my boy suffer and die just to teach a lesson that no one will ever learn.
JESUS	Let him learn peace, Edna. With me.
EDNA	Peace? You've got some cheek, waltzing into this house and using that word, mister! All the slaughtering and hatred and sacrifice made in your name. You call that peace? Once I thought all paths led to you, but I see you for what you really are. You're nothing. Nothing more than a road of sadness. Of despair. Damn you! Damn you and your street of blood!
JESUS	Stop blaming me! I'm tired of being blamed for everything. I'm not to blame. Eden started this, Edna, not me. All I can offer him is the road home.
EDNA	Well that's not good enough for me! Shame on you. I wonder what your mother would think of you now.

She turns away. EDEN looks up.

EDEN	I'm sorry.
JESUS	Shut up, Eden.

YOUNG EDEN #2, wearing the wedding dress, appears in the alley between the stage right and centrestage bridges.

Tell him.

EDEN	Who is that?
JESUS	It's Purse Boy. Washed in blood. Tell him.
EDEN	I'm sorry.

YOUNG EDEN	I forgive you.

> *YOUNG EDEN exits. Intro to "Behold, The Blessed Prairie" starts as underscore.*

EDEN	I forgave myself. Mum? Mum!
EDNA	Shhh Eden, it's all right.
EDEN	Mum, where am I?
EDNA	Oh Edie. You're home.

> *EDNA sings to him softly.*

"BEHOLD, THE BLESSED PRAIRIE"

At dusk the dormant sky turns flame
A gentle breeze stirs wild again
And all around the eyes can see
How this our land is strong and free
Let us rejoice, with grateful voice
Behold
Behold

> *EDEN sings the last line.*

EDEN	Behold, the blessed prairie.
EDNA	Sure is nice to hear you sing again, Edie.
EDEN	Mum?
EDNA	Yes dear?
EDEN	I'm not afraid.
EDNA	That's good, Edie, that's real good.

> *EDEN gasps quietly, thrusting forward a bit, then slumps back into the chair. He is dead. EDNA holds him close.*

My little boy.

> *The tableau is held for a moment, then lights snap out centrestage and up on Ronnie's Jesus special above.*

JESUS	Esmé!

> *Special snaps out as the "Techno Jesus" sound and light show begins again. Ronnie clears the two marionettes and strikes the gallows hanging rods as he crosses to the stage right side tower. The stage manager places a duplicate cross downstage left and hangs (a short-strung) ESMÉ #6 in front of the stage left panel.*

Ronnie jumps off the side tower, enters the acting area stage right, crosses to centre and slams the drawbridge shut.

Why have you done this? He was mine!

He crosses to ESMÉ, taking the control in his hand and playing the scene on her level.

He was lost. And now he's found.

ESMÉ   No darling, now he's dead. In his mama's arms. Oh, that must bring back a lot of memories for you!

Ronnie kneels, grabs ESMÉ by the throat and lifts her straight up to his eye level.

JESUS   Don't you dare!

They are eye to eye for a moment. He slowly puts the marionette down again.

I gave my blood for you.

ESMÉ   I wonder how much I could get for a pint of that.

JESUS   It's not for sale.

ESMÉ   Oh please! The world has been paying the price for your blood for far too long.

JESUS   I gave it freely.

ESMÉ   Look sweetie, that myth may wash with the desperate and discouraged, but I don't buy it. You should stay down here with these people for a while. You won't be crowned in glory. You'll be covered in dirt and shit and blood.

JESUS   It's not time.

ESMÉ   Well, don't wait too long. Comebacks get harder the longer you wait, believe me. And look, there's your cross.

He picks up the cross.

JESUS   What is this, Esmé?

ESMÉ   Home sweet home.

JESUS   Stop it.

ESMÉ   What's the matter? Don't you recognize it?

He throws the cross down.

JESUS   I said stop.

ESMÉ   That's it, isn't it? Oh, I know that most of your history was rewritten to serve the scare tactics of Rome, but you never really died on the cross, did you?

JESUS	What are you saying?
ESMÉ	You are a liar. An illegitimate bastard who invented a fantasy life for himself to protect his whore mother!
JESUS	I'm warning you!
ESMÉ	What's the matter, darling? Finding it hard to turn the other cheek?
JESUS	I died on the cross.
ESMÉ	Liar.
JESUS	I rose again.
ESMÉ	Liar.
JESUS	I am sanctuary. I am forgiveness. I am love.
ESMÉ	You are a liar!
JESUS	What do you want?!
ESMÉ	Proof.
JESUS	Of what?
ESMÉ	Your splendid pain.
JESUS	I can't. Not again.
ESMÉ	Show me.
JESUS	Once. He said just once.
ESMÉ	Show me.

He lifts the cross and holds it, remembering.

JESUS	I was all alone up there. That's why I appear, one at a time. I know the longing. I know the loneliness.
ESMÉ	I want to know your pain. Let me drink from your holy cup.

She crawls onto him. As the following seduction becomes more intimate, her mouth gets closer to his neck.

JESUS	You want my pain?
ESMÉ	Yes.
JESUS	You want my suffering?
ESMÉ	Yes.
JESUS	You want my blood?
ESMÉ	Yes, darling. Give it to me.
JESUS	Then know it. And to hell with you!

> *He raises the cross and violently thrusts it into her. Shrill*
> *music/sound sting. Red light fills the area.*

ESMÉ   Why?!

JESUS   Now you know my pain. And you are free.

> *ESMÉ dies, her control thrown to the floor. Ronnie leans and*
> *kisses her on the lips. He then holds the cross in front of him,*
> *clasps each side with his hands and stares into the audience.*

Fine. I'm back.

> *Music begins, as Ronnie thrusts upward. The stage manager is*
> *above on the stage left bridge and takes the rising cross from his*
> *hands as the "Techno Jesus" sound and light show begins again.*
> *Ronnie clears ESMÉ and hangs her backstage right. He climbs*
> *back up on the bridge level and he and the stage manager*
> *position three rolled-up quilt panels on each bridge leaning rail.*
> *Music changes. Lighting rebuilds to a daytime wash. EDNA #4*
> *enters from the alley entrance stage left of the centre bridge*
> *tower. She is dressed in a hat and coat, carrying her purse.*

EDNA   I haven't slept in days. Needed to finish my quilt. Needed it to be done and out of my hands. But I feel good. I feel calm. Okay dear, let 'er rip.

> *The stage manager unties two cords on the stage left leaning*
> *rail and a quilt panel unrolls, covering the entire area from the*
> *leaning rail to the deck floor. The centre of the panel reads*
> *"Stanley Rural, 1924–1986." There is a cloth appliqué of*
> *a plate of bacon and eggs.*

This is for my Stanley. My bacon and eggs man. A remembrance panel in honour of his life. Hung here for all of Turnip Corners to see.

> *She begins to cross to stage right.*

The whole quilt was supposed to be for Stanley. I guess I figured if I made it so big that it would never be finished then I would never have to acknowledge why it was being made in the first place. But life had another plan, and I had to cut it into a manageable size. I had to hang my quilt up for everyone to see. And if they don't like it, or can't deal with it, or if it makes them angry, well then, as Eden would have said, fuck them.

> *The stage manager unties another panel on the stage right*
> *bridge leaning rail. It reads "Eden Urbane, 1957–2001." There*
> *is a cloth appliqué of musical notes.*

This is for my Eden. I wasn't sure how best to tell the world about him. He was a complex boy. Man. But those notes are music that he loved. The beginning of the chorus to "Midnight in Monte Carlo."

She softly sings:

All I remember
Is midnight and moonlight
You're but a ghost in the mist…

My Edie. He always loved this purse.

She walks toward centrestage.

So here I am, flanked by my men. And forever a part of them. It was a long time in the making, but we were… no, we are the Rural family.

Ronnie unties a third quilt panel which unrolls directly behind EDNA, centrestage. It reads "Edna Rural, 1927–?" There is a cloth appliqué of a fork sewn onto the centre of the quilt, shadowed by the familiar red AIDS ribbon.

Yes, I made my own panel. Can't assume that anyone else will acknowledge how I die, much less care. Turnip Corners is a funny place that way. It's a hard town to be positive in, if you catch my drift. And Lord love a duck, who would care about an HIV-positive old biddy in a Sears housedress anyway!

Special up on Ronnie's face.

JESUS I do.

EDNA turns and looks up.

EDNA I know that. Now. Thanks for appearing in my quilt, Jesus.

JESUS Thank you for recognizing me, Edna. I hope the road is clearer now.

EDNA Oh, I don't know if it's any clearer dear, but at least I know which direction I'm headed in. When you see your mum, tell her I think she should be very proud of you.

The light fades out on Ronnie.

I always thought that when my quilt was done, it would be finished. But I don't think that's true, necessarily. Eventually, hopefully, someone will take that big question mark off of my panel and replace it with a date. I could have left it blank I suppose, but somehow that question mark is reassuring to me.

A great big sign saying, "Well Edna, what's it going to be? What sweet adventure will you take today?"

So I'm going to dance while the music is still playing. And I won't worry if there's no one to dance with. I'm going to turn the TV off and look at things in three dimensions. I'm going to switch off the radio and listen to my own thoughts. I'm going to take a nap in the middle of the day and not feel guilty about it. I'm going to call up Don Divine and ask him for a date. I'm going down to the Red Lantern Café and have myself a plate of french fries for supper. And I'm saving room for dessert, because this time, I'm going to have a slice of the pie!

> *FLUFFER appears in the entrance alley just left of the centrestage bridge.*

FLUFFER   Mrs. Rural!

EDNA   Oh, Fluffer dear, don't you look pretty today!

FLUFFER   Oh, thanks Mrs. Rural. Hey, we got a postcard from Mr. Bishop!

EDNA   Oh, Spanky! How's he doing?

FLUFFER   Well, he lost Miss Häagen-Daz in Montreal, but he made it to Ottawa and he says he's never eaten better in his life.

EDNA   Good for him. I hope he gets to dine at 24 Sussex.

FLUFFER   I've got Eden's Monte Carlo loaded with all the gear, Mrs. Rural. We'd better shake a leg if we're gonna make the show on time.

EDNA   Thank you, Fluffer dear. I'll just say my goodbyes.

FLUFFER   I'll wait in the car, Mrs. Rural.

EDNA   Fluffer, when we're in public, I think you should call me by my stage name, dear.

FLUFFER   Sure thing… Miss Edna Urbane!

> *FLUFFER exits.*

EDNA   Well, I'd best be off. I've taken over Eden's Karaoke Memory Lane business, and Fluffer and I got ourselves a gig at a hospice in the city. Oh I know, I'm just a silly old biddy. But I think it'll work out just fine. And if there's one thing I am, it's positive.

> *Sound of a car horn.*

Did you hear that? It's life calling me again. Wish me luck dear, and remember, no matter what happens to you, keep your fork, because I guarantee… there's pie.

All right, Winnie dear, you can play us out now.

Music in, a piano version of "Behold, The Blessed Prairie."
EDNA exits as acting area light fades, leaving a special on the
fork motif of the centre quilt panel. Ronnie crosses to the stage
left side tower, picks up a miniature blue Monte Carlo and
attaches it to a string running along the "highway" atop the
upstage puppet hanging rail. The stage manager, on the stage
right side tower, begins to pull the string, causing the car to drive
in front of the upstage prairie horizon. Music swells and the
horizon glows as Ronnie waves goodbye. Black.

The End

Stephan and Tinka

Tinka and Dress

Tinka and Mrs. Van Craig

Schnitzel

Carl and Tinka

Carousel Set

Edna Rural and Dolly

Esme Massengil and Dorothy Barker

Eden

Eden and Fetus

Ogden Ramsey and Eden

Happy

Cleo

Drew and Carla

Full Set of *Happy*

Raymond

Antoine Marionette

Vespa Pooperman and Pity Beane

Herschel

Tender

Leda and Dooley

Leda

Pity Beane

Child Leda

Happy

Notes on Staging

The set for *Happy* consists of an octagonal deck one foot above the floor. All other scenic elements and staging take place upon this decking. The central scenic element is a large cabinet, approximately seven feet high by eight feet wide by six feet deep. One side of this cabinet is truly just that, a cabinet. There are three lower drawers, two lower side cupboards, and two frosted glass-front upper cupboards. Between these upper cupboards is a recessed plate rail. In this area, marionettes will appear in a more traditional "puppet stage" setting, with Ronnie manipulating them from above and behind the plate rail masking. Each of the drawers is functional and used for prop and character storage. The top drawer has a false top, opening as a puppet stage. The lower cupboards contain chandeliers for the ballroom scene, and the upper side cupboards contain static figures of Happy's wife and child.

The other side of the revolving cabinet is the stage for The Grey Cabaret. There is a glass bead curtain, cabinet towers to act as wings for entrances and exits, and a clear "glass" (acrylic) floor. Beneath this floor is a dollhouse-scale miniature of the actual rooming house. Each room is individually wired to a hidden control panel in The Grey Cabaret wings, controlled throughout the show by Ronnie. These two wing towers also store the characters used throughout the cabaret numbers.

When not rotated to either the cabaret front or the gray world stage, the sides of the cabinet are used as a netherworld for the scenes between Carla and ghost Drew. There is a two-foot wide "alley" between the two worlds, three feet above the deck.

The staging shifts from various areas and sides of the cabinet unit, as well as the decking floor. There are two chairs that are employed throughout, be it as seating for Ronnie and the stage manager, or as perches for Ronnie during scenes played below. Mirroring these two chairs are forty puppet-scale versions. Several of these are used downstage for setting characters during and between scenes, while the rest are upstage on a three-tiered "amphitheatre" which contains the seated cast of marionettes when not being used. Upstage, behind the seated cast, are seven four-foot wide wooden Venetian blinds. These are the cyclorama and constantly shift in colour throughout the play. These blinds, the floorboards of the deck, the cabinet, and chairs are all stained white. Colour exists only from the ever-shifting lighting design.

Stage directions herein are kept to a minimum. The play is performed solely by Ronnie, and reference to him is throughout the staging directions. Stage Manager Terri Gillis is onstage throughout the play, calling three hundred sound and lighting cues from a wireless headset, as well as revolving the cabinet, doing pre-sets of scenes, and passing marionettes to and from Ronnie.

When a number appears after a character name in the stage directions, such as "Carla #3," it indicates a character replaced by duplicate marionettes. This is usually for costume changes, which requires a separate figure for each. Happy, for example, is represented by five different marionettes; Carla by four marionettes and one handpuppet.

Cathy Nosaty's score and Bill Williams's lighting design are integral to the overall design and performance, although lighting and sound notes within this text are referred to only when necessary to the reading.

The play is performed without intermission, with running time of approximately two hours, ten minutes.

Happy was rehearsed at the University of Calgary Department of Drama's Reeve Theatre in March 2000 and presented at the duMaurier World Stage Festival, Harbourfront Centre, Toronto in April 2000. Produced by Rink-A-Dink Inc./Ronnie Burkett Theatre of Marionettes, *Happy* was a co-production with Harbourfront Centre, Toronto; Festival Theatreformen 2000, Hannover and the Barbican Centre, London with the following company:

Written and performed by Ronnie Burkett

Music and sound design by Cathy Nosaty
Lighting design by Bill Williams
Stage managed by Terri Gillis
Associate producer: John Lambert
Dramaturge: Iris Turcott
Director of lighting: Leo Wieser
Director of sound: Spider Bishop
Marionettes, costumes and set designed by Ronnie Burkett
Marionettes built by Ronnie Burkett
Principal sculptor/assistant designer (marionettes): Angela Talbot
Costumes made by Kim Crossley
Puppet workshop first hand: Larry Smith
Marionette controls/specialty stringing: Luman Coad
Puppet workshop assistant: Charleen Wilson
Scenic carpenter: Wendy Hogan
Rooming house miniature made by Terri Gillis
Music recording produced by Mark Korven
Piano: John Alcorn
Saw: Gene Hardy
Flute: Ron Korb
Dulcimer, electric guitar, autoharp, harmonica, and percussion: Mark Korven
Trumpet: Steve McDade
Piano, electric music design, harp, and percussion: Cathy Nosaty
Banjo: Chris Quinn
Acoustic bass: Steve Wallace
Drums: Ted Warren
Cello: Paul Widner

Subsequent runs include Usine C, Montreal; Festival Theatreformen 2000, Germany; Theatre Network, Edmonton; Canadian Stage Company, Toronto; Manitoba Theatre Centre, Winnipeg; the Barbican Centre, London; One Yellow Rabbit and Alberta Theatre Projects, Calgary.

Characters

HAPPY, a war veteran and pensioner
CARLA, a young poet
DREW, Carla's husband
RAYMOND, caretaker of the rooming house
LUCILLE, a chain-smoking senior citizen
Soldier, the rooming house dog
Mrs. Tom, Lucille's cat
RICKY, a flamboyant shampoo boy
KENNY, Ricky's boyfriend
LILY Maytagwasher, Ricky's mother
Skinny, rooming house resident and Raymond's nemesis
Seamus, elderly rooming house resident
Johnny, another elderly resident of the rooming house
FRANK, a war verteran
HANNAH, Frank's wife
ANTOINE Marionette, emcee of The Gray Cabaret
CLEO Payne, chanteuse
MAUREEN Massey-Ferguson, opera singer
Jacqueline Dupressed, cellist
PERRY Homo, lounge singer
Mae, Happy's wife
Chullie, Happy's son

Setting

A rooming house in a Western Canadian city, and Antonie Marionette's other-worldly Grey Cabaret.

Time

The present.

❧ *Happy* ❧

Music begins. Ronnie and the stage manager enter in pre-set lighting, the stage manager sitting in a chair stage left and Ronnie in a chair downstage centre. Lights up as music ends.

RONNIE   I dream of colour. Not in colour, of it. Closing my eyes real tight, I dream of seeing more than all this grey. But I can't close my eyes. Ever. They're held wide open as witness on this stage of sadness.

Not my sadness. Everyone's. Everyone's but mine. The only sadness I know is something I've never seen through my own eyes. Colour. It's strange to remember something you've never known. Odd to miss a sensation you've never felt. Pretty weird to conjure up a memory that hasn't even happened to you yet.

I wonder.

He stands and picks up the marionette of HAPPY #1.

I wonder at all of them. So colourful, but not really alive. But I wonder what it would be like. To be like them. Painted in colour. Permanently flushed. A crazy rainbow of colour.

I wonder. I'm…

The marionette of HAPPY is swung downstage, and as his feet hit the floor, Ronnie's voice becomes HAPPY's.

HAPPY   …Happy. That's my name, Happy.

I feel great today. Had myself a great big bowel movement this morning. Oh, now don't be getting all squirmy about it. At my age, that's something to write home about. And don't pretend you don't look at the size of your poo, 'cause I know you do. And not just the men. Why, even the ladies lift a cheek and sneak a peek in the toilet bowl. It's natural to wanna see what you're getting rid of. Now usually it's just a lump of poo, but once in a while there's a bit of a surprise. Have you ever noticed that every time you have corn, well there it is in your stool the same as when you ate it? It's the craziest goddamn thing—pardon my French—how some stuff goes into you and comes out all messy, but every now and then something comes out exactly the way it began. I guess you'd call that déjà poo!

He laughs at his own joke and leans back, looking upward.

Look at that sky today. There was this fella, after the war, they called him the Candy Bomber. He started flying over Berlin, dropping parachutes of candy from his airplane to the kids below. And pretty soon there was a whole squadron of 'em, dropping all sorts of things people needed.

I've dreamed of flying my whole life. That's what I remember the most. Looking up, standing on tippytoes, waiting for my turn to spin with no ground to stop me. Flying. Like candy in the sky. Raining down with unexpected sweetness.

I wonder.

HAPPY exits. Ronnie and the stage manager set the stage with the (static) figures of Seamus, Johnny (stage left), and Skinny (stage right). RAYMOND enters.

RAYMOND   I'm off then. I'm off to the store if anyone wants anything. Right. I'm off. Last chance. Don't you lot come crying to me once I've returned. "Oh Raymond, you could have got me this," or "Oh dear, I needed you to pick that up for me from the store, Raymond."

Right then. I'm off. Off to the store.

He walks over to Johnny (seated) and Seamus.

Good morning, Seamus. Hello, Johnny. Nice to see you boys taking a bit of the sun. Lovely day for it, although good to see you've got a cap on, Johnny. Too much light isn't good for the body. Causes all sorts of difficulties. Why, one day you've got a mole, the next day you're riddled with cancer! You can never be too careful. That's why I chose the basement suite. Lovely down there. Nice and dark. Safe from the harmful light.

I'm just off to the store if either of you boys want anything.

He addresses Skinny, seated in his car.

No Skinny, I do not need a ride, thank you very much. And I certainly do not need transportation from the likes of you. A bit of physical activity never hurt anyone. Mind you, I don't expect you'd understand what I'm talking about, by the looks of things. So I'll thank you very much to mind your own business and let me get on with the important tasks of my day.

He walks downstage centre and addresses the audience directly.

Lovely day for a bit of a walkabout. I'm just off to the corner store for rations. Like to keep the larder stocked. Lovely can of pork and beans. You can never have enough pork and beans on hand you know, in case of global disaster, civil unrest, or massive failure of the international telecommunications network. And like my mother always said, "Raymond, be prepared for the worst."

So I'm off. Off to the store. That's why I've got my good walking shoes on. They're made with materials developed for the space program. See that mesh? That's so your feet can breathe. It's very important that your feet breathe, you know, otherwise you'd have a couple of smelly dogs on your hands and goodness knows what sort of infections you might be prone to. And if your feet couldn't breathe, you'd have to change your socks every day, and that would be a terrible inconvenience, wouldn't it? No, it's very important that your feet breathe. Not to mention the support. I've got very weak ankles you see. That's what kept me out of the war. So good shoes are very important. And like my mother always said, "Raymond, you can tell the worth of a man's soul by the soles of his shoes."

Lovely talking with all of you, but I mustn't be waylaid with your idle chit-chat. Oh no, I've got my list you see. A can of pork and beans, a newspaper, and a lovely little bag of Scotch mints. So my breath won't be offensive. I'd offer you one now, but I'm out. So I'm off.

He turns upstage and starts off.

Off to the store in case anyone needs anything.

LUCILLE enters.

LUCILLE	Raymond, pick me up a pack of smokes.
RAYMOND	I most certainly will not do anything of the kind, Lucille.
LUCILLE	Aw c'mon, don't be such a goody two-shoes, Raymond. I need a pack of smokes!
RAYMOND	You need to stop smoking, Lucille.
LUCILLE	What's it going to do? Kill me?
RAYMOND	Have you not heard, Lucille? Cigarettes cause cancer. Cigarettes cause fatal lung disease. Tobacco smoke can harm your children. Smoking during pregnancy can harm your baby. Tobacco smoke causes fatal lung disease in non-smokers. Have you not heard any of that, Lucille?
LUCILLE	And have you not heard that you're an asshole, Raymond?

RAYMOND	I'm doing you a favour, Lucille, because I care about you. I think I deserve a bit of thanks for that.
LUCILLE	I'll thank you when you take your head out of your ass and get me a pack of smokes.
RAYMOND	I am firm in my resolve, Lucille. Nothing could sway me.
LUCILLE	I'll let you see my titties.
RAYMOND	What brand do you like?
LUCILLE	Gotcha!
RAYMOND	You're terrible, Lucille! After all I've done for you. Well I never!
LUCILLE	And you never will. Asshole.
RAYMOND	Perhaps your dear old friend Skinny would drive you to the store. Look at him, sitting there in his fancy car. Parked there all day but never going anywhere. Ridiculous behaviour for a grown man! But I'm sure he'd be more than happy to drive you again, Lucille.
LUCILLE	I'm not getting in that pile of tin. Skinny drives like a goddamn maniac.
RAYMOND	Well then, perhaps time has illuminated who the better man is. And for that very reason, I shall not be party to your nicotine addiction. So unless you need something sensible, Lucille, I'm off. Off to the store in case anyone wants anything.

RAYMOND exits.

LUCILLE	And tell your damn dog to leave my cat alone! Mrs. Tom? Where are you, puss? Mrs. Tom?

She sees the cat sitting atop the cabinet.

Ah, there you are. C'mon sweetie, I'll give you a nice bowl of milk. Raymond! Get me some milk while you're at the store!

RICKY appears.

RICKY	Lucille, do you have to yell? Some people are trying to sleep!
LUCILLE	Ricky, it's the middle of the goddamn morning.
RICKY	I just went to bed three hours ago. I had a very hard night.
LUCILLE	What's his name?
RICKY	Oh honey, I wish! The salon had a hair show at this new club, Primal Queen, and then we partied all night. But I got into a fight with this breeder chick who tried to push me off the speaker I was dancing on. It was ugly, honey.
LUCILLE	You got any smokes, Ricky?

RICKY	Yeah. Kenny! Bring me the cigarettes! Sorry Lucille, they're menthols.
LUCILLE	Christ, what's with you boys and the menthols?
RICKY	I like the cool, refreshing sensation.
LUCILLE	Yeah, well maybe you should get off your knees and suck on a mint for a change.
RICKY	Lucille! You got a dirty mouth for an old broad, honey.
LUCILLE	Thanks. And this dirty mouth is dying for a smoke. Hey Kenny, move it with those menthols! Ricky. Kenny. Christ! What's with you boys always having names that end with a "y"?

KENNY appears.

KENNY	Good morning, Lucille.
RICKY	Not all fags' names end with "y," Lucille. Take Kenny for example. His real name is bitch.
KENNY	At least my name isn't slut!
RICKY	Don't you call me no slut, bitch!
KENNY	Ho!
RICKY	You're just jealous, because at least this ho is gettin' some!
LUCILLE	Excuse me ladies, but a woman is dying here! Where are the cigarettes?
KENNY	Oh, sorry Lucille, I forgot them.
LUCILLE	It's not like you have anything else to do, Kenny.
KENNY	I'm a bit rattled, Lucille. Ricky, the salon called. You're late again.
RICKY	Don't you start with me, bitch. My body is flushing a lot of alcohol right now and I won't be responsible for my actions.
KENNY	The only action you should be taking is getting dressed and getting to work. Ricky, they have clients waiting to be shampooed.
RICKY	I can't be bothered with none of those rich bitches this morning. I fucking hate shampooing those old bags. They're all like, "ooh Ricky, you got magic fingers, baby," and then they don't even tip.
LUCILLE	Maybe your fingers are in the wrong place.
RICKY	Good one, Lucille!
KENNY	I'm serious, Ricky. What will we do if you get fired?
RICKY	Whatever.
LUCILLE	Yeah, well, before you sashay down to the beauty parlour, go buy me some smokes, would ya? Not menthols.

KENNY	Lucille, you're dressed. Why don't you go buy some yourself?
LUCILLE	I can't leave the house. I'm incontinent.
RICKY	I've always wanted to travel.
LUCILLE	Christ. Besides, I can't walk in these shoes.
KENNY	Well Lucille, why don't you get some sensible footwear?
LUCILLE	Gee Kenny, I don't know. Why don't you stop being a pain in the ass?
RICKY	Oh, Kenny hasn't been a pain in anyone's ass in a long time, Lucille.
KENNY	Ricky!

KENNY exits.

RICKY	Don't push me, bitch!

As RICKY is leaving he encounters DREW.

DREW	Hey Ricky.
RICKY	Drew! I have been wanting to talk to you. Could you please turn down your music? I mean really, why do breeders always have guitars in everything?
DREW	Chicks dig it, man.
RICKY	Whatever!

RICKY exits.

DREW	See ya, Ricky. Hey Lu, how you doin', man?
LUCILLE	Not very good, kid. I'm dying here.
DREW	Whoa, bummer. I'll miss you.
LUCILLE	No, for a cigarette.
DREW	What?
LUCILLE	I'm dying for a smoke. You got one for me, kid? And I don't mean the wacky weed that you and the little missus are always tootin'.
DREW	Carla doesn't smoke, Lu. She says it fucks up her writing.
LUCILLE	As if writing poetry wasn't fucked up enough. Christ, none of her stuff even rhymes.
DREW	It's like, y'know, free-form. Stream of consciousness.
LUCILLE	Well I'm gonna lose consciousness any minute now unless I get a goddamn cigarette!
DREW	But you have one, Lu.

LUCILLE	What are you talking about?
DREW	Right there in your hand, man. You've already got a smoke going.
	She looks at the cigarette in her hand.
LUCILLE	Aw Christ! You tell anyone about this and I'll rip your nuts off.
	LUCILLE exits.
DREW	See ya, Lu. Okay, time to get to work.
	He sits on the edge of the stage.
	Perfect location! He should be here any minute, and whatever direction he's coming from, I've got him covered.
	Carla. Hey Carla, c'mere!
CARLA	*(off)* Drew, leave me alone. I'm trying to write.
DREW	Sorry baby, I just thought you'd wanna wait with me for Raymond to come back from the store.
	CARLA enters.
CARLA	I've seen it before, Drew. Why are you so fascinated with him?
DREW	I dunno, I think it's funny. He's so fucked up.
CARLA	Don't be cruel, Drew. I think it's terribly sad.
DREW	You think he's sad just because he's fucked up?
CARLA	No, but Raymond takes things seriously. You shouldn't tease him, Drew.
DREW	You don't think it's funny that he takes that same list to the same store at the same time every day?
CARLA	I think it's beautiful.
DREW	Whoa, Carla!
CARLA	No, I mean it. Raymond has a sense of order. Nothing unplanned, everything precise.
DREW	Baby, you think everything sad is beautiful.
CARLA	I do not.
DREW	Oh come on, admit it, Carla. You love all the old geezers in this house just because they're severely damaged.
CARLA	They're not damaged, Drew. They're…
DREW	What?
CARLA	They're colourful.
DREW	You're such a goof. So, did you write anything?

CARLA	Sort of. Well, a start to something, but I don't really know where it's going.
DREW	Can I hear it?
CARLA	You won't like it, Drew. It doesn't rhyme.
DREW	Come on, baby. If I have to sleep alone when you get these ideas in the middle of the night, at least I should hear why.
CARLA	Okay.

"I always thought I would fall because I was I pushed or I jumped.
The fabled precipice. The ledge. The plateau.
Looking down, wondering whether to choose the fall."

DREW	Cool.
CARLA	Do you like it, Drew?
DREW	Sure baby, it's nice. It kind of sounds like Happy.
CARLA	Happy? It does not. There's not one reference to poo in the whole thing.
DREW	No, but he's always talking about flying.
CARLA	Well this isn't about flying. It's about falling.
DREW	Cool. You know, we could fall down right now.

He reclines suggestively on the ground.

CARLA	No, we could not. Someone would see us.
DREW	No one would see us. Happy's out rambling, Kenny and Ricky are like vampires who never see the light of day, and Raymond's at the store. Come on, Carla. Carla.
CARLA	Lucille's around.
DREW	She'd be cool. I'll bet old Lu fucked like a piston in her day!
CARLA	Drew.
DREW	Although I'm pretty certain Raymond's never been laid. Poor guy. That's probably why he's such a freak.
CARLA	Raymond's a sweetheart.
DREW	Not all the time, Carla. You've seen how mean he is to Skinny.
CARLA	Well, Happy told me that Skinny and Lucille had a thing years ago. I think Raymond's just jealous.
DREW	No baby, he's horny. I bet he'd have a fucking stroke if Lu ever gave him what he wanted.
CARLA	Maybe it's the longing that keeps him alive.

DREW	Oh Carla. What will we do with Carla?
CARLA	Anything you want.
DREW	C'mere, baby.
CARLA	Drew…
DREW	Shhh. C'mere.
CARLA	What if someone sees us?
DREW	It's what they're all dreaming of. C'mon baby, let's prove 'em all right.
CARLA	Drew.
DREW	Come on, Carla. I don't have to be at class for another hour. If you hurry up, we could do it two or three times.
CARLA	I'll be glad when you're an old man.
DREW	Come on, baby.

CARLA slowly kneels down, straddling DREW.

Now tell me a poem.

CARLA	I just did.
DREW	No, one for me. Just for me.
CARLA	Drew, this is stupid.
DREW	Come on, Carla. Just for me. What rhymes with Drew?
CARLA	Poo.

She giggles.

DREW	No. True. True Drew loves you. Indeed I do.
CARLA	And I love you, Mr. Poo.

DREW sighs, and is lifeless. CARLA sits atop him, rocking slowly.

"I always thought I would fall because I was I pushed or I jumped.
The fabled precipice. The ledge. The plateau.
Looking down, wondering whether to choose the fall.
One foot on the ground, one posed in mid-air, the centre of me hovering over the edge."

Do you really like that, Drew? Drew? Oh great, did you fall asleep on me, Mr. Poo? Baby. Drew? Drew, wake up. Come on, Drew, this isn't funny. Drew, you're scaring me. Stop it. Wake up. Damn it, Drew, wake up. Wake up. Wake up. Drew? Drew!

Music in. Loud electric guitar version of DREW's theme. He is dead, and this is staged to the music in a pool of red light. At the end of this sequence, DREW has been placed in a cloth bag and laid in one of the cabinet drawers. His grave.

Until now, the plate rail of the cabinet has been empty. The empty saucer for the cat is now placed in the rail.

CARLA #2 is seated stage left. She is dressed as before, but is now also wearing DREW's sweater.

Cabinet revolves, revealing the grey world. There is a cabaret stage with a beaded back curtain and a transparent stage floor. Beneath the floor is a miniature of the rooming house. ANTOINE Marionette is looking down at the house as his light comes up.

ANTOINE Hello darlings, and welcome to The Grey Cabaret! I'm Antoine. Antoine Marionette.

I am your Master of Ceremonies. A *compère*. A host. I'm here to ensure that this little wooden pageant we parade for you plays out as planned. We know wood. We like wood. Wood remembers, like a muscle remembers a strain. Like a strain of heavenly music. A lot of angels are carved out of wood, have you noticed that? No, of course not. You barely see the angels, let alone notice what stuff they're truly made of. Mind you, wood also fuels the flames of hell. I'll let you be the judge. Just don't be judgmental.

Well, something terrible must have happened in that colourful realm beneath me. An aneurysm I think. For you see my dears, The Grey Cabaret only comes into play when sadness shifts everything into this neutral realm.

He refers to CARLA, stage left.

Oh look! And there she is my friends, the producer of tonight's Grey Cabaret. For every act you witness on our glittering little stage will mirror her stages of grief. Let's see where she wants to begin. Honey, where do you want to start?

Oh, poor thing. Doesn't even know where she is. And if she did, I doubt if she could admit it anyway. Perfect! Stage one, denial. And who better to perform this act for us than Cleo, the queen of denial.

Ladies and gentlemen, I give you now a great artiste. She's tortured, she's troubled, and she's in complete denial, but like all true artists of that caliber she will now come out and share it with you, the paying public. Darlings, please welcome to The Grey Cabaret stage, performing Act One, denial, the incomparable Miss Cleo Payne!

ANTOINE exits as the intro to CLEO's song begins. She enters, a sultry black chanteuse. She sings.

CLEO   The memory of your breathing
Haunts me like a sudden chill
Nostalgia for your quiet laughter
Chokes, a bitter pill
The mirror shows a cinematic close-up of ennui
As I cry
Look at me
Oh so still
You're not gone
Can't you see
What I'll will if I try
Reflections of a heart with no goodbye
The lips can form the pose to speak
The mind can dredge the word
Each try an amateurish sigh
For breath is gone and leaves me weak
Not heard because it's so absurd
This faint frail whisper I deny
Trophies that are testaments
Of our contests once well waged
Like faded, long forgotten diaries
Dead, upon the page
A pallid piece of scenery from a play no more performed
I've gone dry
As I mourn
Centrestage
I've gone mad
So lovelorn
What we had cannot die
Reflections of a heart with no goodbye.

The cabinet revolves. RICKY is found in isolation, standing in front of the plate rail.

RICKY   I don't get that shit. All those fucking love songs, y'know? Whatever. It's like, always so sad. 'Cause, like, it's always about someone who was in love, but then the person they loved left or screwed around or died or something. But at least they got to be loved in the first place.

So I don't get all those love songs. All those, "oh poor fucking lonely me because I was so loved and now it's over shit" songs. I mean, get over it, right? I dunno why those people are always complaining anyway. 'Cause me, I'd be happy to be crying about that shit, honey. At least it would mean that someone loved me enough to fucking leave me. Whatever.

Look honey, I never had me anyone to sing about. But if I did, lemme tell ya, girlfriend, I wouldn't be all sad and shit about it. And I wouldn't be all like, "oh you fucking asshole, you dumped me or screwed around or died on me." No way. I'd be happy. I'd be really happy, y'know? I'd have someone to sing about.

Whatever.

He exits as the cabinet revolves to one side. CARLA stays seated stage left, and the entire scene is played with her voice solely as she stays still-in-repose. Ronnie now becomes DREW, there is no puppet representing him. He sits on the edge of the cabinet.

CARLA   I always thought I would fall because I was I pushed or I jumped. The fabled precipice. The ledge. The plateau.
Looking down, wondering whether to choose the fall.

DREW   Look at her. She's so sad. But that's Carla. My sad little goof, never convinced by anything. She always asked me to tell her. That I loved her. She always had to ask.

CARLA   One foot on the ground, one posed in mid-air, the centre of me hovering over the edge. I thought I would know it when I got there. I thought I would get to make the decision.

DREW   Not that she was one of those annoying, needy girls. It wasn't whiny or anything. It was just, like, she couldn't feel it unless I was looking right at her and telling her. And I told her, man. All the time. And I meant it. I love Carla.

Carla.

CARLA   But what if you don't see the cliff?

DREW   Carla. I love you.

CARLA   What if the bluff blends so seamlessly with the horizon that you don't know it's right in front of you?

DREW   See? She doesn't hear it now. And I don't know if she's gonna remember it from before. I don't know if anything ever lingers for her. I mean, I wonder if she ever just kicks back and smiles at the memory of a fun time, or a good high, or an awesome fuck. Oh sure, she loves stuff when it's happening to her, but afterward, I dunno. I don't know why she can't just know something even after it's over.

CARLA   What if you just walk over the edge of the cliff without knowing.

DREW   Oh Carla, what will we do with Carla?

CARLA	Or worse, like me, what if you amble over the edge of the cliff?
DREW	Carla, you gotta lighten up baby. It's fucking amazing in the light. Carla? Carla.

Light fades on Ronnie/DREW as he moves toward CARLA and animates the puppet of her.

CARLA	Drew?

She runs to centrestage.

Drew.

RAYMOND enters.

RAYMOND	Carla.
CARLA	Drew!

She turns, seeing RAYMOND.

RAYMOND	No, it's just me. Just Raymond.
CARLA	Oh.
RAYMOND	I was wondering if you needed anything, Carla.
CARLA	What? No, thank you Raymond.
RAYMOND	Because if you do need anything, anything at all, I could go to the store and get it.
CARLA	You're very sweet, Raymond. I'm fine.
RAYMOND	I don't mind. Really. I've already been to the store once today, but I could go again. Still got my shoes on.
CARLA	I'm fine, Raymond. Thank you.
RAYMOND	Well that's good then, isn't it?

He starts to leave, then turns back to her again.

Carla…

CARLA	Yes?
RAYMOND	I wanted to say… well, I just wanted you to know…
CARLA	Yes Raymond, what is it?
RAYMOND	Well, as resident caretaker, I wanted you to know that we, all of us, here in the house, we're terribly sorry for your loss.
CARLA	My loss? Is that what you think happened, Raymond? I lost something?
RAYMOND	No, I mean Drew.

CARLA	I didn't lose Drew. You don't lose something you hold onto that closely.
RAYMOND	No, of course not.
CARLA	No. He was taken from me. But he's not going to stay gone. He can't. I won't let him.
RAYMOND	But Carla, he's…
CARLA	He's in a dream, Raymond. Just like this one of mine. It was a nightmare, but now it's just a dream. And I'll wake up. I know I will. I have to. And when I do, I'll wake Drew up and I'll tell him about this dream where he went away. And then he'll cuddle me and tell me I'm a goof. That's how it'll be.
RAYMOND	You're not dreaming, Carla.
CARLA	Yes, I am. And I'll tell Drew you were here and nice to me and he'll love that part, he really will.
RAYMOND	It's not a dream.
CARLA	It is! You're a dream right now, Raymond. You're not real. You're not really here, so I can say things to you I would never tell the real you. Like, no matter how many of those mints you have your breath smells. And that those stupid, cheap, plastic shoes make your feet stink, and that everyone laughs at you all the time. Did you know that, Raymond? Drew only kept telling you about computer problems ending the world so he could watch you go to the store everyday to buy pork and beans.

You and your pork and beans. Your damned pork and beans. I'm wearing Drew's sweater, but all I can smell is your breath and your feet and those fucking pork and beans!

Silence.

I'm sorry.

Oh Raymond, I'm so sorry.

RAYMOND	And formula.
CARLA	What?
RAYMOND	Pork and beans, a newspaper, a little bag of Scotch mints, and formula.
CARLA	Formula?
RAYMOND	I would buy canned formula every day. For the baby.
CARLA	What baby, Raymond?
RAYMOND	Yours and Drew's. In case there was global disaster.

CARLA	We don't have a baby, Raymond.
RAYMOND	I know, but I could hear you trying. Across from my suite in the basement, I could hear you in yours. Trying to make a baby with Drew.
CARLA	Oh Raymond.
RAYMOND	And when Drew kept telling me about computers ending the world, I started to stock up. For all of us in the house. And the baby.
CARLA	We weren't trying to make a baby, Raymond. We were making love.
RAYMOND	Oh.

She starts to leave, then turns.

CARLA	Raymond. I'm sorry.
RAYMOND	I understand.

She leaves. RAYMOND is left alone. Soldier is placed on the ground beside him.

I'm an only child. My mother always said that when I was born I nearly killed her. She almost died because of me. She told me that all the time. So she never had any more little babies. Just me. Just Raymond.

I've always been alone. Always my own man. Independent I am. Just me, myself, and I. Just Raymond.

My mother always said that was important. "Never share yourself, Raymond." That's what she said. Why, my mother let her guard down once and shared herself, and she almost died because of it. She almost died because of me. She told me that all the time.

I started life with an advantage. My mother always said, "Raymond, you're lucky you are. You've got your own bed." See, when you've got your own bed, you're special. It's just you. Just me. Just Raymond.

At night I can think about anything, anything at all, because it's just me. I dream about my life, exactly as I remember it. It's all beautiful in my dreams. Even if it's not all true.

My mother always said that dreams were for fools. But my mother isn't here now. It's just me. Just Raymond.

Just Raymond and his bed. And sometimes Soldier. I pick him up real careful like and put him on my bed. I like that. He's warm. He snores. My mother never let me have a dog, but I don't think she would mind old Soldier on the bed. He's not a person, so it doesn't count. He's an angel I think. And if an angel wants to share your bed, you can't very well say no, can you? Well, that's what I think anyway. But it's just me. Just Raymond.

Soldier is picked up and RAYMOND walks off.

Transition.

Mrs. Tom, the cat, is sitting beside a chair downstage. HAPPY is watching her.

HAPPY   That cat is a funny one. Sits and stares all day, like a preacher at a peep show. Just watches, but never gets too close. And once in a while pukes up a hairball. I've seen her lick it up sometimes. Yes sirree, I've seen her eat her own vomit. Now that's something I can't stomach. Just regurgitating the same stuff over and over.

He starts off, then pauses.

But it's a funny thing. Have you ever noticed that every time you puke, there's carrots in it? Even if you haven't had a carrot in years. It's the craziest goddamn thing—pardon my French. I guess some stuff just takes longer to come up.

He wanders off. LUCILLE is heard offstage.

LUCILLE   Mrs. Tom! Where are you, puss? Mrs. Tom! Here kitty kitty.

Raymond, if your goddamn dog has been bothering my cat again I'll neuter both of you with my bare teeth, so help me God!

She enters, hobbling because of her cha-cha heels.

Christ, I gotta get some shoes I can walk in. These look hot for bingo, honey, but they suck for mobility.

She sees the cat and sits beside her.

Ah, there you are, Mrs. Tom. I was worried that Soldier had chased you up a tree again. Old soldiers after pussy, I know what that feels like, believe me.

Christ. Dogs. Men. They're always after you for something. But no matter how hard they chased me, I always outsmarted them.

Directly to the audience.

Please, men are easy. It's women who are the complicated ones. Look, the pants will always use relationships to get to the sex and the skirts will always use sex to get to the relationship. We can put a man on the moon, but we're still just a bunch of goddamn monkeys. Evolution my ass. That's nature, and that's how it'll always be. Oh sure, we gals love to blame men for all our troubles, don't we ladies. But honey, lemme tell ya, by failing to realize that they need to be diddled and wanked with the same regularity that a dog needs to be walked, we leave men with no option other than to be assholes.

Here's my theory, after years of research in the field. A man's fantasy is a woman who will fuck him like a whore, listen to him like a sister, and nurture him like a mother. Well, that's all fine and well. For the man. But it leaves a woman so busy playing roles for his entertainment that she has nothing left for herself. No wonder men are always saying to women, "Honey, I don't understand you." How can the poor bastards understand us when we don't understand ourselves?

She stands and walks to centrestage.

Girls, here's my advice. Fuck men. They'll be so grateful. They can't be pricks when their pricks are feeling good because they wouldn't want to do anything to wreck the moment. The all-too-brief moment of male happiness when they're waving their flag and the cannon explodes. It lifts them right off the ground, leaving us gals free to get back on our feet.

No ladies, men are easy. Don't make them complicated. They're such little assholes when we make them complicated.

She wanders off.

I gotta get some fucking shoes I can walk in.

Transition.

Cabinet revolves partially to one side. CARLA is standing on the edge, with Ronnie/DREW behind her.

CARLA	I always thought I would fall because I was pushed or I jumped.
DREW	You never trusted me, did you, baby?
CARLA	And now I'm falling. Neither pushed nor leapt.
DREW	Not about other women and shit, but about you and me. You never believed that I would want you. Only you.
CARLA	Falling in slow motion, detached from peak or ground.
DREW	I know you were always worried that I would wake up one day and look at you and go, "Fuck, what an ugly loser! I'm outta here!"
	And that's what you think I did in a way, isn't it? I took the easy way out. I just died. I died on you.
CARLA	Oddly calm as I wonder if I will hit the dirt or begin flying.

DREW	I didn't choose it, baby. I chose you. So don't be pissed at me about this. And don't be a goof, Carla. I would have stayed with you if I could have.
CARLA	Just falling from the edge of the cliff because I walked forward without looking.
DREW	Carla.
CARLA	Without checking a map.
DREW	Carla. Trust me.
CARLA	Who has the map?

Transition.

Cabinet revolves to the grey world. ANTOINE is onstage.

ANTOINE	Listen. Isn't it gorgeous? It's silence. Shhh, savour it while you can darlings, for it won't last long. Not in all this longing. No, it's always calm before the storm. Which is ridiculous, for the tempest is the very thing which leads to the tranquility. But I'm getting ahead of myself, and we don't want to go too quickly. Not while it's dead quiet.

You hate it, don't you?

It's the silence that riles most into the rage of our next stage. The muted indignation that ignites the ego's ire and incites the fight. The peeved pride which feels the pique I'm soon to present. It's vanity, fair or not, that causes this stage. Anger. The conceit of an outraged heart that is left alone. In silence.

I adore this part of our show! It's so frenetic, so foolish, so futile. And fun! Oh, it's such fun to be angry!

Darlings, a candid word, if I may. Personally, I find all this talk of anger management highly overrated, don't you? I mean, without true, unbridled anger acted out publicly we wouldn't have any of the fun things in life. Like clowns. Or religion. Or politics. In short, anything from America.

But I digress. And I hear your concern, I register your dismay darlings. "Antoine!" you cry, "Antoine, you cannot continue! Where is she? Where is the grieving widow, the producer of tonight's Grey Cabaret?"

Relax darlings, I'm a professional. Why, she's backstage right now and she's decided to attack this act herself. Although I'm sure it will be a somewhat amateurish display. But then, isn't anger always somewhat amateurish?

Let me set it up for you.

Ladies and gentlemen, our next act will be a dramatic scene. The tale of a man and a woman, a husband and wife. A lovely couple… once. I knew them well, before the problems began. But they are, within our humble realm, perhaps the most famous stage duo of all time, and truly the most slap-happy couple I've ever known.

Darlings, here to perform the stage of anger, I give you Punch and Judy!

> *He exits. From behind ANTOINE's curtain a handpuppet of CARLA, dressed as Judy, pops up.*

CARLA   Mr. Punch! Mr. Punch, where are you?!

> *DREW, dressed as Punch, pops up.*

DREW   Ah Judy, my beautiful wife! Give us a little kiss then.

CARLA   A kiss?

DREW   A quick caress, my comely consort!

CARLA   You want a kiss?

DREW   Oh yes, my blushing bride.

CARLA   'Tis not a blush you rogue, 'tis anger you see 'pon my cheek.

DREW   And what a lovely cheek it is! Give mine a kiss then!

CARLA   I will brush your cheek, you rake. Take that!

> *She slaps him.*

And another, lest you forget the sting of my passion!

> *She slaps him again.*

DREW   Judy, my shrewish spouse, like, why do you visit these furies upon me, man?

CARLA   Where's the baby?

DREW   The baby, my love?

CARLA   Our baby. Where is it?

DREW   You speak mysteries to me, Judy, for there is no baby.

> *The Punch and Judy act is dropped and they become themselves.*

CARLA   Drew, what are you talking about?

DREW   There's no baby, Carla.

CARLA   Yes there is. I leave the baby with you, you throw it out the window, I come home and get mad and you kill me. Remember? It's in the script.

DREW	I must have a different script, Carla. You don't die.
CARLA	I don't?
DREW	No.
CARLA	Well someone dies, Drew. It's tradition.
DREW	And there's no baby.
CARLA	No baby?
DREW	No baby.
CARLA	Then why am I angry at you?
DREW	I dunno, baby.

She becomes Judy again.

CARLA	Then I will teach you what you need to know, you knave!

She slaps him again.

DREW	Carla, stop!
CARLA	You should know better than to trick your wife.

She hits him again.

DREW	I didn't trick you, Carla!
CARLA	Liar! To think that you could so easily slip from our marital knot. A knot which now chokes like a noose around me!

She hits him again.

DREW	Stop it, Carla!
CARLA	Carla? No, I am Judy, hear me roar!
DREW	No baby, you're Carla. Come on, Carla, forgive me.

She throws him to the ground and stands over him.

CARLA	Why should I absolve you, asshole?!
DREW	Because I died, baby.

The handpuppet of DREW slips off, revealing Ronnie's bare hand.

Carla, I'm dead.

The hand falls limp. CARLA stares at it, then slowly turns away.

CARLA	Then go on. Get out of here. I don't need you. I can do this. Look at me, I can do this all by myself. It's fun being out here all alone. Go! You want to leave, then leave, but you can't stay around like this. Get out of here! I don't need you. I don't even want you here, do you hear that? I hate you. I hate you, Drew!

She begins hitting the bare hand, and as she continues to scream it becomes violent punching with the CARLA handpuppet as a fist against the bare hand.

I hate you! I hate you! I hate you, Drew!

CARLA/Judy disappears as the cabinet revolves. CARLA is asleep. HAPPY #2, dressed in pyjamas and a robe, stands behind her.

To hell with you, Drew, to hell with you! I hate you!

HAPPY	Hey, hey, hey! Carla! It's okay. It's just me, just old Happy.
CARLA	Happy, I was hitting Drew.
HAPPY	No it was just a dream, dear. Just a bad dream.
CARLA	No, it was good! It was good to hit him. He deserves it. How could he do this to me? Fuck you, Drew!

Calmer.

Fuck you.

HAPPY	Feel better?

She nods yes, pauses, then nods no.

Oh Carla, that needed to get out of you.

CARLA	Happy, would you stay for a while? Please.
HAPPY	I'll stick around until you fall back to sleep.
CARLA	I'm not used to sleeping alone. It's too quiet.
HAPPY	Now don't you tell me a young fella like Drew snored!
CARLA	No, it was more like… gurgling.
HAPPY	Oh, I couldn't sleep with that. It'd be like having a tap dripping. I'd have to piss all night—pardon my French.
CARLA	No, it sounded more like the ocean.
HAPPY	Never slept by the ocean. That must be nice.
CARLA	It is. Happy, look at me. I'm falling. I am. I'm falling, and there's no one to catch me!

He leans close to her and begins to sing.

HAPPY	"Lift me up, I fall down Lift me up, I fall down Lift me up to the light Lift me up, I fall down"
CARLA	Why do you always sing that song, Happy?

HAPPY   Well Carla, sometimes you have a hole in your heart, and you
need a plug to stop any more of the good stuff inside of you from
escaping, or to stop any of the bad stuff out there from sneaking
in. And that plug can be the simplest goddamn thing—pardon my
French. Sitting on the swings in the park, or a photograph of
when you were happy, or a little song.

Y'see, Carla, for me, this song is a plug for my heart, so I don't lose
any more of my good, and I don't fill up with the bad. When I sing
that song, my heart gets nice and calm. And then I can work on
fixing what made the hole in the first place.

"Lift me up, I fall down
Lift me up, I fall down
Lift me up to the light
Lift me up, I fall down"

Transition.

*KENNY walks into a pool of light, downstage centre. He talks
directly to the audience.*

KENNY   I haven't been out of this bathrobe since… well, I can't remember
when. It's comfortable. Not that I feel good in it, honey. I mean,
lots of things are comfortable but they don't necessarily make you
feel good. You know. Like television or potato chips or families.
But I don't need to get dressed anyway. I haven't been able to leave
the house in a long time. Oh, it's okay. Really. Ricky goes out all
the time and comes home and tells me about who's popular, or
what people are wearing, or what the dirt is. And hearing about it
is way better than going out into it anyway. Being out there is so
overrated, don't you think? It's just sad and cruel out there, and
I prefer my own company. In my bathrobe. Ricky complains about
it all the time, but I don't think he'd let me go out anyway. I think
he's worried that I'll embarrass him. So why bother putting on
something nice that's uncomfortable just to be the source of
someone else's shame? So I sit at home and watch TV and eat
potato chips in my bathrobe, and wait for Ricky to come home
and tell me all about the real world. He's my family. Oh, he doesn't
love me. I don't even think he likes me. But he's comfortable with
me. And he lets me cook for him.

KENNY exits.

Transition.

*A taps trumpet version of "Lift Me Up" plays. HAPPY #3 enters,
dressed in his veteran's beret and blazer. His tie is a multi-hued
splash of colour.*

HAPPY

I am a veteran. Of many things. But I suppose the thing I am most venerated for is the thing I am least proud of. I am a veteran of a war. See? I've got all these medals to prove it. Not that I am, or ever was, a hero. No, I got these medals for one simple reason my friends. I came back. I survived.

And once a year I put on my beret and blazer and parade with the other lucky ones. Not so I can sit around the Legion afterwards and talk about the glorified best days of my life, because pardon my French, and my English, and Italian and Japanese and American and German, those were not the best days of my life, goddamnit.

But once a year I will put on my beret and blazer. I even brush off these old flannels too. But I refuse to wear my regimental tie, thank you very much. I wear this rainbow instead. So I can remember the boys who didn't come back. In colour.

The figures of (old) Seamus and Johnny are placed stage left. HAPPY walks to stage right and sits.

Seamus and Johnny were there, but these boys don't get dressed up for the parade. They're kind of housebound. Now Seamus there, the standing one, believe it or not, in his day he was quite a handsome bugger—pardon my French—in an Irish kind of way. And Johnny, well Johnny wasn't what you'd call a looker, but he was sweet. Simple. Not stupid mind you, just uncomplicated.

Now as you might imagine, our Johnny wasn't much of a ladies' man. But there was one gal he associated with. Joan. A spitfire if ever there was one! And strangely enough, Joan's get-up-and-go were a perfect compliment to Johnny's sit-down-and-wait.

And when these two boys signed up and shipped off to the conflict, everyone in the neighbourhood knew they'd keep an eye out for one another.

Ronnie is now downstage centre, and without puppets mimes the following action while continuing to speak in HAPPY's voice.

Johnny pined for Joan. And in that loneliness, he wrote. He wrote everything he ever thought or felt or saw in his letters to her. And she wrote back. For a while. And then, nothing. But he kept writing to her, every day.

The boys were seeing active duty during the Italian campaign. It was fierce, but in the midst of all that bloody chaos, there was a miracle. A letter from Joan arrived.

*The head of young Johnny is taken from Ronnie's apron pocket
and held with one hand. The other hand holds a letter.
It is recited initially by HAPPY's voice, which slowly turns into
the voice of Joan.*

Dear Johnny. I have no idea where you will be when this reaches
you, and I pray that you are safe. I have tried my best to keep you
memorized, Johnny, but the distance between us has become too
constant a friend, and my memory of you has dimmed. As this
world rages against itself, I have changed with it, because of it. I've
become a woman, just as this war has made you a man. So forgive
me my dearest, but I must let you go. You are a brave man, and my
hero. Always remember that. Love, Joan.

*The following is enacted simply, with heads of young Johnny
and Seamus (also taken from the apron pocket) being thrust
forward as they run.*

Johnny read that letter once, just once. Folded it up real careful
like, put it in his pocket next to his heart, and ran. Straight into
the mouth of hell. The seamless, shapeless landscape which lies
between two battalions of men at war. Seamus went right after
him, two men running. One completely lost, the other determined
not to lose. And just as Seamus reached Johnny, enemy fire cut
them down. As they died in each other's arms, two boys from the
same neighbourhood became men in a distant no man's land.

The figures of (old) Seamus and Johnny are removed.

When you remember things in colour, not everything's a rainbow.

*The heads of young Seamus and Johnny are placed in the top
drawer of the cabinet, and two plates are placed in the plate rail.*

*A solitary figure of an older man, well-dressed but not in
veteran's uniform, stands off to the side.*

Frank was there too. He doesn't get too close to these things.
Never has. Hey Frank. It's me. Happy.

A quiet fella, he was one of those lads who could pick up a pencil
and draw anything. Give him a paintbrush and that's when he'd
start talking to you. He'd slap colour around until it looked just
like the person did in real life, except more colourful. So given his
artistic talent and all, when Frank enlisted he was assigned to the
Film and Photo Unit.

Frank's job was to help us all remember the war, although he's
never been able to forget it. With those last pictures he took, he
changed in a blink of the eye. And when he got home, he never

drew or painted or photographed anything, ever again. What Frank found at the end of the rainbow was both his blessing and his curse.

> YOUNG FRANK, in soldier's uniform and a skeletal nude of YOUNG HANNAH are taken from the lower cabinet drawer. She is placed in a contained area of light upstage centre. He discovers her.

YOUNG HANNAH
　　　Please…

YOUNG FRANK
　　　Oh God.

YOUNG HANNAH
　　　Please…

YOUNG FRANK
　　　It's okay.

YOUNG HANNAH
　　　Please, don't.

YOUNG FRANK
　　　Don't worry. I won't hurt you.

YOUNG HANNAH
　　　No, don't help me.

YOUNG FRANK
　　　Why not?

YOUNG HANNAH
　　　I'm dead.

YOUNG FRANK
　　　It's okay, they're gone.

YOUNG HANNAH
　　　They're gone.

YOUNG FRANK
　　　Yes, they are. We're here now.

YOUNG HANNAH
　　　No. My family. They're all gone.

YOUNG FRANK
　　　We're your friends. That's why we're here.

YOUNG HANNAH
　　　Friends?

YOUNG FRANK

> Yes. Now come on, take my hand.

YOUNG HANNAH

> You have called too late, sir. My only friend is death. He is a constant suitor. My hand is promised to him.

YOUNG FRANK

> No, you're alive.

YOUNG HANNAH

> I'm alone.

YOUNG FRANK

> I'm here. We're alive.

YOUNG HANNAH

> I'm dead. I'm a Jew.

YOUNG FRANK

> Neither of us belongs here.

YOUNG HANNAH

> Then why are you here?

YOUNG FRANK

> To help you go home.

YOUNG HANNAH

> I have no home. I have no family.

YOUNG FRANK

> Then… I will be your family.

YOUNG HANNAH

> You?

YOUNG FRANK

> Yes.

YOUNG HANNA

> Why do you court a corpse?

YOUNG FRANK

> Because I'm dead too. And no one will ever understand why. Not at home.

YOUNG HANNAH

> I have no home.

YOUNG FRANK

> Neither do I.

YOUNG HANNAH

> Then why do you speak of it?

YOUNG FRANK
> Because I can't remember it anymore.

YOUNG HANNAH
> I can't forget.

YOUNG FRANK
> Home?

YOUNG HANNAH
> This. All this death.

YOUNG FRANK
> Then we must remember.

YOUNG HANNAH
> What?

YOUNG FRANK
> Life. I have seen your other suitor, and I will not let him win your hand. Not this time. Not now. So, I will be your family. What's your name?

YOUNG HANNAH
> I have no name, only a number.

YOUNG FRANK
> What is your name?

YOUNG HANNAH
> Hannah.

YOUNG FRANK
> Then let's go, Hannah.

YOUNG HANNAH
> Where?

YOUNG FRANK
> Somewhere we can remember together. Home.

> *Light fades on them, and they are placed back in the cabinet. HANNAH, old, enters.*

HANNAH   Come, Frank. Frank, let's go.

> *They walk toward stage left. FRANK pauses at the place where the flashback just occurred.*

FRANK   Hannah.

HANNAH   I'm here. Let's go home.

> *She takes his arm, and they exit slowly. HAPPY walks to centrestage.*

HAPPY

I am a veteran, of many things. I've tried to lift my eyes from this blood-soaked earth. I've dreamed of flying my whole life. But until that happens, it's the memories of this ground that hold me close to her while I gaze upward. And neither of us will forget the battleground.

"Lift Me Up" begins to play underneath. He begins to walk out, then turns and salutes. He exits.

Transition.

CARLA is seated stage right, holding a pair of pyjamas in her arms. Cabinet revolves to the grey world. ANTOINE is onstage.

ANTOINE

Let's make a deal, darlings. You want to, I know. I can hear you. I hear it all the time, from all of you. Listen to her right now. "Oh Antoine, the price is too high! I can't possibly pay that price Antoine!" Honey, would you get over it and stop blaming me! Carla, I'm not the owner of this spectacle you're producing, I'm just the manager. All I do is keep inventory. Although it's good to know what you've got in stock, don't you think? No, of course not. You're all like her. You just feel. And of course you feel that the price you're asked to pay for life is far too high.

Well then, go ahead, Carla. Make me an offer I can't refuse. Just remember, all sales are final. No returns.

Oh, she is dreary. But it appears she has moved us into a new stage. Welcome my friends to bargaining, where you will do virtually anything to get back the life you've lost.

I'm actually rather pleased that she's included this stage in tonight's Grey Cabaret. For you see, my darlings, I have a wonderful little number waiting in the wings. It's a song, about a woman not unlike our grieving widow here, who has lost her lover as well, and engages Cupid in a card game to win him back.

And I have a marvellous artiste waiting in the wings. Here to perform the stage of bargaining for you, a true national treasure, a great artiste, and one helluva broad, Miss Maureen Massey-Ferguson.

ANTOINE exits, music intro begins, and MAUREEN Massey-Ferguson enters. When she hits her high notes, her neck extends.

MAUREEN

Life is a cheat
Hold your cards close
Don't let him steal your hand
Love is defeat
The fatal dose

Now I am left unmanned
I played the game
Rules intact
But life must always steal
Love took its aim
But I shoot back
Cupid, here is my deal
Settle up, Cupid
It's time to cash in
I'll pay any price for passion
You're less seraphim than serpentine
For swindling me out of my Valentine
I can't believe you've stolen him
You cheeky, churlish, cherubim
Cards on the table
Now let's make a deal
Pull out your arrow I'm ready to feel
Settle up, Cupid
It's time to cash in
I'll pay any price for passion.

> *Transition.*

> *Cabinet revolves.*

> *CARLA, holding the pyjamas, knocks on RAYMOND's door.*
> *RAYMOND #2 appears, dressed in pyjamas and a robe.*

RAYMOND	Carla, what is it? What's wrong?
CARLA	I have a present for you, Raymond.
RAYMOND	Oh Carla, I don't deserve a present. It's not my birthday or anything special. Is it?
CARLA	They're Drew's pyjamas. He told me you always commented on them.
RAYMOND	Well, I only commented because he wore them during the day. You know, when people should be dressed. Pyjamas are for bed, aren't they then?
CARLA	He never wore these to bed.
RAYMOND	Oh.
CARLA	I'm sorry, Raymond, I didn't mean to embarrass you.
RAYMOND	Oh, not to worry, Carla. It's lovely of you to think of me dear, but I couldn't take these.
CARLA	Please, Raymond.

RAYMOND	No Carla. I can't. It wouldn't be right.
CARLA	Raymond, I killed him.
RAYMOND	What?
CARLA	I killed Drew.
RAYMOND	Now Carla, that's not true.
CARLA	Maybe not the first time, but I'm killing him again.
RAYMOND	That doesn't make any sense, Carla.
CARLA	I took him for granted. I just assumed, just expected that he would always be here. With me.
RAYMOND	I understand that, Carla, but it doesn't mean you killed him.
CARLA	With every minute passing, ticking me further and further away, I can't remember all of him. Parts, pieces, but not everything that made him Drew. And that's my fault, Raymond. I'm guilty.
RAYMOND	Of what?
CARLA	Of not memorizing him. Of not recording him in detail when he was there in front of me. His eyes, his nostrils, the hair on the back of his neck, the softness of his armpit. I think it was soft. I think. His bare white skin. How could a man's skin be so sweet? Or was it? I can't remember. He had freckles on his shoulders. I used to count them when he held me, but I didn't count them well enough because I can't remember how many there were. And that's my fault, Raymond. He'd be on top, his eyes wide open, looking at me, saying "Oh Carla, oh what will we do with Carla?" Am I making that up? Were there two people in that softness? Yes, I think. I don't know. I didn't memorize him. And so he's slipping away from me again. I've killed him all over again. Drew. Raymond. I didn't memorize him.
	Silence.
	Would you put them on?
RAYMOND	What?
CARLA	Drew's pyjamas. Would you put them on?
RAYMOND	Oh. No Carla, that wouldn't be right. Those are Drew's pyjamas.
CARLA	Would you put them on and sleep with me, Raymond?
RAYMOND	I can't sleep with you, Carla. I can't sleep with anyone. My mother always said…
CARLA	They smell like him a bit. Still. Like toast, and beer, and puppies. That's funny, isn't it Raymond? We never had a puppy.

RAYMOND	Soldier smells a bit, but not like a puppy.
CARLA	Put them on, Raymond. Please. Let me fall asleep holding onto a shape that smells like Drew. Let me memorize that before it goes away too.
RAYMOND	Wash the pyjamas, Carla.
CARLA	What?
RAYMOND	Wash them. Fold them up real careful like. And put them under Drew's pillow.
CARLA	What are you talking about Raymond?
RAYMOND	Then they'll be nice and clean for Drew.
CARLA	But he's gone, Raymond. He's gone.
RAYMOND	Not yet, Carla. Not if you don't let him.
CARLA	Raymond, what are you talking about?
RAYMOND	Goodnight, Carla.

He starts to exit.

CARLA	Raymond? Raymond!

Transition.

KENNY is in front of the rooming house. LILY, a small old Chinese woman, makes her way across the stage and approaches him.

LILY	Hey you, mister!
KENNY	Yes?
LILY	You live here?
KENNY	Yes, but there are no rooms.
LILY	What?
KENNY	There are no rooms available. In the house.
LILY	Rooms? I don't want room.
KENNY	No?
LILY	No. You have boy here with you?
KENNY	No.
LILY	I want boy!
KENNY	Oh honey, tell me about it.
LILY	No boy?
KENNY	No boy.

LILY	Then where's Ricky?
KENNY	Ricky?
LILY	Where is he?
KENNY	He's still sleeping.
LILY	That boy, always sleeping!
KENNY	Why do you want Ricky?
LILY	To take him home. City bad for Ricky. He not act like good boy here. Act like girl. I say to him, "Ricky, why you act like girl? Come home to Moose Jaw, marry girl, act like boy."
KENNY	Moose Jaw? No, honey, Ricky's from Puerto Rico.
LILY	Don't be stupid. Ricky from Moose Jaw, Saskatchewan.
KENNY	He told me he was Puerto Rican.
LILY	Ricky see *West Side Story* when he was fourteen. Ever since, he say he from Puerto Rico. Ricky Moreno. Crazy boy. "I want to live in America."
KENNY	That's fabulous! Do you know "I Feel Pretty"?
LILY	Shut up, fat boy.
KENNY	Who are you?
LILY	I'm his mother. Mrs. Maytagwasher.
KENNY	Maytag washer?
LILY	Indian name, like washing machine.
KENNY	I don't understand.
LILY	You very stupid. My husband's name. Ricky's name.
KENNY	Ricky's Native?
LILY	Ricky's father is.
KENNY	And you're…
LILY	His mother. Lily Maytagwasher from Moose Jaw.
KENNY	No, I mean, and you're Chinese?
LILY	What are you? Stupid? Blind? Oh course I'm Chinese. Look at my shoes!
KENNY	So, Ricky is…?
LILY	Not from Puerto Rico.
KENNY	Get me a telephone, this is the best dirt I've ever heard!

LILY	His father waiting in truck. I leave him there. Funny boys like mother better. I heard that on talk show. Ricky! Get out of bed now!
KENNY	Oh, don't worry, honey. I'll get him for you. With pleasure. Ricky, time to wake up, girlfriend!

KENNY leaves. RICKY appears in his dressing gown.

RICKY	What are you doing here?
LILY	We come to take you home.
RICKY	I am home.
LILY	Home to Moose Jaw. Look at you! Why you dress like girl?
RICKY	I'm not dressed like a girl, I'm dressed like an entertainer.
LILY	Ooh, big star! Since when is shampoo show business? Come home, work in store.
RICKY	I'd rather die.
LILY	Don't be stupid boy!
RICKY	Go away.
LILY	Daddy bring truck. I brought food. We take you home now.
RICKY	Fuck off and leave me alone!
LILY	You want to kill me? Listen to you! You kill Mummy with sick city talk.
RICKY	I already killed you.
LILY	What?
RICKY	Look, the day I left that town you both became dead to me.
LILY	Ricky, don't talk stupid.
RICKY	You're dead to me! Now go away and stay dead.
LILY	We talk in truck on way home. Now get dressed. Like boy.
RICKY	I said leave me alone!

RICKY turns away. LILY is silent, turns to leave, then looks at audience.

LILY	He just tired. Not sleeping enough.

She exits.

RICKY	Mum…

Yeah, I know, I guess they mean well. I just wish they'd think it through once in a while. I mean, if they love me so much, why'd they fall in love and fuck in the first place, y'know? If they loved me, they wouldn't have had me. Too late for that now, honey.

Look, I know this ain't Hollywood. But it's a whole fuck of a lot better than Moose Jaw, y'know? There I was… nothing. Just a little half-breed, and both halves were made fun of all the time. "Oh look, it's the little Indian chink from the corner store!"

Whatever.

Look, I'm not gonna get all sad and shit, okay? I figure you get two choices in life. One, you can stay in Moose Jaw and turn into an asshole, or two, you can get out and turn into whatever you want. All you need is Greyhound and a dream! And when I saw that movie when I was fourteen years old—*West Side Story*—it was like God sat on my shoulder and whispered, "Get going, girlfriend!" And let's face it, I look a whole fuck of a lot more Puerto Rican than Natalie Wood, y'know?

I'm not going back there. No way. I'd fucking die if I couldn't be who I'm pretending to be. And take it from me, honey, I'm a somebody now. I went from being just a little Maytagwasher into a top of the line Speed Queen!

> *He exits.*

> *Transition.*

> *Cabinet revolves to one side. CARLA walks to the edge, and leans over. Ronnie/DREW is behind her.*

CARLA   I always thought I would fall because I was pushed or I jumped.

DREW   Carla! Carla, stop!

CARLA   Or did I follow the path to the edge, knowing all the time it was my due course?

DREW   You're doing it again, baby. Stop holding on so tight. Relax, Carla. You gotta relax.

CARLA   Clutching the chart so close that I could not see.

DREW   Sometimes I'd get up in the night to piss, y'know? And she'd be cuddled up to me so tight that she'd be soaked in sweat. But she wouldn't let go. No way. She'd rather sweat it out than cool off. And when I came back from the can she'd be wide awake, waiting for me. And real spooked, y'know, 'cause there was no light on.

CARLA   Too late to retrace those blind steps. My feet are pointless now, there is no ground to touch.

DREW   Me, I could always find my way around in the dark. Bed to bathroom and back again. I could get around the bed and the piles of clothes and through doorways because I knew they were there. I remembered them. But not Carla. If she ever had to pee, she'd turn on the light. Or usually she'd just hold it. So it wouldn't bother me. What a goof. She'd just hold it.

CARLA   I'm falling.

DREW   Carla. I don't want to walk around in the dark anymore.

CARLA   But the dirt gets farther away.

DREW   Carla, let go. It won't bother me.

Transition.

The top drawer of the cabinet is open and the stage floor of same is rolled back. HAPPY #4 is sitting in the drawer, his bathtub. He is naked.

HAPPY   Have you ever noticed that every time you fart in the bathtub, it takes on a greater life than if you had just passed gas in your pants while walking down the street? Why, the force of it can cause still waters to ripple. It's the craziest goddamn thing—pardon my French—but it just goes to show you that when you're naked and in a position where you could possibly drown, even the littlest things become bigger.

He stands up, and looks at his penis.

Well, almost everything. As I said to the missus on our wedding night, I'm a grower, not a shower. Now don't be afraid of my little man here, ladies. This noble warrior was put out to pasture a long time ago. Now he just hangs around and barely pops his head up to notice anything. Oh, he had a mind of his own when he was a working stiff, and this little fella has brought me so much pleasure over the years, I don't mind one bit that he's become as useless as a fart in a windstorm.

The stage manager appears with a towel and dries him off a bit.

Thank you, dear.

He sits.

I suppose I should be embarrassed, sitting here all bare-assed—pardon my French—but I've spent close to eight decades on this planet encased in clothing like a sausage. Look at me now! Wrinkled as a bride's panties. As pink and harmless as the day I was born. But you're not looking at me that way, are you? No. All you see is a naked old fool. Flesh that has ceased to be interested enough in life to even stand firm.

Well, if that's what you need to see, then fine and dandy. But don't think it's what I feel inside this disappointed flesh, because under the skin, there is a heart that beats young and strong. And if this flesh has become a bit distressed because it was the armour that shielded that heart and kept it pumping, then I thank it. And celebrate it. Because now I know it's all connected, and not just one little part rises to the occasion when duty calls.

Laughing, he begins to spin as the cabinet revolves.

Transition.

CARLA is sitting stage right. ANTOINE appears on The Grey Cabaret stage.

ANTOINE   Still a bit lost, aren't you? Well, who can blame you. Look who's producing The Grey Cabaret tonight. A poet! My God, have you heard some of her drivel? "Who has the map?"

To CARLA.

Honey, there is no map!

Back to audience.

Maps are a funny thing though, don't you find? They seem so helpful, so simple, so direct. Yet once you get it laid out in front of you, it's virtually impossible to fold it back up as neatly as it was before you opened it up and looked at it.

But perhaps it's an apt metaphor, for map or not we have indeed travelled to a new stage. Welcome, my darlings, to depression.

Look at her. She's so depressed. Darlings, may I speak candidly for a moment, *entre nous?* Now, I know that when someone is as depressed as our young friend there, we, all of us, can feel empathy and compassion for their situation. But really, after a while it gets so boring. And have you noticed the funny thing about depressed people? They never stay at home and work it out there. No, they always have to take it out in public and spread it around!

Oh, you know the scenario darlings. You're at a cocktail party, for example, canapé in one hand, drink in the other. Someone comes up to you and you say "How are you?" they say "I'm depressed," you say "I have to go," they say "Read my journal," and you say "Stab me in the face with a fork instead!" I mean, really. There's too much sharing!

But she has indeed moved us into depression, and regardless of who's producing The Grey Cabaret, this stage is always included, so it is our most requested and popular act. There will be no singing this time, however. Nothing or no one to sing about.

Besides, it's often important to have something instrumental at this intersection.

I have a great artiste who will now perform it for you, although I will warn you my darlings, you won't understand it and you won't much like it either. But isn't that always the way with art? No need to understand it, as long as it makes you feel sophisticated. Or makes you feel anything at all. Darlings, please welcome to The Grey Cabaret stage an act of depression, as performed by Miss Jacqueline Dupressed.

> *Jacqueline, dressed in white face and the classic (albeit male) Pierrot costume, enters dragging a cello. She sits, spreads her legs, tunes up and begins to play a very sad variation of "Lift Me Up."*

> *Transition.*

> *LUCILLE #2, dressed in a slip and bathrobe, is sitting in front of the house, softly singing. Soldier is sleeping beside her chair. CARLA #3, wearing DREW's pyjamas and sweater, is standing behind LUCILLE, unseen.*

LUCILLE	"Lift me up, I fall down. Lift me up, I fall down. Lift me up, to the light…"

> *She can't finish the lyric. CARLA moves toward LUCILLE.*

CARLA	"Lift me up, I fall down."
LUCILLE	Hey, Carla!
CARLA	Hey, Lucille.
LUCILLE	Haven't seen you in a while, stranger.
CARLA	No, I've been… quiet. I heard you singing. It's funny, don't you think? I mean, it seems so simple, but it's not. Not simple at all. It's a very difficult song.
LUCILLE	Some days I can't even get through the damn thing.
CARLA	It's bullshit, isn't it, Lucille?
LUCILLE	Call me Lu, honey.
CARLA	Lu. That's what Drew called you.
LUCILLE	Lu and Drew. We rhymed, me and that boy.
CARLA	He rhymed with everything.
LUCILLE	No rhyme or reason.
CARLA	It's bullshit, isn't it, Lu?

LUCILLE	Honey, there's so much bullshit going around, could you be a little more specific?
CARLA	That song, "Lift me up." That's bullshit. The only part that makes sense is the falling down. There is no lifting up. I know. I've tried.
LUCILLE	Well, you gotta keep trying, honey.
CARLA	I can't, Lu. I don't want to anymore.
LUCILLE	Better you do the lifting than someone else, Carla. That doesn't count.
CARLA	That doesn't happen.
LUCILLE	Oh, it happens, honey. It happens. You know, I think there comes a time when maybe you're meant to stay down. And just when you should be getting comfortable in the dirt, some asshole comes along and lifts you up. Forcing your eyes wide open when all you really want is a good long rest.
CARLA	No one can force you up, Lu.
LUCILLE	No?
CARLA	No. Who?
LUCILLE	Raymond.
CARLA	Raymond loves you, Lu. He lives for you.
LUCILLE	You depressed, honey?
CARLA	I don't know.
LUCILLE	I think you're depressed.
CARLA	And I think I have every right to be!
LUCILLE	Bingo! Raymond's never been depressed.
CARLA	Raymond's a simple man.
LUCILLE	Raymond has never been depressed, Carla. He never got as far as you have.
CARLA	I've gotten nowhere. I'm just numb.
LUCILLE	Well, that's a few steps ahead of old numbnuts Raymond.
CARLA	Lu, someone on this earth adores you. Raymond loves you. I'd give anything to have that back.
LUCILLE	No you wouldn't.
CARLA	Yes, I would.
LUCILLE	Then you've found the perfect home. This damn place.
CARLA	If it's so awful, why don't you just leave?

LUCILLE	I can't.
CARLA	You never go out. I've never seen you leave the house once.
LUCILLE	I can't. Raymond won't let me.
CARLA	Raymond loves you.
LUCILLE	Raymond won't let me go.

Carla, I should have been out of here a long time ago. But that pain in the ass Raymond won't let go of me. He just keeps holding me up into that light of his. That damned light.

CARLA   I thought the light was… I don't know. You know. Good. Love.

LUCILLE   Right idea, honey, wrong light. Raymond's light is like sunshine through pollution. All that garbage burning your eyes. All that crap when you don't filter things properly. No, it's not the light. It's…. Damn him.

CARLA   What?

LUCILLE   It's grey.

CARLA   That's me.

LUCILLE   No, honey. You're in living colour. Now you stop this bullshit and let Drew rest. He'll thank you for it.

> *She starts to leave.*

Trust me.

> *LUCILLE exits. CARLA sits quietly for a moment. She stands, then slowly lays down on the ground, her head resting on Soldier's body.*

> *Transition.*

> *RAYMOND, dressed in his pyjamas and robe, enters.*

RAYMOND   I can't sleep. I've tried. I've tried everything. Warm milk, counting sheep, holding my breath until I black out. But nothing works. I'm dead tired and wide awake.

That's what you get for thinking right before bedtime. All those thoughts rolling around behind your eyes. Keeping your lids propped open. Very improper at bedtime. Bedtime is supposed to be when you dream, not think.

Not that I think all the time. Oh no. My mind can be totally blank for great stretches of time, and I'm completely happy, thank you very much.

But tonight it's too loud.

It's the noise, you see. The voices. Listen. Walls, floor, ceiling, all in concert. A constant chorus of chattering. All those memories I've made up that won't be quiet and let me rest.

My mother always said, "You're an empty-headed dreamer you are, Raymond. Someday you'll wake up, my lad, and your dreams won't be able to comfort you then. I should know, I almost died because of you." She told me that all the time.

But she did, didn't she? She died because of me. Not almost, like she tells me now, but really. Died, when I was born. A little baby, all alone in all that awful light. But I couldn't be alone. I couldn't be just me, just Raymond. So as soon as I could understand it I started to remember it. But not the real way. My way. Raymond's way. It's better that way, because now no one ever leaves me. They can't.

I remember them all back to life.

Transition.

Soldier enters, walking slowly across the stage. He stops abruptly and sniffs his bum. As he exits, HAPPY enters.

HAPPY Soldier is an inspiration to me. You know, that dog expects very little from life. Oh, he hopes there will be some food in his bowl, some water to drink, maybe an ear scratch or a belly rub every now and then. But he's smarter than most goddamn people— pardon my French. Just watch him. Why, sometimes when he's walking, he'll just stop and turn around to see if his ass is still there. Smart old boy, that Soldier. 'Cause he knows, you can't move forward unless you know what's behind you.

He sits stage right.

After the war, we had a lot of feisty boys coming home. But those boys had become men, and they had but one thing on their minds. It seems that just when all the battles overseas had finished, a new campaign had begun here at home. The birds and the bees were facing off.

To assist in this ritual, one of the fancy downtown hotels would have a dance in their Crystal Ballroom every Saturday night.

The lower doors of the cabinet are opened to reveal two chandeliers.

Now, for boys who had been away from home a long time, trust me my friends, the word ballroom was a loaded gun.

And the main target was Lucille.

Music begins as young LUCILLE enters.

Oh, she was a pistol, that Lu! Now she wasn't what you'd call beautiful, but there was a life about that gal that was like a magnet. Everyone wanted to be around her. If there was a party, she was the life of it. The other gals hated her of course, but the men couldn't get enough of her.

And she saw to it that there was enough to go around.

Now, I'm not saying our Lu was as loose as a whore's knickers. No, I figure a gal has as much right as any fella to enjoy herself. She had waited for all those boys to come marching home, and she saw it as her personal duty to thank 'em all. One at a time. She was having the time of her life.

All the swells got on their knees and begged her to dance.

Ronnie bends to one knee and takes LUCILLE's hand. He stands and she dances and spins to the music, ending in a pose against his leg.

If you hadn't been overseas you were still welcome at these Saturday night affairs, although your place in the pecking order—pardon my French—was considerably lower. And if you were Raymond, well, that would be the bottom of the heap.

RAYMOND #3 enters. He is not young, but the old version of himself, dressed in an awkward suit. In one hand, a flower.

Raymond loved Lucille. He'd never seen anything like her, and his heart went instantly to that place where the butterflies live. But those butterflies inside of him prevented Raymond from ever moving toward that vision which had captured his gaze.

He watches LUCILLE dance from behind Ronnie's leg.

So he watched. And waited for his turn. Hoping that Lucille would notice him. But Lucille was too busy being alive. She had no idea she was a memory in the making.

And then it happened. Raymond received a once-in-a-lifetime gift. A moment of courage that he acted on. He started walking through that crowd toward Lucille, shaking like a bridegroom's boner—pardon my French. And he held up that one single flower like it was a sword, ready to slay any opponent who dared to come between him and the object of his obsession. And just as he reached Lucille there in the middle of the dance floor...

The stage manager places the seated figure of Skinny stage left.

Skinny appeared!

Skinny! The most popular guy in town. A laugh-a-minute star athlete, and he had a big Studebaker. When it came to a good time, he was Lucille's equivalent. And Raymond was no match for that.

LUCILLE dances over to Skinny and kisses him. They are whisked off by the stage manager, leaving the empty chair. On the chair seat is a copy of LUCILLE's dress.

And as Skinny and Lu floated off into the night, Raymond and his flower withered.

RAYMOND slowly begins to make his way to the chair.

But he had already begun his pilgrimage toward that new sacred ground, and could not stop himself now. He followed them to the parking lot and watched as they drove away.

And standing there in that spot in the dark where his vision had vanished, Raymond found Lucille's dress. The butterfly's wings, shed like an unwanted cocoon.

The car and its occupants had raced too fast into that night. Too passionately through a sign that said stop.

The lower cabinet doors are slammed shut.

Skinny's car became a coffin that night. And when they pulled Lucille's broken body from it, she was naked and her mouth was frozen into a laugh.

Who knows what might have happened if Raymond had gotten to that intersection on the dance floor first. Who knows. Only him, because this is the only memory he's chosen to hold onto.

RAYMOND sits on the chair, the dress in his hands. HAPPY stands.

One man's trash is another man's treasure. But maybe some of what we treasure the most should be disposed of. Now, I'm not suggesting that hanging onto something beautiful too long will make it ugly, but I can guarantee you this. Hanging onto something ugly will never make it beautiful.

HAPPY exits. RAYMOND looks at the dress in his hands, and buries his face in it. He stands, and slowly makes his way to centrestage. There is a knock.

RAYMOND   Carla. Carla, it's me. Just me. Just…

CARLA appears.

CARLA   Raymond.

RAYMOND	I know it's late, Carla.
CARLA	It's not too late, Raymond. I'm wide awake.
RAYMOND	I need to do this, now. So I can get some rest.

He holds the dress out to CARLA.

I'd like you to have this.

CARLA	Oh Raymond, it's beautiful. Wouldn't you like to hang onto it?
RAYMOND	No. I've been hanging on long enough.
CARLA	I know.

They are together, but separate now in their thoughts.

It's surprising how calm it is when you realize. That moment when you know that the very thing you've been so diligent in waiting for won't happen. Will never be.

RAYMOND I've held onto this for a long time. I guess I thought that if I held it close enough it would never go away. Something fading in my hands so I could remember the colour of my heart.

CARLA The waiting, oh, the waiting. That's the hardest part. Holding yourself tight, being still. So still, not breathing, pretending to be calm. And so sad because it doesn't come quickly. But you never admit the sadness. That would be defeat. That would be giving up. And a true watcher never gives up.

RAYMOND But just because I have this… thing, doesn't make it real. Not real like it was. Real like I wanted it to be. But no amount of wanting, no amount of time, could ever make it into something it wasn't.

CARLA Until that moment. That tiny little moment when you know. It's not meant to be. Calm. Not pretending anymore. Finally able to breathe.

RAYMOND walks toward his chair, stage left.

RAYMOND I've prayed. I've prayed for death my whole life. With every breath I've thought, please let this be the last one. Because I'm guilty you see. Alive, when so many good people aren't. People who remembered to breathe, to keep living. Not like me. Not like Raymond, who only breathes to stand still. To remember.

CARLA walks toward the chair, stage right.

CARLA I hope there is a God. I do… really do. Because I want to ask him something. I want to know why. Why he would put something, someone, there in my heart and tell me this was right. And then sneak up on me when I was least expecting it and whisper, "No, it's not meant to be."

RAYMOND	So I need to let this go now. I need to let it be what it was, not what I foolishly hoped it might be.
CARLA	I don't know if he's cruel. I don't think so. I don't know. I just want to ask him why. And if he doesn't exist, then who's to blame for all this longing?

LUCILLE enters, and crosses the stage to RAYMOND.

LUCILLE	Thank you, Raymond.
RAYMOND	I love you, Lucille.
LUCILLE	I know.

LUCILLE is placed in a cloth bag, taking one final look at RAYMOND.

Asshole.

She is placed in the cabinet drawer next to DREW. A plate is placed in the plate rail. RAYMOND exits.

HAPPY enters, standing beside CARLA.

CARLA	Happy, they're not real, are they?
HAPPY	Well, real is a funny thing, Carla.
CARLA	I mean alive. Some of the people in this house aren't alive.
HAPPY	Oh, they're alive, Carla. But some of them are kept alive, even though they've gone away.
CARLA	They're ghosts.
HAPPY	No dear, a ghost is the same person that left. Ghosts always stay the same. These people here are different now. They're like me.
CARLA	I don't understand.

CARLA stands and they start walking across stage.

HAPPY	Well Carla, the way I figure it, ghosts stick around a place because they don't want to leave. They don't understand that they're supposed to go. You follow me?
CARLA	Sort of.
HAPPY	But sometimes it's the living ones left behind that can't let them go. So they keep them around.
CARLA	How? Tell me how, Happy. Please.
HAPPY	They never say goodbye.
CARLA	That's all?

HAPPY	That's all.
CARLA	But how do they get old if they're not alive?
HAPPY	Memories get old, Carla. If you hold onto them tight enough they change with you. You look at them differently.
CARLA	So, who's real, Happy? Kenny and Ricky are, aren't they?
HAPPY	Well, I've never been too sure how real Ricky is, to tell you the goddamn truth—pardon my French—but yes, he's alive. And he keeps Kenny alive.
CARLA	But he doesn't even like Kenny.

HAPPY sits.

HAPPY	Ricky doesn't like to look in the mirror, Carla, because what he sees makes him sad. Oh, not that he's a homo. It's all the other stuff. So Kenny became his mirror. Someone who will stand right there in front of him and reflect him, and never leave. Although Kenny did try to leave.
CARLA	Kenny died?
HAPPY	Three years ago. He was so thin at the end. But Ricky never said goodbye. So Kenny still lives here with us. And Ricky keeps him fat.
CARLA	And Seamus? Johnny?
HAPPY	Seamus and Johnny were both killed in the war. Then Skinny and Lucille, taken together that terrible night.
CARLA	Lu left today. Raymond said goodbye.
HAPPY	Then I hope he let Skinny go too.
CARLA	Why would he keep him all this time?
HAPPY	Not all memories are good ones, dear. Sometimes we hold onto the bad ones just to remind ourselves why we're so miserable.
CARLA	And you, Happy?
HAPPY	What do you think?
CARLA	You're too pink. I think you're alive.
HAPPY	Yes dear, I am. And I'm glad for every goddamn minute—pardon my French. But I hope it doesn't last forever.
CARLA	Then why do you stay, Happy?
HAPPY	Because this is my life, Carla. Oh, it wasn't all beautiful, but every minute of it was true. And there's always the thrill of hope.
CARLA	Hope for what. Happy?

HAPPY	That this weary world will rejoice. And I hope Raymond lets me go, if I go first. Maybe it's time you let Drew go. Time to say goodbye.

CARLA sits beside him.

CARLA	He made me happy. There's nothing else to say. I was happy because I loved him, happy because he loved me. All of this, whatever this is, it's all because I was there, at home in the middle of happiness and it went away. I'm not mad anymore. I'm not even sad. I'm just not happy. I know what I'm missing now, and I don't need any more life without it. My home is elsewhere.
HAPPY	You're a young woman, Carla. And there's a whole rainbow of people out there. Someone you could be happy with and love and feel passionate about again.
CARLA	Oh Happy, we had something other than passion. It was… intimacy. We could be anywhere, with anyone, or all alone, and I could just lean into him and know.
HAPPY	Know what, dear?
CARLA	Why I bothered to keep breathing.

Transition.

HAPPY and CARLA stay seated, stage left. Cabinet revolves to the grey world. ANTOINE runs onstage.

ANTOINE	Darlings, would you look at the time! Why, it's almost time to say… well, you know, don't you, Carla?

To audience.

I am so sick of her not saying a word to me. Fine, forget her. This will be for you, my friends. Although, I'm not yours, am I? Your friend. No, best not. Let's keep it professional. Although I know that you will all come running to me one at a time when you need a dose of sadness and memory. Oh don't worry, darlings, I won't out you. I won't tell anyone that you come to visit Antoine on the side.

We have almost reached the necessary beginning that is goodbye. But not quite. We're not finished yet. Our little producer will have to go through one more stage, whether she accepts it or not. Well then, to acceptance.

Now, you will be pleased to know, my darlings, that your patience and perseverance has paid off, for we have fulfilled all the requisite Canadian content for the evening. There will be no more government approved high art, no more faux British accents or classical crap that no one understands. No, now you're going to get what you really want to see when you go to the theatre in this country. Cheap, sleazy, American entertainment!

We have a marvellous entertainer from south of the border, if you will, who will now perform for you. I wondered who best to perform this act for you, and then realized, who better to cram something down our throats and make us accept it than an American?

So darlings, please welcome to The Grey Cabaret stage, in an act of harsh acceptance, the incomparable song stylings of Mr. Perry Homo!

     ANTOINE exits. Perry Homo appears onstage and sings.

PERRY   Fine, you're dead
That's no excuse to leave
Yeah, you've croaked
Excuse me while I cry
Ha ha ha
You've turned so cold
Lying in your bed
I'll never understand the reason why
Well guess what love
Guess I'd better say…
So, you've kicked
I noticed by the smell
Look, a stiff
Who had to go and die
Why why why
You think you're so smart
But I'm not tricked at all
Sorry, doll, but I'm not that kind of guy
Well guess what love
Guess I'd better say…
Faretheewell, *bon voyage, arrivederci,* hon
Pax vobiscum, buenos noches, glückliche Reise
à demain, sally forth, aloha, gotta run
And in case I didn't mention it…
Cheerio, *au revoir, shalom,* and *adios,*
Sayonara, hasta la vista, gotta fly
Auf Wiedersehen, do svidanye, ciao, à bientot
And in case I didn't mention it
I'm sure I must have mentioned it
But in case I didn't mention it…

Transition.

Cabinet revolves. CARLA and HAPPY as before. RAYMOND enters.

RAYMOND Good evening then.

CARLA stands.

CARLA Raymond, here, sit down.

RAYMOND Oh, no Carla. Don't trouble yourself.

CARLA Raymond, I insist. Sit.

RAYMOND Well, I have had my shoes on all day and the mesh is getting a bit moist.

He sits.

That's lovely then.

CARLA Thank you, Raymond.

RAYMOND Oh no, thank you, Carla.

CARLA I mean for the dress, Raymond. Thank you for that.

RAYMOND Oh. I don't know why I hung onto it for so long.

CARLA Because it's beautiful, Raymond. Just like you.

RAYMOND Carla, please, get off with you! Men can't be beautiful.

CARLA Yes, they can.

RAYMOND Did you hear that, Happy? Carla said I was beautiful!

HAPPY I think she was referring to the inside bits, not the outside, so don't be getting your boxers in a bunch there, beautiful.

RAYMOND Oh. Well, that's all right then, isn't it?

CARLA I'd better be going.

RAYMOND No! You're not leaving too, are you?

CARLA I'm… going home, Raymond.

RAYMOND Oh?

CARLA But I'll wear the dress you gave me.

RAYMOND Oh. That's good then, isn't it?

CARLA It's goodbye, beautiful.

RAYMOND Goodbye, Carla.

CARLA Happy…

HAPPY I won't forget, dear.

She starts to leave, and turns back to RAYMOND.

CARLA	Raymond?
RAYMOND	Yes Carla?
CARLA	I'll leave Drew's sweater on your doorknob. He'd want you to have it. You know, in case of disaster.

> *CARLA crosses to stage right. She is exchanged for CARLA #4, wearing young LUCILLE's dress. She sits, and is hung still-in-repose.*
>
> *Transition.*
>
> *Ronnie sits atop one of the high cupboards of the cabinet as it revolves to one side. He is DREW.*

DREW	I never really thought about this much before. Y'know, dying and shit. It's been pretty easy for me though. But then, most things have been easy for me.
CARLA	Freeze-frame, free-falling. Still, in soft focus.
DREW	Not that I didn't care. I cared, man, a lot. About a lot of stuff. But I figured out why it's been so easy for me, y'know, crossing over. It's Carla. She made it really easy for me to do this. Not so much now, but before. When I was with her. It's like she prepared everything, without even knowing it.
CARLA	A shattered lens, but not broken yet.
DREW	I mean, it's not like she packed my fucking bags or anything, but she loaded me up, y'know? She loved me. I always thought she was such a goof because she loved me so much. But she felt what I'm feeling right now, long before I did.
CARLA	With my last pose I see the flash fade, I hear the shutter close.
DREW	I had it easy. Someone loved me big time. I wish I would have thanked her for it.
CARLA	There is no map, no destination. Only destiny. I lift up and fly toward home.
DREW	Carla? Carla. Thanks for loving me, baby. I noticed.

> *Ronnie is off the cabinet as it revolves. He places one of the large chairs in front of the plate rail, and holding CARLA, climbs onto the front of the cabinet. She is standing on the seat of the chair, looking down.*

CARLA	I always thought I would fall because I was pushed or I jumped.

*The stage manager pulls the chair out from under her, leaving
CARLA swinging in mid-air. An abrupt transition begins with
a loud guitar version of DREW's theme as the cabinet revolves to
the grey world.*

*The plate rail opens, as does the back of the cabaret stage.
CARLA passes through from one side to the other, and as she
stands on the cabaret stage the doors behind her slam shut.
ANTOINE enters.*

ANTOINE An interesting choice for a final act, my dear. You're one of us now,
Carla. Go take your place in the wings until someone remembers
you.

She looks offstage.

Go. Fade to grey.

CARLA exits into the wings.

And so, completion. Of a sort. The unmapped journey of
grief. Our young friend chose five stages here in our cabaret,
but darlings, don't be seduced into thinking that's the prescription
for all. Five stages of grief? Highly disputable crap, in my opinion.
Perhaps there's one stage, perhaps a hundred. And who knows?
For some, there may be no stages at all. Shocking, isn't it? But
I've learned that there are some with no need for stages such
as mine. They know that the prism only shows you the colours
when it's held into the light. Not the dark. And certainly not all
this grey.

Oh, I hear you. "But Antoine!" you cry, "Antoine, isn't grey
a colour?" Well, I live in the grey, darlings, and trust me, it's not
a colour. It's a neutral. It's a balance between the harshness of
black and white. And yes, it's necessary. Why, if everything was
remembered in living colours, you'd be blinded. You'd be mad.
You'd be God. Or God forbid, you'd be me. No, grey is necessary,
but not for what's down there. Life wants colour. All the hues of
heaven. On earth.

How divine.

Well, the show must go on. And who knows, perhaps next time
one of you will be the producer. And like the true whore of the
stage I've become after all these years, I'll be here to give you what
you want. Oh, it may not be what you need, but when life's too
much down there, or too cold down there, or the wetness of
despair washes over you down there, come to the grey, wooden
cabaret, sit back, find comfort. And remember.

You'll be back. Sooner or later, the rain must fall.

Transition.

Cabinet revolves. HAPPY #5 enters. He is wearing a bright yellow rain slicker, a so'wester hat, and rubber gum boots.

HAPPY   Y'know, a lot of mothers and fathers tell their little ones that rain is God's tears. Maybe that's why so many people stay inside when it's raining. Afraid they might get stung by all that heavenly disappointment. Me, I can't wait to get outside on days like this. See, I figure that when it's raining, whoever is up there intentionally turns everything grey so he can spot the ones who are living in colour. That's why I got me this jim-dandy slicker. I hope I stick out like a sore thumb, because I want him to see me throbbing with life.

So no need for an umbrella, thank you very much. I'm not bothered by a little rain. I just let it roll right off me. Besides, April showers bring May flowers.

One of the upper glass-front cabinet doors opens, revealing a young woman.

That was her name. Mae. She was the rainbow after the storm that had been the war. And I was an eager young fella, ready to live again. Hold on a second, I've got a photograph.

The stage manager appears holding the head of young HAPPY with a small picture frame around it.

Have you ever seen such a crazy bastard—pardon my French—in all your life? Thank you, dear.

Young HAPPY and frame are removed.

And I was crazy. Crazy in love with that gal Mae.

We did all the normal and right things that were expected of us in that time. We fell in love, we married, we got ourselves a little house, I went to work everyday. And our efforts were rewarded when Mae produced the miracle!

The other glass-front cabinet door opens. Inside, the figure of a little boy, dressed in a cowboy hat and a fringed buckskin, arms spread wide.

We named him Charles, after that fella who flew across the Atlantic. I just had to have a flyer for a son, and Mae wasn't too crazy about the name Icarus, so we settled on Charles. I called him Chullie, because that's the sound he made when he was a baby, sucking on his soother. Chullie chullie chullie. I'd never seen anyone so hungry for life as my Chullie was.

I told him stories, about all the flyers. His favourite was the Candy Bomber, the fella who had dropped them parachutes of goodies. The kids in Berlin had nicknamed him Uncle Wiggly Wings, and my Chullie would spin and twirl in his little cowboy jacket with the fringe a'flying, and he'd say "Look at me Daddy, I've got wiggly wings too!"

The little boy begins to spin inside the cabinet.

My Chullie. I don't know if I put it in his head to fly, or if he had just been born with wings. He was a chip off the old block though. Always spinning too fast. So anxious for the wind to lift him off the ground.

They came and got me at work. I was busy, doing what was expected of me. Producing stuff for the brave new world I had fought for. But that world came crashing down the day my Chullie plummeted from the roof of our house. His fringed wiggly wings melting in the sun around his broken little body on the hard ground. They said he had jumped, pretending he could fly. I knew that wasn't true. He was leaping, upwards, assuming that the sky would greet him as a friend.

The figure of the little boy stops rotating.

I wonder if those parachutes of candy ever smashed when they hit the ground. All that broken sweetness. My Chullie.

Ronnie closes the cabinet door. A plate is placed in the plate rail.

After our Chullie died, Mae turned.

The figure of Mae revolves, revealing her as a bitter old woman.

Nothing ever bloomed in that gal again. She blamed me for this, and instead chose to love an earth-bound God explained in her black and white Bible.

Our home lost all colour when that affair began. She covered all the furniture in plastic. She made the same thing for dinner every night. Meatloaf. I ate meatloaf for years. But I said nothing, because I knew eventually things would change. When one of us died. If it was me first, then I wouldn't have to worry. And if it was her first, well then, I could just continue on like before, because I had already been living alone.

Ronnie closes the cabinet door.

When she died, the first thing I did was rip all that plastic off the furniture. I sat on it, put my feet up, wore it down. Wore it down until I fit into it. Somewhere I could take a load off, so I could start lifting up again.

But it's a funny thing. Sometimes when I miss that woman, I go to furniture stores. And I sit on the brand new sofas and chairs that are covered in plastic. Just to remember her. Just to remember what it was like not to be alone. And some days, some days, I crave meatloaf. Isn't that the craziest goddamn thing?

A plate is placed in the plate rail. HAPPY whispers to Mae's cabinet.

Pardon my French.

He walks downstage, into a concentrated pool of light.

The way I see it, if you want the rainbow, then you've gotta put up with the rain. You gotta get your feet wet. And if the water's getting too high, then head for higher ground. Or better yet, why not hit the sky and fly.

He spins, ending with his arm raised toward Chullie's cabinet.

When I miss my Chullie, I go to the park. Never anyone there when it's raining, so I get the prime seat. On the swings. I love the swings. And when the sky is overcast, it softens everything and lets me think. Lets me dream. Dream of what's behind all that grey. I love swinging into the nebulous sky, because nothing is definite and everything is suspended. Including me. And the higher I swing, the clearer it becomes.

I get a lot of privacy in the park on days like this. I don't know if it's because people are afraid of the sight of an old fart dressed up like a goddamn duck—pardon my French—or if they just know to leave a dreamer well enough alone while he's at work.

I can never get high enough, because the more I go, back and forth, higher and higher, something touches me. And someday I hope I can touch it. Candy in the sky.

The back screens are awash with blazing pink and clouds.

Some people might think that my reach exceeds my grasp. Well pardon my French, but isn't that the whole goddamn point of being alive?

RONNIE   I wonder.

The back screens become separate colours of the rainbow flag and the music swells as HAPPY swings higher and higher.

Blackout.

The End

Provenance

Notes on Staging

The set for *Provenance* is a stylized bar/parlour intended to suggest a brothel. The decor is loosely inspired by art nouveau, and as such, the set is curvilinear and ornamental. It consists of a two-level deck; the downstage main acting area one foot above the stage floor and an upstage level two feet above the stage. These are connected by ramps on either side of the set. Downstage left and right are puppet-scale stair units connecting to the ramps, used by marionettes for entrance into the brothel.

The downstage acting deck is oval, and painted to resemble a swirling mosaic floor. A large bar-like unit sits upstage centre of this deck. This serves not only as a background for the main marionette action, but also as a counter for the upstage manipulation of table-top figures and jointed dolls. The front of the bar unit is painted to suggest an inlaid wood design depicting a forest. At the bottom of this detail are cut-outs faced with pebbled clear acrylic, which are backlit during the show to suggest the lights of Paris and later, a frozen pond.

The ramps and the upstage deck are painted gloss red. Sitting at the furthest upstage point, and running the full width of the set, are nine tall cabinets to house the seventeen marionettes used during the performance. The height of these cabinets varies and creates a wave across the upstage of the set. The fronts are also curved, both inward and out. They are painted in the same style as the bar front, depicting the inlaid wood forest scene. Each door has cut-outs backed with acrylic "glass"

Set slightly off-centre between the cabinets is a large painting. It depicts a young man, nude save for green silk stockings, leaning against a tree. Wrapping around both the figure and the tree is a swan. The background and border are decorative in a post-secessionist style.

A variety of puppet types are used in the performance. In addition to the marionettes in the cabinets, the underside of the bar unit serves as "offstage" storage for fully-jointed table-top figures, the dolls of child Leda and Tender, and handpuppets of Plato, Herschel, and Maybelline. A small shelf sits below the upstage painting and is used for the figure of Pity on a platter and to hold the headrigs. These are headband contraptions holding various character heads directly in front of Ronnie's face. Various characters are represented by a number of figures and types. Leda is shown at four different ages, represented by four marionettes, one headrig, a jointed doll, and two table-top figures. Pity is the same age, however due to costume changes, she is represented by five marionettes, a headrig, a jointed doll, and a table-top figure.

Stage directions herein are kept to a minimum. The play is performed solely by Ronnie Burkett, and reference to him is throughout the staging directions. Cathy Nosaty's score and Bill Williams's lighting design are integral to the overall design and performance, although lighting and sound notes within this text are referred to only when necessary to the reading.

The play is performed without an interval, with a running time of approximately two hours, six minutes.

Provenance premiered at Theatre Network in Edmonton, Alberta in October 2003. Produced by Rink-A-Dink Inc./Ronnie Burkett Theatre of Marionettes. *Provenance* is a co-production with BITE (London, UK), the Canadian Stage Company (Toronto, Canada), Melbourne International Arts Festival (Melbourne, Australia), queerupnorth (Manchester, UK) and Wiener Festwochen (Vienna, Austria). *Provenance* was initiated during the Canadian Stage Company Play Creation group, 2002. Ronnie Burkett's participation as the Canadian Stage Company Playwright in Residence was made possible by a Senior Artist Grant from the Canada Council for the Arts.

Written and performed by Ronnie Burkett
Music and sound design by Cathy Nosaty
Lighting design by Bill Williams
Stage managed by Angie Jones
Artistic associate/production manager: Terri Gillis
Associate producer: John Lambert
Dramaturge: Iris Turcott
Director of lighting: Kevin Humphrey
Director of sound/technical director: Shanna Miller
Marionettes, costumes, and set designed by Ronnie Burkett

PUPPET STUDIO
Marionettes sculpted and carved by Ronnie Burkett
Assistant designer/shop foreman: Dina Meschkuleit
Additional sculpture: Angela Talbot, Noreen Young, Jo-Ellen Trilling,
        Dina Meschkuleit
Studio team: Darren Pickering, Candace Russell, Wini Mertens, Emma Dalziel
Marionette controls: Luman Coad, Frank Meschkuleit, Wulf
Stringing: Charleen Wilson
Studio mascots/supervisors: Charlie and Daisy

COSTUMES
Built by Kim Crossley
Assisted by Elizabeth Copeman, June Crossley, Casey Falardeau, Trish McNally,
        Dina Meschkuleit, and Katri Tahvanainen

SET CONSTRUCTION
Master carpenter: Martin Herbert
Carpenters: Carl Eric Lindgren, Terri Gillis
Set assistance: Werner Karson and Barb Pierce

SCENIC PAINTING
Head scenic artist: Jennifer Hedge
Scenic painters: Corrine Dickson, Kim Stewart

PROPS
Heather Kent, Wulf
Plato's roller skates made by Jeff deBoer
"Tender" painted by Ronnie Burkett
Digital graphic rendering by John Alcorn

Subsequent runs include the Vancouver East Cultural Centre, Vancouver, British Columbia; the Canadian Stage Company, Toronto, Ontario; Alberta Theatre Projects, Calgary, Alberta; BITE:04, the Barbican Centre, London, UK; queerupnorth, Manchester, UK; Wiener Festwochen, Vienna, Austria; Melbourne International Arts Festival, Melbourne, Australia; Queensland Performing Arts Centre, Brisbane, Australia; Great Canadian Theatre Company, Ottawa, Ontario; Manitoba Theatre Centre, Winnipeg, Manitoba; Södra Teatern, Stockholm, Sweden; Kampnagel, Hamburg, Germany; the Brighton Festival, Brighton, UK.

Characters

PITY BEANE, a Canadian art academic
LEDA OTENREATH, the madam of a Viennese brothel
TENDER, a young man in a painting
HERSCHEL FLECHTHEIM, an elderly American
VESPA POOPERMANN, manageress of the brothel
PLATO, the brothel monkey
DOOLEY OTENREATH, Leda's husband
AUNTIE SARI, Leda's imaginary aunt, and a cow
MR. HIRO, a Japanese businessman
MUSETTE, a lady of the brothel
JOHANNA, a lady of the brothel
IRIS, a lady of the brothel
MISS MAYBELLINE, a lady of the brothel

✎ *Provenance* ✎

Pre-set lighting fades as Ronnie enters. He stands centrestage.

RONNIE   Follow my voice.

The painting of TENDER, upstage centre, glows as he continues.

There were trees in the background
Rows of trees, not big but many
Each delicate in their creamy white stance
Thin-skinned bark draped like crepe
There were trees in the background
Rows of them, a fortress of interlocked fingers
A fine fence, gently holding back all intrusion
There were trees in the background
Filtering lace-patterned light
Like snowflakes cut from paper
Skin whiter than ever before
Lace, snowflakes, trees
One would barely notice the blood at all.

A train whistle blows. Light up on LEDA. She is a grand woman, elegant and elderly.

LEDA   I spend my days in vain reflection
Dim the light and the mirror is kind
If you're blind
But never, forever, on closer inspection
Do I see the sight I have in mind.

She removes her dark glasses.

Well, never mind. When one's nose is pressed against the glass, you're bound to catch a glimpse of what those on the other side see. But it's a backward resemblance, nevertheless. Like a painting, viewed upon completion. The final coat of varnish protecting the

surface, the unknown layers of glaze, the first coal smudge upon
the canvas. That primal line, tentative or bold, is the soul of art.
The rest, veneer, added with time. And why shouldn't it be so? But
what of the art of the soul? God himself has it backwards. We
should be born old and dumb, finding our truth as we grow into
youth. Body and mind growing together in knowing and strength.
But no. God doesn't want us that strong. We see ourselves fully
reflected only when the mirror cracks.

> *Light up on PITY. She is in her early twenties, and although
> her clothing is a funky blend of retro and practical (fifties day
> dress and swing coat with brown Blundstone boots), PITY
> is nevertheless clearly and painfully plain.*

PITY   Catalogued wishes mark endless lists
Life as a dream on an empty purse
What is worse
Than to long for a song that can never exist
Or a kiss, that alone, I rehearse.

My dad's boyfriend said there were three important things
to remember. One, always take the Tylenol before doing poppers.
Two, practise sincerity in front of the mirror, you never know
when you'll need it. And three, if you leave a man, take the copper
pots and your good knives. Otherwise, you'll never see them again.
Not in this life. Not the life you're leaving. "Appliances can be
replaced" he would tell me, "but honey, you need your knives." He
wasn't a nice man, which is not to say that he was bad. Uncle
Boyfriend was just different. I guess that's why he left.

> *TENDER is a beautiful young man. He is dressed in a simple,
> cheap suit, the type found in a mail-order catalogue in the early
> part of the twentieth century.*

TENDER   Given a gun and a foreign kilt
A boy-man just beginning to shave
Go be brave
In the stench of the trench where your blood will be spilt
With burnt offerings sharing your grave.

I ran twice. The first time, I took the train. It took me away from
home. The second time, I was trained not to run, but I had to.
I had no choice. I was the train. Heart pounding, breath short,
everything on the sidelines just a blur. It's as though everything
around you were in motion, and you're just standing still. Both
times I ran, and barely moved a muscle.

LEDA	When I was a little girl, the animals talked. Auntie Sari, always a cow. A grand, bovine woman with hooves stuffed into moss-green pumps. The cook, Anna, a bleating old sheep, soft tufts of mad wool bursting from her cap. Daddy, the serious snouted pig, digging through his dealings as if they were truffles, his dark, dim eyes serious and unforgiving. And Mummy, the show dog. Sleek and elegant, erect and alert, obeying every command her breeding demanded. The pig and the purebred, that's where I came from.
PITY	I travelled the world as a child, and never once left home. Uncle Boyfriend cooked, and every year chose a new country to master. At age ten, I was given books on the Orient, Chinese lanterns hung above my bed, and Barbie wore a kimono. That was stir-fry year, and I thought we'd all be found murdered in our sleep if he didn't perfect sticky rice. At eleven and twelve it was Italian, but I didn't dare leave for school without saying "Ciao." I was a willing student in his global game, but my participation never got high marks. "Pity," he would say to me, "you're too bookish. You analyze everything. Less Bette Davis and more Joan Crawford. Feel it girl! You've got to push your brain down to your cunt." To date, I've managed to keep the two quite separate.
TENDER	I was fifteen years old, and I looked it. They allowed me to run and lie and leave. That first train took me away from a tiny still-life in a vast ocean of wheat, and rolled across Canada until there was no more land. Just the ocean. I had seen pirate battles waged upon it in my Boy's Own Companions, but I was not prepared for the beauty of her. I had to cross over this liquid prairie. To kill. To die. Beauty washed me, with salt in every wound. They expected me to walk on water.
LEDA	My nanny Marie raised me better than an English girl should be. She was beautiful, in that way that only French women have, and not even the hint of a slight moustache could detract from her appeal. In fact, it added to her aura I think, for surely her goodnight kisses to my young face conditioned me to swoon in later years whenever a man's facial hair would brush my cheek, scratch my breast, or tickle my fancy. Marie is the only one who was not an animal. She was real and human and beautiful. I was her pet. My hair was strawberry coloured, and she called me her little pink puppy. No man could ever say anything so lovely as that. So I never kissed them back.
PITY	No boy in school was like him. He lived in the library, sleeping in a book. And every time I stole away to him, opening the page with hot, teenage girl fingers, there he was. Awake and looking at me.

I kissed him for the first time, there in the stacks. And now I am
finally travelling to him. My beauty. I'm going to see him at last,
with all his glazed layers revealing his infinite depth. I'm going to
kiss him for real, and finally, lose my brain.

TENDER I have been kissed once. In flesh. I have been kissed a thousand
times, strange lips pressing against some two dimensional version
of what I am. What do they want? What do they expect? I have no
voice but theirs. Yet, they kiss me and wait for an answer that will
never be spoken. I cannot love them back.

LEDA I kissed beauty on the lips. Tender, for a moment. The swan-like
down of youth that brushed my lips but once, now watches them
lie forever. My purgatory is a heart that beats on borrowed breath.
Beauty lives within me, but there is no dreaming when still. It
lives, fully and real in front of me, pressing against my chest with
every step I make. I want to stand still. I can't run anymore.

*A train whistle blows, followed by the sound of steam as if
a train were pulling into a station. Light on TENDER only.*

TENDER There were trees in the background, unseen now
I know they are there, no need to look back
I am captured at last, gazing out beyond the past
The landscape is full, of trees and me
But the canvas is still. Still life. Still blank.
The taut, stretched fabric of my skin empty
Save for snowflake light and blood
It might be beautiful, this
With only one view, that's all there is to see
There were trees in the background
Me in the foreground
But all I see is you
Seeing nothing, looking at me.

*He disappears. Scene shift, rain sounds. PITY is at the foot of the
stairs leading into the brothel. Sound of a bell. VESPA appears
at the top of the stairs.*

VESPA If you're an American, go away. You are not welcome here.

PITY No, no, no. I'm from Canada.

VESPA Same thing.

PITY You Germans are so kind.

VESPA I'm Austrian.

PITY Same thing. *Sig heil, fraulein!*

VESPA	Touché, my dear. I don't know whether to slap or embrace you.
PITY	Neither, please. I'm Canadian, we prefer not to be touched at all.
VESPA	Welcome to Vienna. You'll fit right in.
PITY	May I come in?
VESPA	That depends.
PITY	On what?
VESPA	On what you want.
PITY	I want to get out of the rain.
VESPA	Stupid tourist. Who would travel in Europe without an umbrella?
PITY	I have an umbrella, it's in my bag.
VESPA	Then use it.
PITY	I can't. It's wet, still.
VESPA	That's what umbrellas are for!
PITY	No, it's wet from Paris. See, I was there, before I came here. And it rained so much, but I didn't mind. It seemed… right. Right as rain. And on the train, coming here, I took it out of my bag and I could smell it still. Paris. A real memory.
VESPA	And Parisian rain is better than Vienna's? It's all the same, ja? We've got the Euro now.
PITY	No, not better, just Paris. I plan to have a different memory of Vienna.
VESPA	Then go eat some torte, see a Klimt, tour a palace, take the tram around the Ringstrasse, eat Wiener schnitzel until you explode! I don't care! Just leave me alone. Well, what are you waiting for? I said go away.
PITY	I won't. I'm expected here. I have an appointment.
VESPA	Ja, I doubt it. We don't cater to women. The Madam is very particular about which specialties she allows. Try Frau Wieser down the street. Her girls will do anything.
PITY	No, Mr. Flechtheim told me to meet him here.
VESPA	You know Herschel?
PITY	Well, not exactly. We corresponded, and he told me to meet him at this address. Please let me in, I'm soaked to the bone. I don't want to get sick.

VESPA	Ja, but then you could take a romantic European illness home with you.

PITY rings the bell.

What are you doing?

PITY	Look, I've come a long way and I will not be turned back now.

She rings the bell again.

VESPA	Stop that. You'll wake the Madam.
PITY	I've no idea who the Madam is, but clearly she's in charge and I would like to speak to her.

She rings the bell again.

VESPA	I'm in charge. I decide who gets in and who doesn't.

PITY rings the bell again.

Enough!

PITY	I am to meet Mr. Herschel Flechtheim at this address. Now, will you let me in, you mannish shrew?
VESPA	You little American bitch!
PITY	Canadian bitch, thank you very much. Now will you let me in, or do I have to kick this door in and you down with it?
VESPA	You wouldn't dare!
PITY	Lady, I was raised by two gay men. You have no idea what this bitch is capable of. Well? May I enter, gentle woman? Or do I have to open a fresh can of Liza and Judy's whoop-ass?
VESPA	Don't drip on anything.

VESPA steps aside, allowing PITY to enter.

Tourists.

Music and lights reveal the brothel. PITY stands in the centre of the room taking it in.

PITY	Vienna!
VESPA	*Willkommen zum Affenkaffee,* or, as the Yankee doodles call it, The Monkey Bar.
PITY	Uncle Boyfriend would love this place.
VESPA	Uncle Boyfriend?
PITY	He's my step-father. I swear he'd shit himself if he saw this room.

VESPA	Ja, well, good thing for the floor he's not here. Wait, I'll find Mr. Flechtheim. Your name, fraulein?
PITY	I'm Pity. Pity Beane.
VESPA	Of course you are.
PITY	And you?
VESPA	What?
PITY	Your name?
VESPA	I didn't say it.
PITY	That's why I'm asking.
VESPA	Poopermann. Vespa Poopermann.
PITY	Of course you are.
VESPA	You can hang your coat in here, fraulein Beane.

VESPA exits, hung in a cabinet. The marionette of PITY is put into the cabinet as well, as Ronnie exchanges her for another version. It is PITY in the same costume, without the coat. PLATO the monkey enters on roller skates. He wears a little tuxedo and a fez. He sings.

Ah Beauty

PLATO	Ah beauty! Ah beauty!
	Will you light upon my heart
	And if thou art, let my soul be awed
	Ah beauty!
	Settle here and steal my gaze
	Nestle close and spend your days
	And waken me to God
	Oh beauty! Oh beauty!
	Take my hand and lead me there
	And show me where there's no blindness
	Oh beauty!
	Help to halt my backward pace
	Turn me toward the radiant grace
	Heaven's kiss of kindness.

The song ends and PLATO exits. HERSCHEL enters.

HERSCHEL	I see you've met Plato.
PITY	Hello. Plato?

HERSCHEL	The joint was named in his honour. Herschel Flechtheim. You must be Miss Beane, from Canada.
PITY	Yes, Pity Beane.
HERSCHEL	Well, that's an interesting name, my dear. Tell me, is it short for something else?
PITY	Pittance, which is short for everything. But I've always been Pity.
HERSCHEL	Then I have a new shoulder to cry on.
PITY	Thank you for seeing me, Mr. Flechtheim. I've come a long way to find you.
HERSCHEL	An exciting adventure then!
PITY	Yes, it is. I've never travelled alone before.
HERSCHEL	And how are you finding the world, thus far?
PITY	Oh, pretty much as I'd imagined it. Except with people, of course.
HERSCHEL	And how has the European branch of the species been treating you?
PITY	Oh, people here have been great. For the most part, they just ignore me. Except for that woman who let me in.
HERSCHEL	Don't let Vespa scare you. She's our watchdog. Only the truly brave or foolish get past her.
PITY	I think I used up all of my bravery just getting in the door.
HERSCHEL	Well, it's a funny thing, isn't it Miss Beane. Why is it always assumed that brave people aren't terrified too? The only difference is that brave people have feet that can keep up with their heart.
PITY	Or vice versa.
HERSCHEL	Exactly. And here you stand, my dear. Feet on the floor, heart through the door. An heroic act indeed!
PITY	I'm hardly a hero, Mr. Flechtheim.
HERSCHEL	Who knows? The best ones always go unnoticed. Maybe you're just not looking at yourself in the right light.
PITY	I'm not here to look at me. Myself, I mean.
HERSCHEL	Me, myself, and oy! You're an Anglican, aren't you, Miss Beane. So, what brings you here? Your two letters were very mysterious.

PITY	I'm sorry about that. It's just that it took me so long to even find you, I had to be sure you were…
HERSCHEL	That I was still alive.
PITY	Yes, I'm sorry.
HERSCHEL	Don't be. I'm alive! Schnapps for everyone!
PITY	As I told you, I'm searching for the painting known as "Tender." Now, I've been able to track it somewhat during the early-to-mid part of the last century, although there are still great holes in the provenance of this piece.
HERSCHEL	Provenance?
PITY	I'm sorry. The history of ownership pertaining to a work of art. That's what brings me to Vienna and why I need to see you, because, Mr. Flechtheim, the last known owner of the painting is you.
HERSCHEL	Fascinating. I'm famous in the art world! Oy, I should buy a beret.
PITY	Mr. Flechtheim, please, where's the painting?
HERSCHEL	Now, patience, Pity. You've just come in from the rain. You're still wet behind the ears. Relax. Take a coffee. You're in Vienna now. It's beautiful here.

> *HERSCHEL leaves and is placed in his cabinet. LEDA enters from hers, upstage left.*

LEDA	Vespa, I heard the bell. Is it him? Did you let him in? What did you tell him? You should have come for me. I wasn't expecting him so soon. Really, it's madness, what sort of person arrives in daylight. Vespa, please keep them away, don't let anyone in. I can't see anyone now. Look at me, I'm not done. Vespa, I hope you haven't… oh, hello.
PITY	Hello.
LEDA	You're… not him.
PITY	I'm sorry.
LEDA	No, please my dear, you mustn't be. The sight of you is a relief. I was worried it was him, and I haven't got the answer yet. And I can't receive anyone, look at me. I'm still in my morning dress. Oh God, mornings are so difficult for me!
PITY	I love the morning. It's the least disappointing time of the day.
LEDA	You must forgive me, my dear. It's so lovely to see you again.

PITY	But we've not met.
LEDA	Exactly, each day is a new beginning, isn't it? Where on earth have you been?
PITY	Um, Canada.
LEDA	I'm so sorry. And how did that go?
PITY	It's not… done. I mean, I've come here, now.
LEDA	And I couldn't be happier! Let me look at you. Darling! How exciting! When are you due?
PITY	What are you talking about?
LEDA	The baby. When shall we expect it?
PITY	I'm not pregnant.
LEDA	No, of course not. You've just let yourself go natural. So many girls do, these days. That's why I didn't recognize you. Well then, let me have a good look. Stay there, don't move! That light, it's perfect for you. You must never leave it.
PITY	I've never been able to stand still.
LEDA	Then you must learn. That's the secret, isn't it?
PITY	Of what?
LEDA	Of everything, dear. Light. Now, granted, this is daylight, never preferred, that. No, artificial evening light is much more easily controlled, nevertheless, you look quite… what is it? Innocent. Very marketable, that. But as I'm sure you already know, when you're not beautiful you must find the other. And for you, in this moment, it's purity in light. You must never leave it.
PITY	Well, I can't just stand in one place.
LEDA	Why not? It's done all the time. Have you ever wondered why beautiful people are always the centre of attention?
PITY	Because they're beautiful.
LEDA	No. Because they always find the best light.
PITY	I don't have those instincts.
LEDA	It's not instinct dear. It's an art. Studied and practised. Next time you're at a party, look for the most beautiful person in the room. I guarantee they'll be standing in the best light, never moving, just letting the rest of the world come to them. I don't know you, do I?
PITY	I'm Pity Beane.

LEDA What a sad name. Did you live up to it?

PITY My parents are the sort of people you talk about. Beautifully lit. It was assumed I would be the same.

LEDA It's a curse to be the plain child of beautiful parents, I know. Better to be deformed or feeble-minded, shockingly ugly, or spectacularly wrong in any way. Only two things are noticed in this world. The beautiful and the grotesque. Pity, indeed, the rest of us born plain.

PITY Who are you?

LEDA I'm Leda Otenreath. This is my house. What do you want, my plain little girl?

PITY I've come for the boy.

Scene shift.

Art Slide

A microphone on a small stand is placed on top of the bar. Ronnie speaks for an unseen character.

VOICE And now, Pity Beane, a master's degree candidate in the art history, theory, and criticism program, will speak on works of missing provenance and institutional responsibility toward original ownership claims. I'm sure this will be quite fascinating. Miss Beane, when you're ready.

Ronnie wears a headrig with PITY's face in front of it. His hands and the rest of his body are used in conjunction with this face, as if it were a miniature mask. PITY's voice is amplified during her speech, as if in a lecture hall.

PITY Thank you, Professor Turcott. While I am hardly an expert in the field the professor mentioned in his introduction, my current course of research centres around a specific painting, the provenance of which becomes somewhat dubious after World War II. Further hindering the historical tracking of this painting is a lack of information regarding the artist himself. Steve, may I have the slide now, please.

Sound of a slide projector. A rectangle of light frames the painting behind PITY.

Known simply as "Tender," this word being the only marking on the back of the canvas, it may be speculated that this is the title of the piece, or, could indeed be the signature of the artist himself. Personally, I've always believed it to be the latter, although no,

I don't have the data to confirm that at present, Professor. Research, working, getting there. If, however, the word "Tender" represents a title for the canvas, it may be speculated that perhaps the piece is a work unto itself or part of a grouping, not unlike, say, the seven deadly sins or an artistic representation of the virtues of which, one may conclude, tenderness would be considered most admirable indeed.

We know that the work was painted in 1921, information obtained from records at a London gallery show of new—and therefore unknown—artists. The first owner was Mr. Baltan Fazood, an importer of artifacts from the Middle East. We know that the painting remained in Mr. Fazood's possession until the early 1930s, a mention of it appearing in a 1934 article on his new London townhouse, noteworthy for its stark all-white gallery-like interiors, no doubt a predecessor to the present loft condo craze.

Mr. Fazood was found murdered in that townhouse in 1936, victim of a liaison with a gay-for-pay piece of trade named Angus MacNamara. At the time of the police investigation, the only "artwork" found were pre-Pollackesque spatters of blood on the previously pristine white walls. Mr. MacNamara was tried and convicted of Fazood's murder, and shortly thereafter, and finally true to his profession, I guess you could say he was quite well hung indeed.

VOICE	Miss Beane, please!
PITY	I'm sorry, Professor Turcott. The painting resurfaced in London in 1993 as part of an auction of art and antiquities released from Moscow after the dissolution of the USSR in 1991. The painting was purchased by Mr. Herschel Flechtheim of Chicago, Illinois, for £21,000. For the time, this price was considered somewhat of a record given not only the mystery surrounding the artist and the missing provenance from 1934 to 1991, but also because of the subject, composition, and somewhat sentimental rendering.
	Which naturally has shocked the serious art world, which all too frequently has deemed this painting and other works like it as derivative post-Secessionist decorative illustration, or, as Professor Turcott himself has called it, "Romanticized crap to match the couch salon painting."
VOICE	Miss Beane, I'm warning you. Tread carefully. No such words may be attributed to me.
PITY	Well, not in print, sir. But you did indeed dismiss "Tender" as exactly that when I first proposed this painting as my course of

research. Do you not remember chuckling at your own clever re-titling of the piece as "Laddie and the Swan"? Personally, I believe it's the obvious beauty of this painting that is indeed its downfall, sir, because it has no need for an academic to dissect and objectify it like a whore spread-eagled for our pleasure.

VOICE Miss Beane, sit down please.

PITY Oh, come on, Professor! You know, I know, all of us here in this room know, that if any one of us could paint even remotely like that artist, hell, we wouldn't be twitching, bitter academics. No, we would speaking to the world through the end of a paintbrush, not out of our assholes.

VOICE You will stop now and sit down, Miss Beane!

PITY What is art, Professor? To you. Only you. Your personal definition? And don't you dare tell me it's your job, your career, your tenure, your pension. I won't hear that! No, art is the personal contribution to the ever-continuing conversation about life. And I'm having that conversation here today, even if I can't render it on paper or canvas, I want to talk about art, it's my turn. But I will not stand up here and do what all these other monkeys in this department do for your pleasure, Professor. I will not stand here and tell you what I think about art. No. I want to talk about how I feel about art, and how it makes me feel. But I'm on thin ice, I know that, Professor. Because ever since I've been in this department, sir, my feelings have been a source of ridicule, and dismissed as mawkish and sentimental. And why is that, Professor? Are you so afraid of my feelings, are they so dangerous to you? Well you should be afraid, sir, because art is dangerous. And I will tell you, here and now, with my colleagues to bear witness, that this painting is dangerously beautiful to me. And why? Because it makes me feel. It makes me feel something I get nowhere else in the world. It makes me feel love. I love this painting. I love that boy!

When all the real people in your world are just so... three-dimensional. And they can't help it, but they just keep letting you down. Your dad. Your dead mum. Even Uncle Boyfriend. The fairy fucking godfather who, with all his bitchiness was actually the only one who ever did me any good, but what does he do? He leaves. He left me. And why? Well maybe, Professor, because he finally figured out that having all the beautiful things in life that you think and talk about all the time means nothing if all you do is dream of something more. The unspeakable beauty. You know what his note said? The note he left my dad on the kitchen counter? All it said was, "It's just not beautiful anymore." He left me an envelope too. A cheque for $100,000 and a note that said, "Pity, squander this on beauty." That was all he wanted for me, that I would find my unspeakable. But I failed him. I let him down again. And how? What did I do with that money? I used it to come here, because I thought this would be the most sensible road toward art and beauty. But no, all I am met with, day after day, are hearts and minds more blank than a post-modernist canvas.

My God, is growing up in the art world achieved only by embracing the ugly and the unpolished? Is that the road I have to take to be taken seriously? Well, I can't. I won't. Life is already grotesque. Don't tell me to find more ugliness. I don't want to look at ugliness. I don't need to look at it, I already have a fucking mirror, thank you very much. And stop pushing the weird on me. Stop telling me it has to be weird to be art, it has to be weird to be beautiful. I don't need any more weird. And it's not like I don't know weird, I grew up with two gay daddies, for fuck's sake, I know weird shit when it splats on my face, okay?

VOICE Miss Beane, you will come to my office. Now!

PITY No Professor, the only reason I would ever come to your office again is if you plan on bending me over your desk, lifting my skirt, dropping my panties, and fucking me from behind. But that's not what you're going to do, is it, Professor? Because I'm just a plain, silly girl, not even attractive enough to dismiss as a beautiful object, and you're just going to kick me out of this department, aren't you? Oh no, it's okay. I think we've both seen this coming, Professor, so why don't we just skip that little meeting in your office, sir. You're a very busy man and I'm sure you have lots of things to think and talk about, and it's not like I don't have things to do. I still have a little bit of money left from Uncle Boyfriend and I should just go find my unspeakable. Him.

She points at the painting.

The real thing. That's what I'm going to do. And you know what you can do, Professor Turcott? You can go to your office, and you can fuck yourself.

She turns, as if to leave. Simultaneously, the lights shift, placing us back in the present time in the brothel. PITY sees the painting of TENDER.

There you are. Thanks for waiting. I'm sorry it took so long to find you, but beauty, I'm home now.

Ronnie removes the PITY headrig. Shift/transition.

Lunch Menu

Music in for the introduction of "The Ladies," the four whores of the brothel, JOHANNA, MUSETTE, IRIS, and MAYBELLINE. Each is taken from an upstage cabinet behind the bar. Ronnie dances them individually to their hanging spots in front of the bar as they are presented to the audience. When all four are in position, and as the music comes to an end, VESPA enters from her stage right cabinet.

VESPA   Girls, our gentlemen will be arriving soon for lunch, and so, a final inspection, ja, before the buffet is laid.

Ah Johanna! How nice to see, Frau Pfefferkuchen, that your slip is clean and that yesterday's *schlagsahne* has been wiped clean from your breast. Ah ah! No arguments, please! Now Johanna, I've decided to lock up the trolley of cakes until after your first appointment. The lawyer will be arriving soon, and he has some briefs that need your immediate attention.

Iris my dear, you, on the other hand, could stand to eat something. I know, you cannot put anything into your mouth and enjoy it. It's the curse of your ballet training. Luckily, I've been able to book you with a British tourist. A few quick pounds and it'll be all over.

Miss Maybelline, *meine kleine schwartze princessin*! How nice of you to join us. Your presence always adds such elegance to our menu, even if the dish is sold out, ja. As usual, Miss Maybelline, your time has been booked exclusively by Mr. Flechtheim once again.

Musette, you are a naughty girl. I've heard you conversing with your customers again. How many times must I remind you, my pet, it's so impolite to talk with your mouth full. The banker is coming today. He wants to liquidate your assets again.

So ladies, those are the reservations for lunch. This evening's menu, however, is a catastrophe. Not that you're to blame. How could you be to blame? You're beautiful. You're the most beautiful girls in all the world. But tonight, we have had a request for a special feast. Mr. Hiro, a businessman from the East, will arrive soon, and his tongue is not used to the spread we provide. No, this gentleman from the Pacific Rim would like a virgin to serve dinner to him.

PITY is standing upstage.

VESPA   Ah, fraulein Beane. How can I help you?

PITY   Who are these women?

VESPA	These are the most beautiful girls in all the world.
PITY	They're whores.
VESPA	Ja, is that a problem for you, fraulein Beane?
PITY	I believe you're the one with the problem, Frau Poopermann. You need a virgin.
VESPA	Ja, it's true.
PITY	Let me do it.
VESPA	You? Ha! Why?
PITY	I'm a virgin. And you need a virgin, no?
VESPA	Ja...
PITY	So?
VESPA	Is it money you're after, fraulein Beane?
PITY	No. Something priceless.
VESPA	What?
PITY	To be the object of desire, anyone's desire, just once. I want to know what that feels like.
VESPA	Why?
PITY	Because I can't give it away. So, what do you say, Frau Poopermann? I have something you need, and you have something I want. You let me be one of your most beautiful girls in all the world for one night in my life, and I'll do it for free.
VESPA	That's a very interesting offer, fraulein Beane, but I'm afraid we'll have to discuss that later. With the Madam.

Doorbell sound.

Ach du leiber! Our gentlemen have arrived. Girls, take your places. Ladies, assume your positions!

> *Music in, a faster and shorter version of the theme which first introduced the girls. JOHANNA, IRIS, MUSETTE, and MAYBELLINE are quickly removed and placed back in the cabinets. VESPA is returned to her cabinet. In exchange, HERSCHEL enters.*

HERSCHEL	A fascinating house, this, wouldn't you say, Miss Beane?
PITY	Mr. Flechtheim, please. It's a brothel.
HERSCHEL	No, Miss Beane. This is a refuge.

PITY	From what?
HERSCHEL	Child, please. You know, Miss Beane, I've spent most of my time on this earth just waiting for my life to start. Standing still, hoping it would find me. Oh yes, I always thought that one day, life would tap me on the shoulder and say, "Come on, Flechtheim, here I am, it's life, let's go, let's be alive at last, old man!" But let me assure you, my dear Miss Beane, life will not come knocking on your door. No. Which is why I had to come back here and ring that bell.
PITY	Why?
HERSCHEL	Why? To have lunch.

HERSCHEL   I met Miss Maybelline in 1937. I was sixteen at the time. Oy, this house was so different then. Schrammel music, cabaret artists, laughter and light, drinking and dancing all through the night. And into all that brightness came the darkest beauty I had ever seen. A dancer from America. Maybelline! Oy, she caused a sensation in this pale, proper town.

We were different as night and day. But even they meet and fold into one at dawn and dusk.

But the following year, my dear Miss Beane, Vienna threw a parade to welcome Herr Hitler. Needless to say, I had to get out of town. I fled to Paris, she was to follow. She never appeared. So I fled further still. To America, her home. And I never saw her again.

PITY	I'm sorry, Mr. Flechtheim. Why didn't she follow you?
HERSCHEL	Her movements would have been a little too obvious, my dear, not so easy for her to disappear in the white heat that was Europe in those days. But your painting there, Miss Beane, saved my Maybelline.

You see, the Gestapo had discovered that champagne was on ice in this house, and girls who never considered it gave into vice just to survive. And one of those men, who only knew how to destroy, took a fancy to beauty one night. Your white, gleaming boy. In order for that German officer to be colour-blind, Leda gave him the painting so Maybelline would be spared.

PITY	Mrs. Otenreath owned the house even back then?
HERSCHEL	No, no, no, she had abandoned her married name back in those days. But, she was greatly loved by all those who had not deserted hope. A star in those darkening skies, she was known as Leda Lichter then.

*Music in, the intro for LEDA's wartime song. All light onstage
shifts to a concentrated pool, suggesting a lone spot in a cabaret.
A younger version of LEDA turns into the light and sings.*

Until the Sun Returns

LEDA   The sun has closed its eyes
Without the light, the world is grey
And into night we fall
As storm clouds fill the skies
In frosty shrouds, so still we lay
Awaiting springtime's call
Till I thaw on that bright day
You are what my heart must learn
Your arms are warm, so I will stay
Until the sun returns
Hold me through this winter day
For it's you my blue heart yearns
The moon and stars will lead the way
Until the sun returns

*She is returned to the cabinet from which she came, and time
shifts back to present.*

PITY   Oh my God. He came here. After disappearing from Fazood's
London townhouse, the painting came to Vienna. Okay,
I can track that, it's an A to B. There's got to be a trail. But
Mr. Flechtheim, what you just said, no way, that doesn't make
any sense. Okay, I get the part about Mrs. Otenreath giving the
painting to the Nazi guy, but he would have taken it with him. It
would have gone somewhere else. But it's here now, and I'm here,
and I'm so close but I don't understand any of this.

HERSCHEL   My dear, you don't understand the times. That painting was
loot, like everything was back then. And after the war, hidden in
mountains of art, it was stolen again. Taken off to Russia. Hidden
in grey rooms without any light, until the wall came down. That's
when I heard about it, so I bought it at auction and brought it
home. And when I rang the bell after a lifetime away, Leda was
here—Mrs. Otenreath again—and so was the dream I had left
behind sixty-three years before.

PITY   So, are you going to marry her, Mr. Flechtheim? Make Miss
Maybelline an honest woman at last?

HERSCHEL   My dear, I was married to an honest woman for fifty-two years. Marry Maybelline? No. I have her hand in mine at last. Till death do us part.

PITY   But Mr. F, don't you have to pay for her company in this place?

HERSCHEL   You've obviously never been married, Miss Beane.

PITY   So, do you... you know. Do you and Miss Maybelline have... more than just lunch?

HERSCHEL   At my age, lunch is a highlight. But if you're asking if we make love, well, that's none of your business. But I'll tell you this, my inquisitive little Canadian research travelling girl. Miss Beane, please, I'm old, I'm not dead. Of course, all those years, when we were apart, I did have a somewhat special little—how do you say—fantasy.

During the following, HERSCHEL and PITY are hung on the downstage chairs. Ronnie uses handpuppets of HERSCHEL and MAYBELLINE to enact the scene.

I would dream of returning home to Vienna. And she would be waiting for me. And the streets would open up to our joy, as we reclaimed the city as ours. Everything had changed. All the horror and secrets of the past forgotten in the dawn of a new day. Neither she nor I were looked at as different, as less, as disposable. We were simply part of the heartbeat of Vienna, hand in hand.

Music in, and HERSCHEL and MAYBELLINE dance. As the music ends, the handpuppets are removed.

PITY   That's a beautiful story, Mr. Flechtheim. So, did it happen? Did your fantasy come true after all those years?

HERSCHEL   Oh, Miss Beane. To these eyes, she continues to be the greatest beauty ever seen. Vienna however, while beautiful still, is perhaps unchanged at heart. And so, no, we do not venture out. All we are and all we need is within these walls. This refuge.

He is placed inside his cabinet, as Ronnie continues to speak his voice.

And now, if you'll excuse me, Miss Beane, I do believe I have a luncheon date.

LEDA enters.

LEDA   Vespa! Vespa, I've been thinking about our young visitor's offer of assistance. It's madness, she has no experience whatsoever, yet she's willing to hike up her skirts and help however she can. Very

Canadian, I suspect. But he wants a virgin to serve him dinner and Vespa, we must be pragmatic, where on earth are we going to find a virgin in Europe at this time of year.

She sees PITY.

Oh, it's you.

PITY	You're Leda Lichter.
LEDA	I've had many names. That was one. It served its purpose, for a time. But that time is long over.
PITY	But it lives on. I've seen your song—"Until The Sun Returns"—performed many times. A very popular drag queen does you.
LEDA	So that's the point of living a century then? To be parodied by transvestites.
PITY	Oh no, she does it very seriously. It's like, total homage.
LEDA	It's ridiculous.
PITY	You're an icon. The song is timeless.
LEDA	The song only meant something because it was specific to its time. And those who heard it, needed it desperately. But it was not unto itself. It was part of a movement. But how could you understand? That's the problem with today. There are no new movements.
PITY	That's not true.
LEDA	Really? Look at you, suddenly interested in me because I'm someone worthy of reproduction. Leda Lichter, alive again and appearing nightly in the artless male drag queen's grasp!
PITY	Or alive, without your permission.
LEDA	She was not the most interesting version of me.
PITY	Then why is she the version who is remembered?
LEDA	She was selfish enough to survive.
PITY	She was a hero.
LEDA	She was a runaway, a fraud, a disappointment.
PITY	To who?
LEDA	To herself. Not this old woman, Pity. I don't care what I have become. But the first incarnation, the original version of me as a woman. The wild girl. She would have cared about what I became.
PITY	Why was she wild?

LEDA   Child, the times were wild. I simply listened, and the rhythm of it all changed my heartbeat.

Wild Girl

LEDA   I had been raised a proper British girl, taught to keep myself straight and narrow. For a moment, in my youth, I had escaped the constraints of the cage, but it was a brief lick of liberty. Even after I had been found wandering in the wood, I was returned home and scrubbed clean of the wild. And so I waited for fate's next offer of elopement. Silent, save for pencil, chalk, crayon, and brush. Anything to extend my reach and touch what was hidden behind my downcast eyes and frozen smile.

And so, in those endless days between child and adult, the brush was tamed, my hand steadied, and my heart at peace with art. I was becoming a woman, as I learned to speak in a world without ears. I longed to be an artist, for a world without eyes.

It was my saviour, and at seventeen I painted my dedication. I was gifted, said some. Showed promise, said others. Unoriginal and derivative, said the critics. A blasphemous whore, said my father. When he heard that my painting was to be exhibited in a London show of new painters, I was banished from his home and finally free from his prying hand.

Music in, an early 1920s jazz rhythm, beginning softly and simply, building throughout the following scene.

So I ran again, knowing this time that no one would try to find me. I ran, with money of my own from the sale of that irreligious image. I ran to the temple of all who are wounded yet alive, dead but unable to sleep, penitent to wasted youth, and fevered to waste the rest. To find, to feel, to fuck, to forget.

I ran. To Paris.

A marionette of LEDA as a young woman in her late teens appears. Her clothing is of the time, with cloche hat and a straight, unfitted coat, cut just below the knee. This garment will open completely down the front during the scene, exposing her bare breasts and satin knickers. The scene is enacted between Ronnie and the marionette, all set to music.

An awkward, rigid girl in an elegant, curvaceous city. Lady Paris taught me well, for she held my hips, rubbed against me, let me taste her salty sweat and smell her sweetest secrets. And whispered in my ear. "Jazz," she purred, as we began to dance.

And as my posture relaxed and my morals laid to rest, men stood at attention, eager and erect. Their arms flung open, waiting to be crucified by my youth. She watched, my lover Lady Paris, and smiled as these tasty men taught me how to move them. Every night was a heavenly ride to hell and back, and oh, how we danced!

Some were Spaniards, slippery as olives and sharp on the tongue. Some were Germans, all meat and potatoes, deliciously disconsolate. Some were Americans, sweet as pie, proud and loud and up for anything. Most were French. Oh, the French! Bastard baguettes, dipping into whatever they wanted, mouths reeking of smoke and self-importance. It was a smorgasbord of men, and while they thought they were consuming me, I was devouring them.

I never held a brush or stared at bare canvas again. I had painted what needed to be said, and found instead my calling by being not the painter, but the painted. The anointed muse to the drunken tribe of lost boys. I was their model, their inspiration, their comrade, their lover, their mascot, their saint. I became absolution through paint. And oh, how I danced!

I danced with Cubists, who were fading by the time I arrived, but the few who remained were fun. I felt they really saw me, as they looked from all angles, trying to capture every side simultaneously. The finished canvas was usually flat, but on softer sheets, as they flipped and fondled me in search of my whole, they were brilliant to have around.

I danced with Expressionists, who were brutes and loved to torture me. Not in reality, but as a representation of the afflictions they so longed to possess. They worked from their inner state, and when that failed them or proved to be uninteresting, I was splayed on the bed and painted as a mutilated whore, or propped on a crutch, posed as a maimed veteran. They were cynical, socially critical, and sobbed uncontrollably when they came.

I danced with Surrealists, who painted fantastic images from their subconscious minds, none of which made any sense. I understood them completely. They were degenerates, hooligans, layabouts, and onanists. The kind of fellows a girl that age should meet. They knew as well as you that you'd never marry them, but chances are they're who you'd close your eyes and dream about once you had found Mr. Right and settled down.

Music ends. Ronnie toasts the audience and drinks.

To art! And the bad boys who make it. And finally I stopped dancing. Not because the music ended, but because a new song began playing. Some people have a fork in the road to choose from, all I did was pause. Damn our need to breathe, for as I stopped to catch my breath, he caught my eye. He had been staring at me for a long time, I know. But I made the fatal mistake that all doomed lovers commit. I looked back at him. And while I had no intention of following his level path while the mad dancing laughed around me, he froze me with his stare. He was like a song that you don't really like, yet you know all the words and against your will, you sing along.

DOOLEY enters. He's handsome, in the old Arrow-shirt ad kind of way, although a bit too serious and sad. He's dressed in evening wear.

DOOLEY   I am a guest in a ghost town. A town of ghosts, not my own, but haunting me without end. Former lovers, not mine, but hers, in numbers almost too many to bear, be it three or three hundred, it matters not, I imagine one set of frozen, foreign lips the same as a thousand. I wander her streets filled with named ghosts, and the undead greet me with their smirking glances, their rotting smugness, their sealed, dead youth and their corpse cocks frozen in memory's *rigor mortis*, the ever-present reminder that they were here first. I am alive, surrounded by all the history that touched and kissed and knew her before me. But I am the only one who loves her. I know that, because I dare not reach for her, even though we are the same in this alien grave. She is beautiful, and I am haunted. Oh, to die in her arms just once, or forever! Beauty, kill me. One kiss to smother me, please, for I am dead, living in your ghost town and cannot return home until you take my breath away.

LEDA approaches DOOLEY.

LEDA   Why do you stare at me?

DOOLEY   I wasn't aware that I was staring.

LEDA   Liar.

DOOLEY   I'm sorry.

LEDA   Don't be. I like it.

DOOLEY   Why?

LEDA   Because otherwise I would go unnoticed.

DOOLEY   Were you making sure I noticed?

LEDA	No. That's why I can't figure you out. You're different.
DOOLEY	It's quite natural to be drawn toward beauty.
LEDA	Shall I sit for you then? So you may capture my beauty for all time.
DOOLEY	I'm not an artist.
LEDA	Have you tried?
DOOLEY	No.
LEDA	Then how do you know you're not?
DOOLEY	I'm a collector.
LEDA	Of what?
DOOLEY	Of beauty.
LEDA	So you are an expert, Mr…?
DOOLEY	Otenreath. Donald Leopold Otenreath.
LEDA	Swanky. What do your friends call you?
DOOLEY	Dooley.
LEDA	I like that. It makes you less sad.
DOOLEY	If I'm sad, it's simply because I don't know who you are.
LEDA	Leda Swann.
DOOLEY	· Very clever.
LEDA	Your appreciation should be directed toward my parents, Mr. and Mrs. Swann. Naming me thus, with their tongues placed firmly in their classical ass-cheeks, was perhaps the only mirthful thing they ever did. Although whimsy certainly was not the intent. I was to be beautiful, as befits the name.
DOOLEY	They are proven then to be prophetic. I shall have to thank them.
LEDA	That will only be possible if you're visiting hell. They're finally dead.
DOOLEY	I'm sorry.
LEDA	Don't be. At last the ugly duckling has the freedom to fly home, pardoned from her exile of disgrace. Not that I'm in any great hurry. I'm at home here.
DOOLEY	Home is the language in which you think. And you don't think like these people, no matter how hard you try.

LEDA	What do you want from me, Mr. Otenreath?
DOOLEY	What does anyone want from that which they find beautiful? Simply to be recognized.
LEDA	As what, a fellow countryman? Very well, God Save the King! Now on your merry way.
DOOLEY	No, not that.
LEDA	Then what? To be seen as beautiful in return?
DOOLEY	No. As worthy.
LEDA	Of what?
DOOLEY	Of gazing toward the light.
LEDA	You're blind.
DOOLEY	You're right. But what a sight.
LEDA	Shall I be part of your collection, sir, is that what you propose?
DOOLEY	No, a different proposal for you, I think, Miss Swann.
LEDA	Please, I hate that name.
DOOLEY	Then change it.
LEDA	To what?
DOOLEY	Mrs. Otenreath.
LEDA	My word. Can you afford this acquisition, Mr. Otenreath?
DOOLEY	Name your price.
LEDA	Eternal devotion.
DOOLEY	Sold.

> *Transition. DOOLEY remains, hung in position. LEDA is taken away and hung inside a cabinet. The following is spoken by Ronnie without a marionette.*

LEDA	Well of course I married him. Who wouldn't? He was handsome enough to cause others to wonder how I would have snared him. Rich enough to afford my bohemian fantasies. Patient enough to suffer my constant reinventions. Smart enough to not delve into my past. Sure enough to believe that I was satisfied with his considerate lovemaking. Sad enough to remain interesting to me. Although my careful devotion to him is no doubt what made him sad. For we were clever, Dooley and I. We did everything right, thinking of one another, when really all a lover wants is

thoughtless desire, not kindness. But I convinced myself that Dooley was the one, because, you see, in certain light, he looked like the one. A manly version of the first boy I kissed. In those moments I loved him, completely, without reason. And then he would move, or be Dooley again. And I would pretend to love him still, because he was good enough to deserve that.

> *Transition is complete. We are now in the London townhome of DOOLEY and LEDA Otenreath. This is played by Ronnie sans marionette(s), as DOOLEY standing at LEDA's door, her voice as if offstage.*

DOOLEY   Leda, darling, are you ready?

LEDA   In a moment.

DOOLEY   Whatever are you doing in there, Mrs. Otenreath?

LEDA   A final inspection of the damage in the mirror.

DOOLEY   Shall I be your mirror instead?

LEDA   Away with you, Mr. Otenreath, while I make my final adjustments.

DOOLEY   Really darling, it might be more interesting if you allowed me to make a few adjustments of my own.

LEDA   Dooley, don't be scandalous, we've a full house this evening. And if their host is not downstairs to ensure that their drinks are filled, you will have a riot on your hands, sir. Darling, you know they can only discuss art through the bottom of a glass.

DOOLEY   I thought they only discussed themselves.

LEDA   Dooley, don't be a bore. They bring some fun into the house.

DOOLEY   Do hurry, darling, I'm lost without you.

LEDA   Dooley, don't.

DOOLEY   I don't deserve you, Leda. But I vow, I will do anything to stay with you forever.

LEDA   If you stay on the other side of that door forever, I'll never be finished. Trade your melancholy for a martini, darling. I'll be down before the first sip burns the blues from your lips. Now run along, Mr. Otenreath.

> *DOOLEY exits. Marionette of LEDA walks into the playing area. She is now in her late twenties, although her elegant coiffure and gown suggest an older, more refined woman.*

Anton! Darling, you are so sweet to lie. No, I've gained, actually, look at me, I'm a house. No inspection required, darling, best keep those hands for the piano. You're playing for us tonight.

Freddie, I knew you'd be here, old thing. Really? Which one? He's a bit old for you, isn't he? He must be enjoying his first pair of long trousers. Yes, yes, I'm sure he's very intelligent, Freddie.

Charlie, what are you doing here? We heard you were exiled in France until the play was finished. Oh darling, congratulations. Now we really have cause to celebrate! Help yourself to anything liquid.

Hello, I don't believe we've met. I'm Leda Otenreath. Thank you, we find it cosy. A cunning little cage for the primates at play. Yes, they are an amusing lot aren't they. So madly artistic. Which one of these clever monkeys brought you tonight? Really? I didn't know Dooley had friends of his own.

DOOLEY joins her.

DOOLEY	There you are. I was worried we would have to send Ginger up to lure you out of your lair with his gin-soaked sweet talk. He's quite drunk already you know. He's decided to create a mural in the kitchen using whatever he can get his hands on.
LEDA	Good. We can sell it for a fortune in the morning.
DOOLEY	Ah, I see you've met Mr. Fazood.
LEDA	Just. A pleasure. Mr. Fazood is a friend of yours, Dooley.
DOOLEY	Our paths cross from time to time. Galleries, auctions, that sort of thing. He has quite an extraordinary eye, haven't you, Baltan? Although he's caused me considerable grief in bidding at auction, Leda, I don't think you should favour him with any more of your attention.
LEDA	You must be a keen lover of things to be such a formidable foe, Mr. Fazood. Dooley always gets what he wants, don't you darling?
DOOLEY	Only the things that matter.

He puts his arm around her.

LEDA	You see, Mr. Fazood? I am one of Mr. Otenreath's trophies.
DOOLEY	No Leda, you are my prize for being alive.
LEDA	So sweet. Regardless, I trust that you will be gentlemen this evening and not engage in battle over me. Why, if blood were to

be spilt I'm afraid Ginger might dip in and continue his mural right into the salon.

DOOLEY You see why I'm mad for her, Baltan? Never fear, darling, no fisticuffs tonight. For I've already won.

LEDA Whatever are you talking about, Dooley?

DOOLEY Our friend Fazood here has possessed a treasure that I have admired for a long time. And due to his kind heart and generous spirit, I am now the owner.

LEDA I see. So you named a price, Mr. Fazood?

DOOLEY He was brutal, darling. But the cost is immaterial. I wanted it. I have it. Although I shall be sad to part with it.

LEDA Such mystery, Mr. Otenreath! Are you selling it so soon?

DOOLEY No Leda. I'm returning it to you.

As though DOOLEY has clapped his hands, he calls the guests to attention.

My friends, your attention for a moment if you please. As you all know, today is my wife's birthday.

LEDA Dooley!

DOOLEY I have been warned under penalty of death not to mention this, and so, before I make my final walk to the hangman's scaffold, I would like to thank her. Thank you, Leda. For being the most wonderful woman on earth. For tolerating me and making me want to be better for you. But most of all, my darling Leda, thank you for looking at me in the first place. And now, because you are my love, and a beauty who loves art, here is something beautiful for you to look at. Again. Happy Birthday, Leda!

Immediately after DOOLEY's last line, the painting of TENDER—which has obviously been visible on the stage throughout, but not specifically lit during the previous scene— is suddenly and prominently lit. As they turn upstage, sound of glass shattering. Transition. The marionettes of LEDA and DOOLEY are whisked away and hung in a cabinet. PITY enters.

Sensory Recall

PITY I discovered the boy in the painting when I was thirteen. A pivotal age, a seminal time, an instance that has influenced the entire life of Pity Beane. He lived in a book—*Trends in twentieth-century*

Art—forgotten in the school library, and I was only too happy to have him there. He was safe and untouched by others. The art section of my school library was no man's land, small and tucked away, better still for me, so no one could see as I kissed him, day after day after day. And so it was for three years. Secret and perfect and ours.

As I matured and turned sixteen, I felt that I did not know my boy as well as I should. I knew a smell to assign to him, but it was musty and somewhat weak, like the pages of the book in which he lived. If I was going to carry him with me, I would have to find a way to marry all my senses to this angelic boy. So, to liberate him from that tomb-like tome, I decided to create a fragrance and a whisper all his own.

I would pretend to be looking in another direction, intentionally brushing up against boys in the hall, or walking right into their chests. And before they would push me aside, or worse, just ignore me, I would inhale.

I would take them into my lungs and know their scent. The jock gods reeking of soap and Dentyne, the slackers oozing of tobacco and booze-stained T-shirts. Asian boys wafting through the halls in a haze of ginger and hair gel. Christian kids, like salt and vinegar chips, brainiacs and geeks who always smelled like fast-food litter left in the back seat of a car. And once, by mistake, a teacher. Mr. Van Ryn, tart and familiar like mayonnaise. But the best were the Italian boys in their rayon shirts, smelling sweet and sweaty like sausages hung in the sun to dry. My beautiful boy in the painting could not have smelled like that, but when I morphed them together in my head, I thought I would die.

His voice, of course, was another matter. And although in my fantasy we rarely spoke—we didn't need to, you see, we simply understood everything—still, once in a while he would want to tell me how beautiful I was, or how much he loved me. So I needed to hear him. But the problem with modern culture is that every sound has a visual. And I already had the picture. No, hearing my boy was not easy, or perhaps he had nothing to say. And just as I was about to give up, there was a miracle. There was a school play.

My high school had this drama teacher, Mr. Garfinkel, who apparently had studied at a lesser institution of higher learning in a suburb of Toronto and that made him, like, this total theatre expert. He was always doing collectives and student-created work. That's a step up from musicals and murder mysteries I suppose, but, just the same, they were always so lame. But not to Mr. G. In his mind they were totally relevant to our teenage angst.

Anyway, there was a play—or rather, a student collective—called *Beautiful Voices*, a hodgepodge of melting pot stories reflecting the diversity of teenage experience and the one-ness of our global village, blah, blah, blah. It was a series of monologues and choral chanting with yoga-based movement, and featured the usual cast of characters. Amy Tamblidge, this totally annoying born-again with giant tits talking about her dreams for global peace, as if Miss fucking Universe! Randall Betrick, ranting on about his parents' divorce, again. Trey Fergusson and Amber Witherspoon in this really embarrassing dialogue about teenage suicide without having the courtesy to actually perform it for us. Oh, and get this, Blaine Harker confessing that he was gay—oh puh-leese, like that was news, and now we were all supposed to like him even though he was just as annoying as before but out, and on and on and on. But near the end, there he was. My miracle. A boy who had never dipped his toe into the cesspool of drama club before, but had been coerced into the group by Mr. Garfinkel because of his brooding intensity and sullen mystique. Which meant he was totally hot, in that damaged and dangerous kind of way.

The boy's name was Angelo Bajrektarevic. He was the son of Yugoslavian immigrants, and although he had been in school as long as I could remember, no one seemed to know him. I stood next to him once on the football field during a weekly bomb threat, and he smelled divine. Like cheese. Not wholesome and annoying like cheddar, or stinky like Stilton, no, kind of foreign and funky, like Camembert wrapped in cashmere. I'll admit I had a minor crush on him, but I already had a boyfriend. The angel in the painting. And like Uncle Boyfriend always said, fantasizing about someone real only leads to disappointment.

I have no idea why I went to see *Beautiful Voices*, but I'm really glad I did. Because somewhere near the end, after all the whining drama club assholes had tortured us, Angelo Bajrektarevic came out into a pool of light, set his gaze beyond the audience and then he did it. He spoke. He spoke of loss, of grief, of the sadness that he would never know the homeland his parents had fled. And why? For what? Invisible lines, that's why people bled. Erecting borders between brothers where none had been before. Drawing lines in the sand, that's what men call war. And then he levelled his gaze with ours—no, not ours, with mine, I swear—and he simply, softly, surely said, "This school is full of stupid assholes. Nothing is beautiful, but you only know that when you're dead." And then he took a gun out of his jacket and pointed it at us. No, not us, he pointed it at me. Like he was going to shoot me through the heart with his truth. I don't know if that was the end of the play or not, because everyone started screaming and rushing for the exits. But I just sat there, frozen.

Fuck that was a good play.

Rumour had it that Mr. Garfinkel actually shit himself backstage. Angelo, of course, was expelled, and he never came back to school. I think about him though. He's going to have a hard life, because he figured things out far too soon and that's no way to get along. But I wish I could have told him that part of what he said that night was wrong. There is beauty in the world. You just have to know how to make it up. Like, whenever I close my eyes and dream of my angelic, painted youth whispering in my ear, it's always and forever Angelo's voice I hear.

> *PITY leaves. Transition. Interior of a train, moving. On top of the bar, LEDA (as a table-top figure) sits alone.*

Wicked Winter

LEDA Wicked winter
Despised and scorned
Find me now and find within
A warm reception to your
Simple chill
You cannot take my heart
For others have tried
And all have failed
It beats, but only to mock life
Not sustain it
So, like a lover
Place your cool lips on mine
Let me inhale you
Feed me with your frost
And freeze me
My useless heart and empty breath
Already a wasteland
Waiting, for you
Wicked winter
Despised and scorned
I will not love you, I promise that
But give instead this gift
Of frosty respect.

Cattle Car

Ronnie puts on the headrig of AUNTIE SARI, the cow.

SARI   I loathe travelling by train. Too much time for reflection in the glass, watching the world pass you by.

LEDA   Auntie Sari. What are you doing here?

SARI   I was about to ask you the same thing, my dear. This is a rather common means of transportation, Leda. Surely you might have arranged a private car. You're married to a very substantial man.

LEDA   I shall have to employ thrift for awhile, Auntie Sari. Besides, I've had quite enough luxury. Travelling first class can be costly to a woman.

SARI   You are quite the most ridiculous girl. I don't know why I bother with you.

LEDA   Then why do you?

SARI   Because you can see me. And hear me. You rarely listen, mind. I don't know why I waste my breath.

LEDA   Perhaps because I give it to you.

SARI   And, as such, I feel a duty to use it in your interest.

LEDA   My conscience is a cow.

SARI   You could do worse, my girl.

LEDA   I have, Auntie Sari.

SARI   Then let's just enjoy the ride. Leda. Leda, where are we off to?

LEDA   Vienna, I think.

SARI   Vienna? Not Paris?

LEDA   I'm known in Paris.

SARI   Precisely, we could have some fun.

LEDA   I want to be unknown. Besides, I thought you loathed Paris, Auntie Sari.

SARI   I do! But Paris is a place you can love and hate at the same time. Like a real lover. That's the beauty of it. But Vienna? Oh Leda, it's all waltzes and cake and memories of a lost empire. There's nothing to do!

LEDA   Vienna is a beautiful old dowager, exiled from reality. She'll teach me to fade gracefully as we crumble to dust.

SARI	And what does Dooley think of this madness?
LEDA	I don't know, I didn't tell him. I left without saying goodbye.
SARI	Leda! Scandalous girl! Why must you visit another outrage upon our family name?
LEDA	It won't be on your name, Auntie Sari. Nor Dooley's. I've taken Mother's maiden name. Lichter. Father couldn't bear it of course, it sounded so Germanic. But dear Mother has finally done me a favour. Leda Lichter. I'll fit right in.
SARI	I thought you wanted anonymity.
LEDA	You are only left alone if you appear to belong in the first place.
SARI	And are you alone now?
LEDA	Apparently not, Auntie Sari.
SARI	You know what I mean. Don't play games with me, my girl.
LEDA	But Auntie Sari, you are a game. My childhood imagining. That's why you exist.
SARI	And you imagine me a cow. Such cheek!
LEDA	Why complain? I dress you well.
SARI	Yes, you've always had style, I give you that.
LEDA	It's all a plain girl can aspire to. The stylish, elegant hostess.
SARI	Then why such an inelegant move as this?

LEDA looks out of the window.

LEDA	Dooley loves me, Auntie Sari. The version I gave him. The object of his affection. I want him to remember her.
SARI	Ah, so that's it.
LEDA	What?
SARI	The point of this folly. Running from age.
LEDA	No. From youth.
SARI	Then why have you brought it with you?
LEDA	You sat next to me, Auntie Sari. I didn't invite you.
SARI	I'm not referring to me. It's that painting, isn't it? Youth. You've brought it with you.
LEDA	I cannot escape him.

SARI	A maiden aunt must learn to chew her cud at times. But Leda, mark my words, that painting has never brought you happiness.
LEDA	I am happiest on my own, Auntie Sari.
SARI	Wicked gibberish! You delight in shocking me, don't you? Leda, you can't be alone. You're a woman! You need someone to take care of you. Which is why I've brought the monkey.
LEDA	What are you talking about you silly old cow?

Ronnie places a handpuppet of PLATO on his hand.

SARI	What are you, deaf, blind, dumb? This monkey! I'm gifting you with a little monkey to accompany you on this mad adventure.
LEDA	I can't take care of a monkey.
SARI	Of course not. He'll take care of you. He's very clever, as monkeys go. He sings you know.
LEDA	Monkeys can't sing.
SARI	And maiden aunts shouldn't be cows. But that's your gift, Leda. You can hear us. And my gift to you is this little singing monkey. Sometimes it's nice to hear a song from the past. Just to remind you of where you've been, my little woman of mystery. Well, time for tea. I hope they have scones. They go so nicely with my clotted cream.
LEDA	What's his name? The monkey.
SARI	You're the one who's so very clever with names. Leda Swann. Leda Otenreath. Now, Leda Lichter. Haven't you one to spare?
LEDA	Come on, old thing. I know you've thought this through. Otherwise you wouldn't be giving him to me.
SARI	Call him Plato. Perhaps with time, he'll help you find the reality of your ideals.
LEDA	Thank you, Auntie Sari.
SARI	You're welcome, my dear.

SARI kisses her.

Safe passage to you, Leda.

SARI leaves. PLATO sings to LEDA.

Say Goodbye

PLATO Let me go, if you leave
Say goodbye, then be gone
Do not stand in the wings, do not linger on
Let the fire's final hiss
Die away, like your kiss
Say goodbye when you leave
Then be gone.

LEDA You're a funny little thing, aren't you? Like a man in a monkey suit. So, this is my destiny then. To travel in the company of a beauty and a beast.

> *LEDA and PLATO are put away. Transition. PITY approaches the elderly LEDA, singing the last lines of the song.*

Animal Crackers

PITY Say goodbye when you leave, then be gone.

LEDA Plato, how lovely.

> *She turns and sees PITY beside her.*

Oh, hello dear.

PITY I like your monkey. He sings beautifully, I think.

LEDA You can hear him?

PITY Well sure. Can't you?

LEDA Yes. But I thought I was the only one. Have you always heard the animals sing?

PITY No, I was taught.

LEDA How?

PITY Uncle Boyfriend. He was like you, in a way. At some point he just decided that animals were better. Easier.

LEDA Angels.

PITY Yes. I suppose. And he could hear them. Not converse really, not communicate, but hear. And he taught me.

LEDA To speak.

PITY To follow the voices. I was seven when it began. We started with dogs of course, because they're easiest to understand. And generally the nicest, on the whole. I love listening to dogs, don't

	you? And, over time, I became fluent in mice, birds, even some large zoo animals.
LEDA	Elephants are so droll, *n'est-ce pas?*
PITY	And hippos, oh my God, bitter as hell but fucking hilarious!
LEDA	Did you master cat?
PITY	Not really. Cats are difficult. Except when they're in trouble. Then they're totally understandable.
LEDA	What else do you hear?
PITY	Thoughts, warnings, crying, the usual.
LEDA	Crying? Whose?
PITY	Animals, mostly. And sometimes, boys. Whole choirs of them, crying.
LEDA	Dying.
PITY	Yes.
LEDA	I've never heard that.
PITY	You're lucky. It's not as romantic as it sounds. But it's been increasing lately. I hear crying choirs of boys more often than animals. Sometimes you just want to sit and have a pigeon whisper to you, or listen to a rabbit giggling.
LEDA	You'll be mad one day. You know that.
PITY	I hope so. Personally though, I don't know if I would have dressed him up. The chimpanzee. Plato. I don't know if I would have put him in that suit. It seems a bit humiliating, dressing him up like a devolved little man.
LEDA	He came to me that way. Who am I to monkey with evolution?
PITY	That cow is a piece of work. Has she been around long?
LEDA	Oh God, don't tell me you can see and hear Auntie Sari too?
PITY	She's kind of hard to miss.
LEDA	You can see my memories?
PITY	Your memories are totally cool. It's like watching sad old black and white movies on TV with Uncle Boyfriend.
LEDA	But you barely know me.
PITY	Well lady, I know you talk to a cow.

LEDA	I made her up. When I was a little girl. She helped me through some very unpleasant times. Plato was a gift from Auntie Sari.
PITY	Whoa. Your imaginary cow gave you a real monkey? Fuck, that's good.
LEDA	Oh stop, it's nothing, really.
PITY	Shut up, you're fabulous! I mean, Uncle Boyfriend was pretty good, but even he couldn't make his imaginary world interact with physical reality.
LEDA	Now Pity, if you can hear the animals talk and see my memories, I suspect you've already dabbled in forging fact with fancy.
PITY	A bit.
LEDA	I knew it!
PITY	Don't get too excited, it was a complete disaster. I created a lifeless shape and then tried to give it breath.
LEDA	Rarely successful, that. Breathing life into static icons. Only the Pope or select puppeteers can do it, but even at best it's still just sleight of hand. Better to begin with one's reality and layer on top. I was a pink puppy for a while. And how? My hair. Strawberry blond, you see.
PITY	I was a beaver.

Beaver Tales

PITY	Queen Elizabeth High School had a football team. The Queen Elizabeth Beavers. The obvious cheap comedy of the name was seemingly lost on school officials. I, however, had the distinct cultural advantage of being raised on show tunes, *Carry On* movies, and classic animation, so my sense of humour was as camp as a boy scout tent.

I've never had much team spirit, because frankly, no team ever wanted me. But it seemed a glaring omission to my refined aesthetic that the football team didn't have a mascot. Queen Elizabeth had no beaver, and I made it my personal mission to rectify the situation.

In his heyday, Uncle Boyfriend was a bit of a Miss Thing when it came to clothes, and luckily for me, the entire history of men's fashion excesses for the last thirty years was stored in our basement. From that stash, I chose a long, loose-fitting, grey

Italian wool overcoat, circa 1984, with shoulder pads the size of a small Cessna's wingspan.

Mr. Kelecki at the Budget Upholstery Barn gave me a garbage bag full of foam rubber scraps, and with assistance from the *Muppets Make Puppets* book and a hot glue gun, I fashioned a reasonable facsimile of a modern character mascot. Okay, it wasn't exactly *Disney on Ice* quality, but if you squint you can detect the obvious parallels to contemporary Czech stop-motion animation. And courtesy of a brief flirtation with Goth culture in the eighth grade, I had a floor-length, black, crushed velvet cape at the back of my closet, perfect for reincarnation as a tail. And thus, Queen Elizabeth's beaver was born.

> *PITY appears in a beaver costume. It is threadbare, obviously homemade, and somewhat nasty. The cartoon proportions hint at cuteness, although the rather demented beaver head held under her arm, with maniacal teeth and eyes, creates a creepy picture. The quilted velvet tail trails behind her.*

I think a lot of people actually liked having a mascot, although admitting that wouldn't have been cool. So, at every opportunity, someone would push me over. I quickly learned that mascot work affords limited peripheral vision, so there's never a hope in hell of sensing an attack. Luckily, the peanut shaped foam underbody of the costume padded my fall. But I would just pick myself up, clench my two front teeth—metaphorically speaking, of course—and soldier on.

The combination of foam rubber, wool, and perspiration very quickly resulted in a really ripe rodent. And it didn't take long before I began to hear the snickering in the halls, or as I entered class, "Hey, isn't that the chick with the smelly beaver?" followed by the chortle and snort punctuation so adored by underachievers and athletes. But it didn't make me want to stop, in fact, it was even more reason to put on my stupid costume and become something other than myself. Besides, I had already clued into the ugly truth that I was never going to be beautiful, but at least in this suit, I had the potential for cute.

We had a game against the Wailers from Our Lady of Perpetual Sorrow, a Catholic high school across town. I wasn't invited exactly, but I schlepped my beaver in three big garbage bags on the number 57 bus. I got to the school before any of the team, and a custodian told me I could suit up in one of the locker rooms. I'd finally clued into the heat factor, and decided to wear the costume with nothing on underneath. So, there I was, naked in my beaver suit, all alone in a strange locker room. I put the head on, checked myself in the mirror, and sat down on the floor. And apparently fell fast asleep.

When I woke up, I knew I wasn't alone. The team had arrived and were going at it in full teenage boy throttle. Swearing, goofing around, snapping towels, the usual. But even with my limited visibility through the mesh strainer eyes, I could see them. Undressing, partially clothed, naked. C'mon, it's not like I hadn't seen a guy naked before. I mean, the boy in the painting was naked, but, okay, yes, this was the first time I'd actually seen a real guy without clothes. And there was something so, I dunno, sweet about the way their bums danced under the skin, how their boy chests spread like butter on a hot knife when they moved their arms, and the wholly new view of those penises just, well, hanging there. They weren't as big as I had been told they were, but they were cute. I had a hunch that penises and I were going to get along just fine. I wanted to tell Uncle Boyfriend about this, but I knew I never would. How could I? How could I admit that all these boys saw was a big, lumpy, foam rubber costume just lying in the corner. How could they know that I was already inside, that I had very slowly, and almost automatically, drawn my right hand up inside the sleeve and down into the round cavern of the body. How could anyone know that I was rubbing myself inside that beaver suit. How could anyone know, when I wasn't even aware of it myself?

This was the moment. Mum, can you see? My unwitnessed passage from child into woman. And just as I was about to come to that beautiful, new threshold, I heard someone say, "I dare you to kick that fucking beaver," followed by "No fucking way, that thing stinks. Besides, I hear it has AIDS." Peels of laughter rang out. "No shit man, I heard that chick has two fags instead of real parents." Hoots and howls all around. "Yeah, my dad said they're total cocksuckers, man. I bet that girl isn't even a real girl. She's probably, like, a fag too. I mean, come on, she's too fucking ugly to be a chick, man." And, like a scene from *Lord of the Flies*, crazy chanting "Kill the fag! Kill the fag!" began. I didn't have time to be afraid, I was still verging on my impending first moment of bliss when they started kicking. Kicking me, kicking what they thought was an empty costume lying on the floor. Naked wild boys, tight skin stretching like rubber bands, snapping into me. Mr. Kelecki's foam rubber couldn't cushion that much hate. I felt every blow, and clenched my teeth so as not to cry out. "Kill the fag! Kill the fag! Kill the fag!" until heat and pain shocked me unconscious.

In my fantasy of this story since, I awaken finally, bloodied but brave, and find my way to the playing field, game already underway. And my paint stick teeth become knives, my foam rubber claws are real and deadly, and I take my revenge on boys and cheerleaders. Their shoulder pads and pompoms are no match for the natural armour given to me by nature, and they die. They die horribly, knowing in their final moments that behind the mesh strainer eyes is the girl, now made woman by all this blood.

Actually, the custodian discovered me during the game. He heard some whimpering from the beaver suit on the floor and found me inside, naked and bleeding. My crossing over into womanhood did not occur by orgasm, but with three broken ribs, a dislocated shoulder, two broken fingers, and severe trauma to the head, back, and hips. I was in hospital for three weeks, in bed at home for a long time after that, and finished high school by correspondence courses and tutors. No charges were ever laid. The team had made it to playoffs. And that was all that mattered.

> PITY beaver is placed in a cabinet. Another version of PITY is taken from the same cabinet. She is now dressed—awkwardly—like one of the whores. LEDA, still centrestage, speaks.

LEDA Where did you find that ridiculous costume?

PITY Up there. In that room.

LEDA My room. No one in this house is allowed in there.

PITY But I'm working for the house tonight, and I wanted to find something so I would be beautiful for Mr. Hiro.

LEDA You miss the point of his request, my dear. He does not want a painted whore. He desires your naked innocence.

PITY But how shall I greet him?

LEDA You will not greet him. Stay silent. You must be an object beyond his grasp. He will pay simply for the pleasure of knowing that.

PITY But I thought he wanted a virgin to deflower.

LEDA No, Pity. He will not touch you. Keep your eyes closed, do not look at him. If he finds you beautiful, it is to remind himself of how unworthy he is. Beauty never looks back at us, we stare at it and hope. Surely you know how that feels.

PITY Can I at least wear the stockings?

LEDA Oh God. How did you find those?

PITY   I didn't mean to snoop, honest. But I couldn't resist. They're like the ones he's wearing in the painting.

LEDA   Those are the ones he wore.

PITY   You knew him?

LEDA   I was there.

PITY   Where?

LEDA   Inside that scene. Against that tree.

PITY   I can't see that memory.

LEDA   It's not a memory, you stupid girl! He's alive! He's my breath.

PITY   Who is he?

LEDA   He is Tender.

PITY   Artist and subject were the same?

LEDA   No. I signed his name to my witness of him.

PITY   You're the artist.

LEDA   I am an old whore. My brush became silent a long time ago. I painted him, then no more.

PITY   Why?

LEDA   So he could continue to speak.

> *LEDA and PITY are left downstage in front of the bar. Ronnie goes behind the bar and reveals a doll figure of child LEDA. The whole scene (undressing, travel by boat across the channel, etc.) is played on top of the bar with this single jointed figure. The voice is LEDA's, in present time.*

I stopped being a girl in 1917. The world was at war and I was thirteen. Marie was my nanny, she called me her puppy. Her little pink puppy with strawberry hair. And that was enough at that age in between. Neither child nor adult, I would lay in my bed and wonder what being a woman would mean. In the shadows above, I imagined my husband or lover or both. They looked like my father and smelled just the same. That was my game at night and those were my dreams, when I was thirteen.

Wide awake, I would see him, but my eyes forbade me to look. Quiet now, in the dark, I would stroke my own hair, reach down into my nightgown to feel breasts that were not there. I could not wait for them to grow, but I was just a girl. Daddy's little girl. And these were not my hands.

My nanny Marie in the doorway, watching me feel where breasts
should be. But I was not moving as the room sprang to life. No
words, only breath, gulping and short above me, a gasp at the
door. Hands disappeared, the breathing stopped, and my feet hit
the floor.

Marie stole me from my bed, without a word, nothing said.
Just a look, hurry now, this is not a game. Plucked from the
china cabinet world of childhood, never to be prized porcelain
again. Trousers on my legs, scissors hurriedly hacking at my curls,
concealed in a truer version of myself than when I was a girl.
My hair was cut short, and childhood left behind in a puddle of
tendrils and frills on the doll house floor. All was left behind as we
ran. The little pink puppy looked like a boy and ran like a man.

I never asked why. She never explained. We knew, woman and girl,
that men are horrible, be they at large or at home. And so we ran,
into the warring world, together. Alone.

Passage by night across the channel, illegal and daring and foolish
and heart-in-your-throat exciting. I do not know what lies or
truths Marie had told to gain our place upon that merchant vessel.
What did she pay for our passage that night? No woman's freedom
is without a price. No hand extended unless a coin or a breast is
placed in it, no knight in armour appears until a damsel lies, he
does not take a shining unless there is a prize. I slept in her cloak
and did not see the journey, shrouded from sight I did not witness
the fare being paid as England grew dim in the darkness and to
France we were conveyed. There were no stars, only salt air in the
black.

We did not walk on water. We ran, and never looked back.

On land at last again, our feet never stopped. My first taste
that running does not make one free. Simply fugitive from the
inevitable sentence. We ran like open prey all day until, at last, we
were surrounded by trees. I did not know which wood it was, nor
did I know what would become of us there, only that no fate
could be so great as that which lay in wait in Britain. Of that
I was certain. The indecorous hand of the incubus. My father.
No passage by wartime sea, nor flight through unknown, scarred
terrain could be as frightening as he, who stood over my bed and
breathed. Shallow, short, spurting over me. No tree in unknown
wood could threaten more than this. And so we ran. My hair, cut
short, shorn of all female propriety. I looked like a wild boy. And
was hungry like a man.

But sounds of other hungry men thundered through this place. For war was near and we could hear the guns and cannons scream. Come with me, said Marie, but as night's fingers covered the wood, I lost grip of my nanny's hand. Marie, Marie, where are you? Don't leave me, Marie! Your little pink puppy is lost, alone in this strange land.

There was no sight to see, just sounds and smells. No light. No Marie. Just me and fallen leaves. I dare not move in darkness, for every crunching step revealed my place. My feet had touched the water, not the sea nor river, but something wet and still. I drank and fed my thirst from the awful, fetid swill. And so I sat and waited, in the bed of leaves I'd made. All the distant thunder dead, I held my breath and prayed. Not to God, oh no, not him, but to my father instead. Oh Father, please let me come home. Where I can be warm and you can touch me in my bed. My hair will grow back, Daddy I promise, I'll keep myself for you. My little hands, my secret mouth, my not yet woman's breasts. Just come and find me, Father, and do what you must do. And as I prayed this terrible hymn to the horrible he who hurt me, that he would not desert me, as I had done to him, sleep came at last and on this leafy bed I laid my head to rest.

The doll of LEDA is curled into a sleeping position. A doll of TENDER, dressed in his Highland Battalion uniform, is revealed and acted on top of the bar.

TENDER Little toy soldiers, all in a row. Perfect pewter playthings pushed to the front, mapped on a board like a game. Some to fall, some to advance, to retreat is defeat, so push into France. Little toy soldiers, all in a row. To battle, to battle we go.

A little toy soldier dressed for the game, to run and jump and crawl in unknown fields of death. But I am young and full of breath, and so my country sent me, like a perfectly wrapped bequest. Wed to this war in my tartan trousseau. To battle, to battle I go.

A little toy soldier dressed like a man. Don't think of me as real, that would cause you to care. What then if I fall, to die in the mud, another land's hands stained with my blood. No, don't think of such things, make me a toy. A poster, a stamp, a song filled with joy. Speak of your flag or your country or king, speak of every ridiculous thing but the truth. Sit on your hands and make war while your youth die. Keep me a lie. Don't sing of me, for then I am real. Don't say my name, don't think, don't feel. I'm just a toy, and when broke I'll be gone. That's the beauty of war. We only remember the posters, the stamps, the songs filled with joy. I'm your little soldier toy dressed like a man. How can you mourn a boy you don't know? To battle, to battle I go.

If you must play at Remembrance Day, let go of your God and let the devil win. For there is no sense in war. The smell of burning flesh and hair, like sour toast, bonfires of boys left to roast. Keep your homefires burning if you can, the kindling has been sent to other lands. You must never hear the screaming or the moans. The gurgling of your son shot in the throat. Clutch that last letter he wrote, make him a song, he won't sing anymore. No mother, sing, for you sent him to war. And whatever his last words might have been, forever you never will know. For your honour, madam, to battle, to battle we go.

It was beautiful. It was silence and stillness, and I thought I was home. I dreamed of the prairie, wished for that sky, people who knew me, but I was not there, I was here on my own. I lifted my head, wanting angels above, but they only lay dying around. This moment had found me alone in the trench, bodies of comrades still, by my side.

Cushioned on impact by boys like myself. A little toy soldier alone on the shelf, the others all toppled and red. Warm from the last moment of life, from urine and feces and chests opened wide. An army of toys, all dead. Wild-eyed boys, staring at me, begging for one last look. There was no singing then, I didn't hear a thing. Didn't hear the second blast as poison shell was lobbed my way. Only saw the air become death as the cloud hovered and fell. Forget the smell. Ignore the sounds, the constant ringing. This devil had yellow fingers. Die. Die. Dichlorethylsulphide. Mustard gas, the blistering touch, reaching out and dragging me down below. "Take my hand," the devil said, "and to Hades, to Hades we'll go."

No.

Does a boy decide to be a man? Or does nature simply take his hand and guide him? Can a man decide to be afraid? Or is the softer heart's destiny made when simply pushed in the opposite direction that heroes choose. There were no shoes for me to fill, no footsteps clearly marked. I simply ran, in the twilight yawning somewhere between boy and man. Shell-shocked out of all senses, I ran, I ran, I ran, until I could run no more. I ran. Until the devil's fingers could not reach me.

Mum!

At last my gulping breath was calm, and night pushed closed my
eyes. When I awoke I saw the dawn, the ringing in my ears was
gone, and morning's mist was all around. There was no sound, but
this. The crunch of fallen leaves under footsteps coming near. Not
an army like before, nor the sound of distant war, just one man
walking toward me as I lay there on the forest's floor. "Are you
hurt?" he asked, and I said no, simply taking rest. "I will not be
addressed that way, stand up, salute, explain yourself, what have
you to say?" I stumbled to my feet to find a man whose age and
rank were greater than my own. Not a boy, nor soldier toy, he was
an officer from the army of men, different, better, higher, yes, but
also from my home. He was me, he was mine, familiar and living
and true, but when I reached out for his hand he struck me down
again. "Look at you!" he spit, his foot was on my chest. "A coward
running through the woods, a runaway, no less. You will not defile
those clothes anymore, will not ridicule these garments of war.
Stand up, strip down, undress!" I tried to speak again, to tell the
hell I saw, but when I moved my mouth his fist was swift and hit
my jaw. I bled at last in war, beaten by my own. "Coward, coward,
coward," he crowed, as my uniform hit the ground. Blood and
leaves and tartan swirled all around. I was not his brother, his
comrade, or his friend.

A naked boy in foreign wood, cloaked in shame and autumn air.
Not a man, nor a toy, neither soldier, just a boy. Shivering, hairless,
pale, and lost, waiting for this jury of one to speak the price,
extract the cost for running from death to this. From his rucksack
the man took something soft, something green, and threw it in my
face. It smelled of something beautiful, the city, a woman, powder,
life lived far from this strange place. "If you can't be a man," he
said, "then you must be a girl. Hairless and pale and afraid. But
you're less than a girl, so put on these stockings and then you'll
be made like the whore I took them from in Paris." And for a
moment, he smiled and was delicate as I fumbled with the silk,
embarrassed by his game. I was not a toy soldier, but a doll yet
again. He knelt between my legs and smoothed the green shroud
as it enveloped my skin, touching only stocking, never flesh, no
part of me on him. And slowly standing, turned me round and
bent me toward a tree. The bark was rough against my cheek, but
not so coarse as his trouser's wool, scratching at my back, rubbing
against me.

And then, I bled again. Ripped wide by what, I did not know.
Oh no, oh no, not that, not him in me. His hands on my hips,
pounding from the rear. I screamed, but no one heard, only trees
were near. "Coward, coward, worse than a girl," he whispered as he

took me at the tree. This was not love, this was not sweet, a little toy soldier's final defeat. This was not beautiful, I am not your Christ. No god cried for me as this son paid the price. No poppy grows to resurrect me, as my countryman fucked me and finished my youth. Who was the coward now, there is your truth. Brave soldier he was, and honoured back home, butchered a boy, buggered his own. Sing him a song, he knows all the words. And a secret verse you never have heard. "Coward, coward, worse than a girl," everyone sing along.

The melody of me will not linger on. You will not remember my name.

Arms overhead, left for dead, forgotten little soldier boy, tied up to the tree. Cast-off broken soldier's whore, toyed with in the leaves. A carpet of red and gold underneath my feet, branches blazing with their dead ready for release. But I cannot return to dirt and rot into the ground, for I am held against the bark, no earthly grave to mark the spot where the little toy soldier fell down.

> TENDER *stays tied against Ronnie's chest as the doll of sleeping* LEDA *awakens.*

LEDA | And then, I awoke, frozen from the night before. My skin so white, my fingers blue, transparent in the light. I have never thawed since that day when I woke up alone and lost. All the past behind me, and across the pond a vision sent to show the way. Through the mist an angel, dying by a tree. A final sign to prove that God was dead inside of me. I stood and walked on liquid ground, the water froze and all around the air was filled with snow. Neither wild boy nor girl, nature's hand escorted me to the other side. I was woman as I walked on water toward the wingless angel guide.

TENDER | Lace-patterned flakes danced around head. But if to hell I go and I am dead, there were no flames as fires hissed, but from the snowy waters' mist rose a creature soft and white. My God had not forgotten me, but came down as a swan. Let life's last touch not be the hand that took my will to live, but your sweet kiss to forgive and lift me toward the light.

LEDA | He bade that I should kiss him before his life was gone. "I am Leda," said my nearing lips, but he said "No, you are the swan." This angel boy had skin so thin I felt I could see inside of him. Surely he was beauty, surely he was love, surely he was good. What had he done to heaven to be cast out, left bleeding in the wood. If heaven's mercy could not hear an angel's final plea, I understood, from that day, it never would find me.

TENDER	This swan was my lone Valkyrie, standing in the wait. And trees and leaves and snow and she were witness to my fate.
LEDA	Drawing close to him I touched the skin of the angel nearing death. And as my lips received his kiss, he shared his final breath.
TENDER	I am Tender.
LEDA	He said, and then there was no more. His closing breath became my first, at last I was as woman cursed as my body cramped and bled. Pray Valhalla greet him, as to final battle, like chattel, he'll go. Angel dead and dying swan, bleeding in the snow.

> *Ronnie blows a handful of small white feathers above the scene, and they float onto and around TENDER and young LEDA. The jointed figures are removed and Ronnie returns to LEDA and PITY in front of the bar.*

PITY	You're wrong, you know.
LEDA	How so?
PITY	You said beauty never looks at us. But he looked into you.
LEDA	And saw a swan, not me.

> *Sound of the doorbell.*

It appears that Mr. Hiro has arrived. Pity, you don't have to do this.

PITY	Let him in, Mrs. Otenreath. Let him look. Make him pay. He won't touch me.
LEDA	Pity, wash your face. Don't drown yourself in paint.

> *LEDA and PITY are placed in cabinets. Doorbell sound.*

> *Ronnie presents a tray and places it on the bar. We see a nude doll figure of PITY, flat on her back. Taking a small serving dish, he places a small piece of food on her body. The tray is rotated so that her head is downstage on the bar. Turning upstage, Ronnie puts on the headrig of Mr. Hiro. He turns and bows toward PITY, then, placing his hands on the bar, leans down to smell her. His hand above her face, as if caressing but without touching, it travels down the length of her body, his breath audible throughout. He takes the piece of food and slowly raises it to his mouth. Ronnie thrusts his head back and puts it into his own mouth. Hiro puts his hands together, bows, and takes out a money bill and throws it onto PITY. He bows, turns, and leaves. Removing the headrig, Ronnie turns back toward the*

bar. PITY sits up, and as she is lifted by Ronnie, faces the
painting of TENDER, upstage.

PITY   Now I know how it feels.

She turns toward the bar.

Poor you.

The doll and tray are removed. Ronnie puts on a headrig of
(old) LEDA. It has a "dress" of flowing chiffon hanging from it.
His hands become hers.

Holes

LEDA   There are holes in my shoes
That's provenance, dears
Age-hardened leather grows thin through the years
For too many dances
Blister the soul
And covering your tracks in the dirt takes its toll
How droll, I admit
Counterfeit, a fraud on the stroll
I've traded the past, squandered my history
Always well-heeled but shrouded in mystery
With no one to know, no one will miss me
Oh dear
No, running's my best-suited role

There are holes in my heart
This provenance, alone
A beating, bloodless fist chewed to the bone
Bludgeoned but not beaten
Buried alive
Pounding bloody marvel willed to survive
Revive, it dares me
It wears me and will not be deprived
My heart isn't true, but one truth I've known
Red goes with everything, blue's best alone
Heart on wing, the ugly cygnet has flown
So alone
No, this is my secret swan dive

There are holes in the story
This provenance, mine
Gaps in the journey forgotten with time
Beginnings unfinished

Endings not met
Bushels of middles I choose to forget
And yet, I cannot
I forgot to bury regret
I've dampened my laughter, dried all my tears
Smothered the gasping for breath through the years
I've danced with the devil, and still I am here
It's mine
No, this is the version you get.

PLATO (handpuppet) joins her.

Plato, constant friend. There you are.

PLATO I've been with you all the time.

LEDA I'm sorry I broke your heart. I don't know what I was thinking. I should have let you be a man again, Dooley.

PLATO I once told you that I would do anything to stay with you forever.

LEDA But Dooley, like this?

PLATO I don't mind being a monkey.

LEDA Which is why you're such a good man. Dooley, I'm done. This portrait is complete. Here then are the last snowflakes of my long winter, to rest upon my lashes and freeze my eyes shut.

PLATO Then curl up my little pink puppy, and sleep.

Ronnie removes the headrig of LEDA, placing it on the bar. PLATO sings.

Hold me through this winter day
For it's you my blue heart yearns
The moon and stars will lead the way
Until the sun returns.

The handpuppet of PLATO is removed and rests beside LEDA. Transition. PITY and HERSCHEL are taken from a cabinet.

HERSCHEL Leaving us so soon, Miss Beane?

PITY Yes, Mr. Flechtheim. I'm done.

HERSCHEL You think so?

PITY I know the provenance of the painting.

HERSCHEL I've been thinking of this word of yours, my dear. Provenance. My own has a gap of sixty-three years, and while not stolen, it was hidden away. My heart unseen by the one for whom it beat.

PITY	You'll stay then.
HERSCHEL	Indeed. And what of you, my dear? Where will you go now?
PITY	Where I began. Home.
HERSCHEL	Has the thrill of travel worn off so quickly?
PITY	Seeing the world at large has made me feel quite small. And that's really good, Mr. Flechtheim. I don't need to be larger than life.
HERSCHEL	You've come so far to see your boy in the painting. It would be a pity to leave without him. Let me make a gift of it to you, please.
PITY	Thank you for your generosity, Mr. Flechtheim, but no. I have seen him, at last, in the best possible light. So he will be forever real in my mind's eye whenever I need to feel him. But he does not gaze on me, nor should I sit before him in vain, waiting for his breath on my cheek, or to speak Pity's name. If I take him with me and return home clinging to him still, then I have not travelled at all. I love him, but I am changed.
HERSCHEL	And what do you desire now, Miss Beane?
PITY	Less. There are so many people in the world. Beauty, the kind you stare at, the kind that makes you lose yourself in your own plainness, that's rare. Which is why it stops you in your tracks. But what about the rest of us, Mr. Flechtheim? Millions of plain people who don't look at each other. If one plain man were to look at me now, I would embrace him. It would scare him, but I would hold onto him. I just want one man to look at me. Just one plain man.
	And not a beauty, please. Not a man who looks at himself in mirrors.
	A plain man, simple. A man who will dance with me. A simple, wrinkled man. I'll be his reflection, and he mine. And we'll dance, plainly. We'll be one another's mirror, but not in vain.
HERSCHEL	I think it would be a shame to leave Vienna without a waltz. Miss Beane.
PITY	Mr. Flechtheim.
	HERSCHEL takes PITY in his arms, and they slowly begin to dance. When done, they walk up the ramp together.
HERSCHEL	I know you Canadians think you can walk on frozen water. But be careful, my dear. Something tells me the ice will melt the moment it feels you. I am so glad I lived long enough to meet you.

| PITY | Goodbye, Mr. Flechtheim. |

She kisses him on the cheek.

There's a freebie. On the house.

| HERSCHEL | Godspeed, Pity Beane. |

HERSCHEL leaves, is put into a cabinet. PITY looks upstage at the painting.

| PITY | It's unspeakable, this view |

It's unspeakable, this view
Unthinkable loveliness in the plain, simple scene
All I have been cannot compare to this
I am better for finding you and leaving
No farewell glance, no parting kiss
No vow to meet again
You will not notice as I go
So close yet distant still
Look
There are trees in the background
Me in the foreground
Fading from view
But when snowflakes fall, I'll close my eyes
And you'll be there to warm me
Tenderly, as I remember you.

PITY walks to one of the cabinet doors.

Goodbye, Vienna. You've been a beautiful hostess.

PITY is placed in the cabinet, exchanged for another marionette version of her. She is wearing a knitted pink hat and ice skates. The decorative frosted glass around the bottom of the bar is now blue, and she skates in a circle.

It's unspeakable, this view
There, in the distance
Will familiar trees bend to greet and shade me
We will never meet again, but last in remembrance, fondly.

| TENDER | I have been passed, lonely still-life unchanged |

I have been passed, lonely still-life unchanged
But not unmoved. I see too
There is no riddle to solve
No provenance of my own
Please lead me home, as I follow your voice
I am a record of you
There were trees in the background
Me in the foreground
And there, in the distance

This unspeakable view
Beautiful, there you are
All this beauty
All of you.

> *PITY continues to skate for a moment, and as the underscore builds she jumps into the air. Lights snap to black.*

The End

photo by Trudie Lee

RONNIE BURKETT has been captivated by puppetry since the age of seven, when he opened the *World Book Encyclopedia* to "Puppets." He began touring his puppet shows at the age of fourteen and has been on the road ever since.

Recognized as one of Canada's foremost theatre artists, Ronnie Burkett has been credited with creating some of the world's most elaborate and provocative puppetry. Ronnie Burkett Theatre of Marionettes was formed in 1986 and has stimulated an unprecedented adult audience for puppet theatre, continuously playing to great critical and public acclaim on Canada's major stages and as a guest company at international theatre festivals.

Ronnie has received numerous awards as a playwright, actor, and designer for his work with Theatre of Marionettes, including the prestigious Siminovitch Prize in Theatre, a Village Voice OBIE Award in New York for off-Broadway Theatre, and four Citations of Excellence in the Art of Puppetry from the American Center of the Union Internationale de la Marionnette. His latest creation, *Billy Twinkle*, is the eleventh production from Theatre of Marionettes, and follows the now-retired international successes *10 Days on Earth*, *Provenance*, and the Memory Dress Trilogy.

When not touring, Ronnie can be found surrounded by more than 1200 books on puppetry, two dogs, Plasticine, and woodworking tools in his Toronto studio, where he is creating yet another new show.